JSP Examples
and Best Practices

ANDREW PATZER

Apress™

JSP Examples and Best Practices

Copyright ©2002 by Andrew Patzer

ISBN (pbk): 1-59059-020-1

Printed and bound in the United States of America 12345678910

Trademarked names may appear in this book. Rather than use a trademark symbol with every occurrence of a trademarked name, we use the names only in an editorial fashion and to the benefit of the trademark owner, with no intention of infringement of the trademark.

Technical Reviewer: David Czarnecki

Editorial Directors: Dan Appleman, Peter Blackburn, Gary Cornell, Jason Gilmore, Karen Watterson, John Zukowski

Managing Editor: Grace Wong

Project Manager: Alexa Stuart

Copy Editor: Kim Wimpsett

Production Editor: Kari Brooks

Compositor: Impressions Book and Journal Services, Inc.

Indexer: Carol Burbo

Cover Designer: Tom Debolski

Marketing Manager: Stephanie Rodriguez

Distributed to the book trade in the United States by Springer-Verlag New York, Inc., 175 Fifth Avenue, New York, NY, 10010 and outside the United States by Springer-Verlag GmbH & Co. KG, Tiergartenstr. 17, 69112 Heidelberg, Germany.

In the United States, phone 1-800-SPRINGER, email orders@springer-ny.com, or visit http://www.springer-ny.com.

Outside the United States, fax +49 6221 345229, email orders@springer.de, or visit http://www.springer.de.

For information on translations, please contact Apress directly at 2560 9th Street, Suite 219, Berkeley, CA 94710.

Phone 510-549-5930, fax: 510-549-5939, email info@apress.com, or visit http://www.apress.com.

The information in this book is distributed on an "as is" basis, without warranty. Although every precaution has been taken in the preparation of this work, neither the author nor Apress shall have any liability to any person or entity with respect to any loss or damage caused or alleged to be caused directly or indirectly by the information contained in this work.

The source code for this book is available to readers at http://www.apress.com in the Downloads section.

I'd like to dedicate this book to my wife, Beth, and our daughters, Ashley and Emily. Once again, they've been very supportive of me as I took on another book. I know it's been difficult at times to put up with me not being around because I had more writing to do. Thank you for your love and continued support.

I'd like to give special thanks to both my mother and my mother-in-law. They've both had to deal with cancer this past year and continue to fight. I've learned a great deal personally from both of them about courage and strength. I pray they continue to enjoy life to its fullest each and every day.

Contents at a Glance

Contents

About the Author

Andrew Patzer is a web architect for the Centare Group, a consulting firm located in the Midwest. His first book, *Professional Java Server Programming* (Wrox Press, 1999), is a best seller and one of the first books to cover J2EE technologies. Andrew recently served as a lead systems architect for a leading application service provider in the insurance industry, and he was directly involved in designing and building a J2EE development framework upon which the company's key product was built. Andrew has delivered several presentations over the years to local user groups as well as national conferences.

About the Technical Reviewer

David Czarnecki is a computer scientist in the Advanced Computing Technologies lab at the GE Global Research Center in Niskayuna, New York. He's involved with various projects ranging from the development of application frameworks to the use of natural language processing techniques. He's the coauthor of *Java Internationalization* (O'Reilly, 2001), and he regularly provides expertise on how to properly internationalize software. David is also a speaker at national conferences such as JavaOne.

Acknowledgments

I BELIEVE STRONGLY that a person can only go so far unless they surround themselves with good people. Over the years, I've had the pleasure of working with some outstanding people. I'd like to specifically mention a few that I worked with at Workscape (now Riverwood Solutions). Mike Schenk, Mike Connor, and Craig Wohlfeil are each extremely talented architects who not only taught me a great deal, but also pushed me to achieve more than I could have on my own.

Dave Glyzewski, owner of the Centare Group, has always been a friend and has done his best to support me over the years as my career has taken me many different places. I'd like to thank Dave for being in my corner and always believing in me. Thanks, Smithers!

John Carnell, my perpetual coworker, has been there to keep my competitive juices flowing. We always seem to push each other to new heights (although I can't seem to push you past that five-foot mark—sorry, I couldn't help myself). Seriously, thank you for being a friend, as well as competitor, throughout my career.

I'd also like to thank my friend Scott Borth. Scott is the only person I've found who will laugh at my jokes and find humor in the same things I do. When your job has you sitting in front of a computer screen all day, it helps to talk to someone who not only allows you to be yourself, but actually encourages it.

Introduction

WHEN I WROTE MY FIRST BOOK covering JavaServer Pages and Java Servlet technology, there was a great deal of uncharted territory to cover. Today, much of what I wrote is not only outdated, but completely obsolete. The technology has grown tremendously fast and, with it, a legion of Java developers eager to stay on the cutting edge of Java development. Although this is certainly a good thing, it does however create a problem. Quite often, in a rush to implement the latest technology, little thought is given to good design and architecture.

This book attempts to provide a framework for developing quality software using JavaServer Pages technology. Chapters 1 and 2 lay the groundwork for using JSP. Chapters 3 and 4 explore the separation of roles between page designer and Java developer using both JavaBeans and custom tag extensions. Chapters 5, 6, 7, and 8 present several design patterns for the presentation tier. These patterns are applied using JavaServer Pages and Java Servlets. Chapters 9 and 10 walk through the basics of testing and deploying web applications using open-source tools. The book concludes with the development of an application framework along with a complete reference implementation in Chapters 11 and 12.

I hope you enjoy this book as much as I've enjoyed writing it!

CHAPTER 1

JSP Foundations

Developers have seen great improvements in server-side web development in the past few years. We've gone from complex, non-scalable Common Gateway Interface (CGI) scripts to some elegant enterprise-class solutions using technologies such as Active Server Pages (ASP), Java Servlets, and JavaServer Pages (JSP). Unfortunately, with this explosion of new technology come a lot of misguided efforts by well-intentioned developers.

It's easy to simply learn the skills you need to accomplish a specific task and then move on to something else. When you revisit that same task, you may learn a little bit more to make necessary modifications, but it's still not quite right. What eventually happens is that you end up with a system of "patchwork" that needs to be supported and maintained. Wouldn't it be nice to do things right up front and avoid creating this mess in the first place?

This book's purpose is to educate those of you who may have developed several JSP applications but have never really thought about concepts such as role separation, frameworks, and enterprise development patterns. Having developed several server-side Java applications over the past few years, I'd like to share with you some of my ideas as well as some best practices that I've arrived at while working alongside some of the best and brightest developers around.

This chapter will lay down the basics of developing a web application using JSP. It'll explain the fundamental concepts behind web development, J2EE (Java 2 Enterprise Edition) applications, and simple JSP development. If you're already a JSP expert, then you may still want to skim over the chapter. It'll include information helpful for setting up a particular JSP environment and laying the groundwork for the book's examples.

Developing Web Applications

It may seem a bit trivial to discuss the elements of a basic web application in an advanced JSP book, but I think it warrants attention when I see numerous people claiming to be web developers who know nothing about HyperText Transfer Protocol (HTTP) or even web servers. It reminds me of my client/server days, when I was surrounded by Visual Basic developers who had no understanding of the Windows operating system. They were certainly capable of producing a working application, but they could have done so much more had they understood the basic foundation upon which they were developing.

Web developers, for the most part, tend to get caught up in their specific technology and then do exactly what they need to do to get their programs to work. Quite often, there just isn't any time to learn anything more about it. With a proper foundation, developers can make better decisions before diving into development. So, let's start this book by reviewing HTTP and how each component of a web application plays a part in the overall interaction with the user.

Understanding HTTP

HTTP defines the way in which web browsers interact with web servers. HTTP uses TCP/IP, the network protocol of the Internet, to communicate standard messages between machines across the Internet. By using standard protocols such as these, you're able to communicate with any web server from a variety of different web browsers and expect similar behavior.

At the heart of HTTP lies a request message and a response message. This is the fundamental way in which a web browser communicates with a web server (see Figure 1-1). The user types in the location of a document in the URL box, the browser issues a standard HTTP request for the document, and the document is located and returned to the browser as a standard HTTP response.

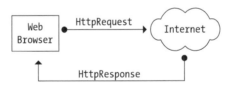

Figure 1-1. Basic HTTP exchange

The HTTP request consists of a series of standard headers along with any parameters, or form data, necessary to fulfill the request. The web server, for which the request is intended, is able to read these headers and respond accordingly. There are two common types of HTTP requests, GET and POST. A GET request will append form data to the requested URL and send it as one packet. A POST request will first send a packet containing header information and then send a separate packet containing the form data. A common question I'm asked is, "Which type of request should I use in certain situations?" A good rule of thumb is that you should use POST requests to modify a resource on the server and GET requests to simply retrieve information from the server. You may find that this doesn't always apply in every situation, though.

The HTTP response consists of standard response headers such as content-type and content-length, along with an HTTP version number and an HTTP status code. In addition to the header, chunks of data are sent immediately following the response message. The browser uses the response headers to determine the best way to render the data and then displays it accordingly. Most of the time, the response consists of HTML content, along with a few images. Sometimes, however, the content-type may be something like application/pdf, which is known as a *MIME type*. The browser will match this against its own list of MIME types and determine which helper application to load. In this case, the Adobe Acrobat Reader would render the response data.

Table 1-1 shows the log file of an HTTP tracer program that tracks every HTTP message sent between your browser and the Internet. You can see how the POST request issues two separate messages. What you can't see in this particular log is that the second message contains all of the form data (notice the size of the message). The response that is generated contains a header of HTTP/1.1 200. The first part (HTTP/1.1) is the version number. The last part is the status code (200, which means OK). This also contains any response headers such as content-type and content-length (not shown in this log). The remaining lines show how the browser receives the response data. The browser will take this data, along with its content-type and content-length, and render it appropriately for the user to view.

Table 1-1. Example of a Single POST Request and Subsequent Response

TYPE	ID1	ID2	BYTES	RESPONSE TIME	DATA
SEND	735	1	741	0.000	POST /marketplace/default.html
SEND	735	2	1489	2.799	POST /marketplace/default.html
RECEIVE	735	3	172	2.720	HTTP/1.1 200
RECEIVE	735	4	2048	0.005	2048 bytes
RECEIVE	735	5	7680	0.035	7680 bytes
RECEIVE	735	6	512	0.002	512 bytes
RECEIVE	735	7	2560	0.019	2560 bytes
RECEIVE	735	8	63	0.018	63 bytes

Components of a Web Application

A typical web application involves a web server, an application server, and a database server. Each of these servers listens to a specific TCP/IP port for incoming messages containing requests to carry out. These listeners are sometimes called *daemons*. They're threads of execution that wait for TCP/IP messages to appear for a specific port. For instance, the web server will, by default, listen to requests addressed to port 80. Because web servers default to this port, there's no need to specify it in the URL, it's just implied. If you were to request `http://www.apress.com`, the request would be sent to port 80 of the machine on which the web server is running. To specify a different port, let's say port 7100, you would add it to the URL like this: `http://www.apress.com:7100`.

Ports provide an easy way in which a company can limit access to its network resources. A network administrator can simply shut off outside access to all ports other than port 80. This ensures that the only way someone will get in is through the web server. Application servers listen on a port that is typically private to the outside world. The web server is configured to forward specific requests to that particular port. Database servers operate in a similar fashion. The database server may be listening on port 3306 for requests. The application server would then establish a database connection with that port. Figure 1-2 shows this *chaining* of servers through port mappings. It's important to note that each of these servers can be running on the same machine or multiple ones. If they're running on separate machines, then you would need to specify the machine name in front of the port name (machine_name:port).

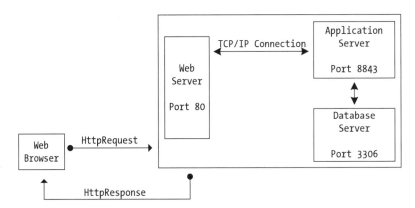

Figure 1-2. Web application architecture

The typical flow of handling a request starts with the browser issuing a request for a specific resource. The web server picks up this request off of port 80 and determines that the application server should handle the request. The application server receives the request and executes some code to handle the request. Within the code, the database may be called by making a connection to whatever port to which the database server is listening. Once a response has been assembled, it's sent back to the browser from where it originated.

Developing J2EE Web Applications

You've seen how HTTP has made it possible for various web servers and web browsers to communicate with each other regardless of the underlying technologies. In a similar fashion, the J2EE specification has made it possible for applications to be deployed in a wide variety of environments with little or no modifications necessary. An application server that is said to be *J2EE compliant* can fulfill a "contract" between the application itself and the services the application server provides. Popular J2EE-compliant application servers are BEA WebLogic and IBM WebSphere. Some open-source options are Enhydra and JBoss.

The J2EE specification defines the use of several services with which a typical enterprise application is concerned. These services include transaction management (JTA), naming services (JNDI), messaging (JMS, JavaMail), distributed object handling (RMI-IIOP), and database management (JDBC). In addition to these services, a J2EE-compliant application server provides both a web container and an Enterprise JavaBean (EJB) container (see Figure 1-3).

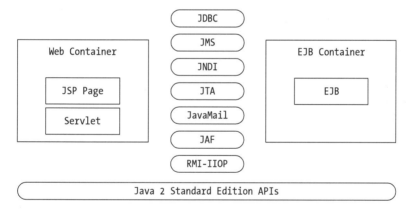

Figure 1-3. J2EE architecture

Understanding Web Containers

A J2EE application server provides a standard container that can handle the execution of both Java Servlets and JSP, along with any services that may be needed by these components. This container is the *web container* because the components within it are responsible for page navigation and presentation.

Java Servlets

A few years ago, there were not many options for delivering dynamic content through the Web. Most people had to write Perl scripts to be used through CGI. Although this approach worked reasonably well, it was not very scalable (a new process is required to service each request). Sun introduced Java Servlets to provide a scalable solution that brought with it the many advantages of the Java platform.

Servlets are nothing more than Java classes that implement the HttpServlet interface of the Java Servlet API. This interface defines a set of lifecycle methods that can be overridden to provide dynamic responses to HTTP requests. A J2EE-compliant application server provides an environment for servlets to reside and handle incoming requests.

The web container can load and manage multiple servlets within the same Java Virtual Machine (JVM). Once a servlet is loaded, it handles each incoming request by spawning a new lightweight thread to perform its task. This enables the application server to service a great number of requests without significant degradation of performance.

JavaServer Pages

The biggest problem with servlets was that they required the Java developer to assemble the HTML-formatted output from within the Java code using a series of `out.println()` statements. This not only created some ugly code, but it also made it difficult to create a decent user interface. If you wanted to use a tool to visually design a page, you needed to copy the HTML into your Java code and wrap the `out.println()` method calls around each line. In short, there was no clear separation between the application code and the user interface. To change one, you invariably changed the other.

JSP was introduced as a way to separate the content from the presentation of the content. A JSP page is typically an HTML page with special tags for including Java code. The page dynamically compiles into a servlet behind the scenes and executes as such. This makes it possible to write pure HTML (and use HTML tools) without regard to the Java code in the page.

There are many ways to further separate content from presentation using both servlets and JSP pages. Chapters 3 and 4 discuss these techniques in depth.

Understanding EJB Containers

In addition to a web container, J2EE-compliant application servers provide an EJB container. The web container will typically communicate with the EJB container to access business logic contained within one or more EJBs. It's often through EJBs that the web container accesses enterprise resources such as databases, message queues, and distributed objects.

EJB containers provide an environment to host EJBs as well as a set of system-level services such as transaction management and security. An EJB makes itself known to its container by publishing a home and remote interface. It's through these interfaces that client objects communicate with the EJB and invoke the business logic contained within them.

Structure of a J2EE Application

All J2EE-compliant applications must follow a specific deployment structure. This structure helps to minimize the differences in deploying an application to different application servers (in other words, WebLogic vs. WebSphere). The directory structure is as follows:

```
app-name (.html & .jsp files, along with any subdirectories required by html)
    web-inf (web application deployment descriptor, web.xml)
        classes (application classes, servlets)
        lib (3rd-party jar files)
        tlds (Tag library descriptors)
```

The web.xml file contains configuration information for the web container to use. For a complete description of this file, see the Java Servlet specification at http://java.sun.com/products/servlet/download.html.

Patterns for Web Application Development

Web applications written in Java typically follow some kind of development pattern, whether or not the developer realizes it. The idea of patterns has its origin in Object-Oriented (OO) programming. A development pattern defines a *best practice* for a common situation. For instance, a common OO pattern, called the *factory pattern*, defines a standard structure for dynamic instantiation of objects that are unknown at compile-time. By using this repeatable pattern, the developer is able to solve their problem with a proven technique.

Although OO patterns define best practices at the language level, web development patterns provide best practices at the system level. When developing Java applications for the Web, there are three basic patterns to follow. Beyond these basic patterns, a series of J2EE patterns have been defined to address many of today's web application issues. These patterns go into greater detail, utilizing much more of the J2EE component set. The J2EE Blueprints are available online at http://java.sun.com/blueprints/ for you to peruse and become familiar with enterprise application development patterns. Later in this book, I'll introduce several presentation patterns as you develop a complete request-handling framework.

Introducing the Servlet Model

The first of these models was the simple servlet model. Not too long ago, this was the only option for developing a server-side Java application. This model is simple in the sense that everything is contained within the servlets. For this same reason, this model is also complex. The servlet, or servlets, contains navigation code, business logic, and presentation code (see Figure 1-4). Although this was a fine solution a few years ago, there are better ways available to us now.

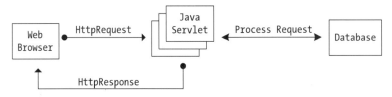

Figure 1-4. Servlet model

Moving to JSP Model 1

The introduction of JSP created a massive shift from the servlet-centric model to a JSP-centric model. Although this may have eased some of the pains relative to servlets, it's still a combination of presentation code, navigation code, and business logic. The developer writes the entire application as a set of JSP pages (see Figure 1-5). The majority of today's JSP-based applications follow this model.

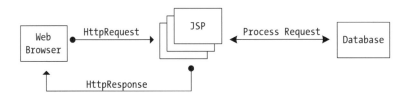

Figure 1-5. JSP model 1

Moving to JSP Model 2

This pattern implements the typical Model-View-Controller (MVC) pattern. In an MVC architecture, a controller handles system navigation, a model stores a set of data, and a view (or multiple views) presents the data stored in the model. This enables you to present a single set of data in multiple formats. For example, the Swing library in Java makes extensive use of the MVC pattern. Visual components separate their data from their presentation. This enables an application to completely change its look-and-feel with a single line of code.

Web applications implement an MVC pattern using a Java servlet for the controller, a JavaBean (or EJB) as its model, and JSP pages as the view (see Figure 1-6). There are many benefits to this pattern. These include better role separation, single point-of-entry, high scalability, and the ability to present content in multiple formats such as HTML or Wireless Markup Language (WML).

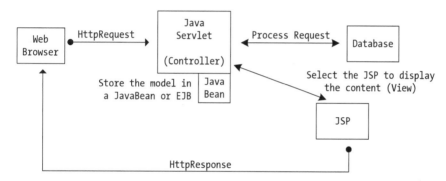

Figure 1-6. JSP model 2

Introducing Enterprise Patterns

The J2EE patterns catalog defines a series of patterns that make full use of the J2EE technology suite to help ease the burden of enterprise application development. These patterns are separated into different sections based on the type of application with which you're concerned. For these purposes, I'll discuss the View patterns in Chapters 5–8. Each of these patterns elaborate on the JSP model 2 pattern previously discussed.

Learning JSP Basics

This section will review the basic foundations of JSP. It should be enough to get you started and enable you to follow along throughout the rest of the book as you dive into more advanced techniques. Those of you who are already skilled JSP developers, feel free to skip ahead to the next section of this book, where I talk about setting up your development and runtime environments.

JSP Processing

Although it's possible to write a working JSP application without any knowledge of the way in which it's processed on the back end, there's so much more you can do once you understand the inner workings of how a JSP page generates a response to a simple request. Without this knowledge, it's nearly impossible to deal with issues such as application management, scalability, and persistence.

 NOTE *Throughout the text, the phrase* JSP page *or* JSP file *refers to a page that will be processed by a J2EE web container conforming to the JavaServer Pages specification. This may seem redundant at first to say* JSP page *if you think of it as* JavaServer Page page. *However, when I use* JSP, *I'm referring to the technology as a whole, not a literal expansion of the abbreviation.*

Let's start with the basics. A JSP page is simply an HTML page that contains special instructions to execute Java code throughout the page. A J2EE web container capable of processing servlets and JSP pages handles the page. The web container has a servlet engine that will go through a series of steps to deliver the results of the JSP page (see Figure 1-7).

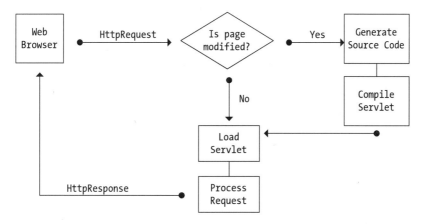

Figure 1-7. JSP processing steps

The first time a JSP page is requested, the servlet engine will read the file and generate source code to create a servlet. The code compiles and the servlet loads. Once loaded, it handles requests in the same manner as any other servlet. The only difference is that each time a request is made of a JSP file, the timestamp of the file is checked against an embedded timestamp in the servlet. If the JSP file is newer, then it has to be compiled into a servlet and reloaded.

This can have performance implications in many situations. For instance, let's say you have a web application that consists of a series of 40 different pages. The first person to use the application would have a horrible experience if they had to sit through the compilation of every page as they navigate their way through the system. Most J2EE web containers allow you to precompile your JSP files to avoid this performance problem. This also helps to alleviate the problem encountered when a page has compiler errors. You certainly would not want the user to see that!

As you can imagine, a JSP page goes through a lifecycle similar to that of a servlet. When it's first loaded, the jspInit() method is called. Once loaded, the _jspService() method is called to generate a response to the request. This method contains the servlet code that will output the HTML along with the results of the Java code contained in the JSP file. Before the servlet (JSP) is unloaded from the web container, the jspDestroy() method is called.

The jspInit() and jspDestroy() methods can be overridden in the declarations section of the JSP page. The _jspService() method cannot explicitly be overridden because it's a system-generated method that corresponds to the body of the JSP page. I discuss this further in the next chapter, but here's a look at how to override the jspInit() and jspDestroy() methods in a JSP page:

```
<%! public void jspInit() {
        // Initialization code (DB initialization, login to resources)
    }
    public void jspDestroy() {
        // Cleanup code (close system resources, cleanup filesystem)
    }
%>
```

Structure of a JSP Page

A JSP page follows a simple structure that makes it easy for the servlet engine to translate the instructions into a corresponding servlet. In addition to HTML (referred to as *template text*), a JSP page consists of directives, declarations, expressions, and scriptlets. Each of these elements can use either standard JSP syntax, or they can be expressed as XML tags. The one caveat, however, is that you cannot intermix the two. The exception to this is that you can use the include mechanism to insert a file that may use a different syntax.

NOTE *I discuss each of these elements, along with a brief code example and the corresponding XML syntax, in the following sections. Keep in mind, however, this is not intended as a thorough examination of basic JSP. I'm only reviewing the basics so you can all have a similar understanding as you move ahead toward more advanced ideas. There are many good books that cover JSP in exhaustive detail. If you're new to JSP, I recommend going through one of these as a supplement to this text.* J2EE Frontend Technologies *by Lennart Jorelid (Apress, 2001) is an excellent guide to JSP technology and Java Servlets.*

Directives

JSP *directives* appear at the top of the page. They contain special processing instructions for the web container. The most common directive, the page directive, contains many different attributes you can set. Here's an example of the page directive:

```
<%@ page import="java.util.Date, java.io.*"
        extends="myJSPpage"
        buffer="32k" autoflush="false" %>
```

This page directive tells the web container to import the java.util.Date class and the java.io package. It also instructs the web container to create the corresponding servlet by extending the myJSPpage class. Other attributes shown here set the buffer to 32k and turn off autoflushing. Here's what this would look like using XML syntax:

```
<jsp:directive.page import="java.util.Date, java.io.* "
                    extends="myJSPpage"
                    buffer="32k" autoflush="false" />
```

Another important directive is the include directive. This enables you to import the contents of another file into your current JSP page. Because this effectively replaces itself with the text of another file, this directive can appear anywhere throughout the page. Here's an example of an include directive (both standard syntax and then XML syntax):

```
<%@ include file="/legal/disclaimer.html">
<jsp:directive.include file="/templates/footer.html" />
```

The other JSP directive worth mentioning here is the taglib directive. This enables you to load and identify a tag library for use throughout the rest of the page. I discuss tag libraries in depth in Chapter 4.

Declarations

Variables and methods can be *declared* using the <%! and %> tags. Anything declared within these tags will be visible to the rest of the page. Think of this as declaring variables at the class level outside of any particular method. This is also where you can override the jspInit() and jspDestroy() methods. Here's an example of a few declarations, followed by the corresponding XML syntax:

```
<%! int balance = 0; %>
<%! public int getAccountBalance() {
        return balance;
    } %>

<jsp:declaration> int balance = 0; </jsp:declaration>
<jsp:declaration>
    public int getAccountBalance() {
        return balance;
    }
</jsp:declaration>
```

Expressions

An *expression* is an instruction to the web container to execute the code within the expression and replace it with the results in the outputted content. Anything placed inside of the <%= and %> tags is first evaluated and then inserted in the final output. What this really does is insert the expression within the output string in the generated servlet. For example, consider the following expression:

```
Hello, my name is <%= getName() %>. How are you?
```

The servlet code will look something like this:

```
out.println("Hello, my name is " + getName() + ". How are you?");
```

This is effective for maintaining continuity within your HTML template text, rather than writing a scriptlet (see the next section) every time you want to retrieve a single value. There are some performance implications with expressions to consider, however. You can see how the generated servlet performs several string concatenations to achieve the desired result. If you were writing the servlet yourself, you'd probably prefer to perform this concatenation using a StringBuffer instead. This would be more efficient than creating several String objects. Keep this in mind as you liberally sprinkle expressions throughout the page and try to think of some alternatives. One such alternative would be to build the entire line inside a scriptlet like this:

```
<%  StringBuffer sb = new StringBuffer();
    sb.append("Hello, my name is "");
    sb.append(getName());
    sb.append(". How are you?");
    out.println(sb.toString());
%>
```

The XML syntax for an expression uses the <jsp:expression></jsp:expression> tags in place of the <%= and %> tags.

Scriptlets

You can use *scriptlets* anywhere in the page. They're fragments of Java code that get inserted into the _jspService() method of the generated servlet. Anything that can be done inside of a servlet can go inside of a scriptlet. To create a scriptlet within your page, surround your Java code with <% and %>. Here's an example of a simple scriptlet followed by its XML equivalent:

```
<%  for (int n=0; n<10; n++) {
        out.println(n);
        out.println("<br>"); // Line break
    }
%>


<jsp:scriptlet>
    for (int n=0; n<10; n++) {
        out.println(n);
        out.println("<br>"); // Line break
    }
</jsp:scriptlet>
```

Setting Up a JSP Environment

You have many different options to choose from when setting up an environment to develop and deploy a JSP application. The important thing to keep in mind is that everything should be J2EE compliant. This will ensure that the web server, application server, and database server will be able to work together to deliver JSP pages, Java Servlets, and Enterprise JavaBeans using Java DataBase Connectivity (JDBC) as a standard protocol to interact with the database.

The environment I chose to use for the development of this book is JBoss for an EJB container, Tomcat for a web container, and MySQL for a database server. Each is a free, production-quality server. You may choose to use something different. As long as it's J2EE compliant, feel free to do so.

Choosing a Development Environment

You can develop JSP applications with nothing more than a simple text editor. However, many tools can ease development tasks significantly. Selecting a tool is really a matter of personal preference, so I'll walk through my development process, and you can decide if it makes sense for you.

When developing a JSP page, I prefer to design the page first using a web authoring tool such as Macromedia Dreamweaver. Whenever the page requires some dynamic data that will be generated from some Java code, I insert some kind of stub. This helps generate a visually appealing page that at least looks like it wasn't built by a programmer. Once the page has been designed, I take the source code and open it up in a code editor such as Macromedia HomeSite. This enables me to insert the appropriate JSP tags and Java code.

For JavaBeans, Servlets, and EJBs, I like to use a Java Integrated Development Environment (IDE). It really doesn't matter which one you use. I prefer to use an open-source development tool called jEdit for all of my Java development. jEdit is highly extensible, allowing you to customize it well beyond what commercial vendors can offer. For more information about jEdit, or to download the tool, visit `http://www.jedit.org`.

Picking an Application Server

You have several options to consider when choosing an application server to host your JSP and servlet applications. The popular commercial vendors are IBM, BEA, and iPlanet. The price tag for these products is quite high because they're intended for large-scale corporate use. It's possible in most cases, though, to obtain a 30-day evaluation copy of each product. I've always been a big fan of BEA WebLogic and recommend it highly to anyone considering an application server for their company.

The alternative to an expensive commercial product is to simply download a free one. I like to use JBoss for hosting EJBs and Tomcat as a web container. It's extremely simple to set up (see the next section), and it performs quite well. Again, the important thing to look for here is J2EE compliance. There are several free, open-source application servers from which to choose.

Setting Up Tomcat

Because this book focuses on JSP and servlet development rather than EJBs, it would be best to simply install the Tomcat server at this point. The Tomcat server is an open-source servlet container available from the Apache-Jakarta project (`http://jakarta.apache.org`). It's the reference implementation for both the Servlet and JSP specifications and, best of all, it's free!

The examples in this book require that the servlet container implement version 2.3 of the servlet specification. Therefore, you will need version 4.0 of Tomcat at a minimum to follow along in later chapters. Once Tomcat has been downloaded and installed, you must configure for use. You do all the configuration in either the startup scripts located in the `\bin` directory or in the `server.xml` file located in the `\conf` directory. At this point, there's no need to modify the startup scripts. To add an application to the server, however, you must first create an appropriate J2EE directory structure underneath the `\webapps` directory and then add a context entry to the `server.xml` file.

In preparation for the examples in this book, you'll need to create the following directory structure underneath the \webapps directory:

```
\tomcat
   \webapps
      \jspBook
         \WEB-INF
            \lib
```

In the \tomcat\conf\server.xml file, add the following context entry:

```
<context path="jspBook"
   docBase="webapps/jspBook"
   crossContext="true"
   debog="0"
   reloadable="true"
   trusted="false"
</context>
```

Now you'll be able to access your JSP files by entering **http://localhost:8080/jspBook/** in the browser window preceding the filename (Tomcat listens to port 8080 by default). You'll be adding files to the \jspBook directory inside of subdirectories for each chapter. For instance, the next example will be customers.jsp and will be stored in the \ch1 subdirectory. To access this file, you would type **http://localhost:8080/jspBook/ch1/customers.jsp**. For further information on setting up and configuring Tomcat, refer to the documentation included with the installation or located at http://jakarta.apache.org.

Selecting a Database

Database Management Systems (DBMS) provide efficient and manageable access to large amounts of application data. The most popular form of a DBMS is a Relational DBMS (RDBMS). A relational database stores and retrieves data using tables tied together with common fields. Another widely used form of a DBMS is an *object* database. An object database stores data as objects, much like you use in your Java programs. This is sometimes more efficient than a relational database because you may need to do some complex joins of relational tables to get the data required for use in your Java code.

For this book, I'll use the relational DBMS called MySQL. It's an open-source database that you can freely download from http://www.mysql.com. When downloading, be sure to get the MySQL server and the MySQL client administration tools. You'll need both to successfully host and manage your database.

Once installed, you'll need to create your database and add some tables. To create a database, go to the command prompt and move to the \mysql\bin directory. Enter the command **mysql** and press Enter. This will take you into an interactive scripting environment where you can issue commands to the database. Now type in **CREATE DATABASE quoting;** to create the database I'll use for these examples. To exit, just type **exit**. Here's a summary of the commands:

```
c:\dev\mysql\bin> mysql
  mysql> CREATE DATABASE quoting;
  mysql> exit
```

To create the necessary tables, along with some test data, type in the following commands using the mysql utility or save it to a file for batch execution. To execute the commands in batch mode, save it to `dbcreate.sql` (use any name you like) and issue the following command:

```
c:\dev\mysql\bin> mysql quoting < dbcreate.sql
```

Here are the commands used to populate the database:

```
DROP TABLE IF EXISTS customer;
CREATE TABLE customer (id int not null, lname varchar(30) not null,
                fname varchar(20), age int, sex char(1),
                married char(1), children int, smoker char(1));
INSERT INTO customer VALUES
        (1, 'Smith', 'Jane', 26, 'F', 'Y', 2, 'N');
INSERT INTO customer VALUES
        (2, 'Doe', 'John', 47, 'M', 'N', 0, 'Y');
INSERT INTO customer VALUES
        (3, 'Johnson', 'Michael', 36, 'M', 'Y', 0, 'N');
INSERT INTO customer VALUES
        (4, 'Brooks', 'Susan', 24, 'F', 'N', 1, 'Y');
INSERT INTO customer VALUES
        (5, 'Inman', 'Bernard', 34, 'M', 'N', 0, 'N');
DROP TABLE IF EXISTS product;
CREATE TABLE product (id int not null, description varchar(75),
                base float, lt30 float, lt50 float, gt50 float,
                m float, f float, married float, children float,
                smoker float);
INSERT INTO product VALUES
        (1, 'Preferred Healthcare', 75.00, 1.0, 1.1, 1.3,
        1.1, 1.2, 1.8, 1.4, 1.2);
INSERT INTO product VALUES
```

```
      (2, 'Premium Healthcare', 65.00, 1.0, 1.1, 1.3,
        1.1, 1.2, 1.8, 1.4, 1.2);
INSERT INTO product VALUES
      (3, 'Value Healthcare', 50.00, 1.0, 1.1, 1.3,
        1.1, 1.2, 1.8, 1.4, 1.2);
DROP TABLE IF EXISTS quote;
CREATE TABLE quote (id int not null, custID int not null,
                prodID int not null, premium decimal(9,2));
```

Now that the database has been created and populated, the only thing left is to obtain a JDBC driver. You will use the JDBC driver to access the database through your Java code in a database-independent manner. You can download the JDBC driver from the MySQL website. Unzip the file and move the mysql_uncomp.jar file to the \tomcat\webapps\jspbook\WEB-INF\lib directory. This will enable your JSP pages to automatically find the driver. All .jar files in a web application's \WEB-INF\lib directory are automatically added to the web application's classpath.

To run the database, simply execute the mysqld command from the \mysql\bin directory. You may also want to run this as a service. Refer to the included documentation for instructions on setting it up as a service. The mysqld program listens for database requests on a specific port. The default port is 3306. This is where I'll establish the JDBC connection.

> **NOTE**   *Any relational database will serve your purposes here. The only requirement is that you obtain the appropriate JDBC driver for whichever database you choose. Some people prefer to use Microsoft Access while learning JSP. To do this, you'll need to use the JDBC:ODBC bridge from Sun Microsystems. The script given here should work with just about any database, but a few vendor-specific modifications may be necessary.*

Building a Simple JSP Application

Throughout the book, you'll be developing pieces of a health insurance quoting system. The intended user of the system is a sales agent looking to issue quotes for personal health insurance. The agent will enter customer information, select an insurance product, and generate a quote based on the customer's age, gender, marital status, number of children, and smoking status.

For the first example, you're going to simply display the customers that have been entered into the system. This will eventually be the main screen for an agent. The idea is that the agent will be able to click on a customer and view existing quotes or generate a new one. For now, you'll simply build the list of customers and the appropriate links required by the application. This example will demonstrate the basic elements of JSP discussed in this chapter. You'll revisit it later to improve upon it significantly.

Designing the Page

The first step when developing a JSP page is to lay out the desired end result. As I said before, I like to use Macromedia Dreamweaver for this. Use whatever tool you like (even a simple text editor) and assemble the HTML that will display your page. Wherever dynamic data is required, put in a stub to be replaced later.

The page should list each customer and include the customer ID, last name, and first name. In addition to that, you need to include actions on each row that enable us to edit the customer, delete the customer, or add a new quote for the customer. You can do this using hyperlinks to another JSP with the appropriate action tagged onto it. In later chapters, you'll see a better way to do this, but this will suffice for now. For a preview of what you should expect of the page, see Figure 1-8.

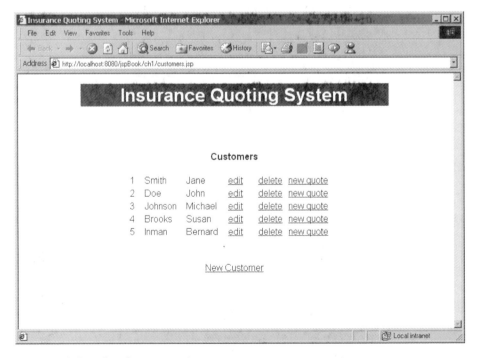

Figure 1-8. Results of `customer.jsp`

Establishing a Database Connection

Now that you have all of the HTML layout complete (referred to as *template text*), you'll move on to editing the source code to include the appropriate JSP tags and code. The first thing you need to add is a page directive to import the java.sql package for the database code:

```
<%@ page import="java.sql.*" %>
```

You'll use a single ResultSet object to hold your database results. Because you'd like this to be available to the entire page, the next thing you do is declare it in a JSP declaration tag:

```
<%! ResultSet rs = null; %>
```

Finally, you establish a connection to the database and retrieve the required data. For now, you handle exceptions by simply outputting them to the system log. I'll discuss better methods for dealing with errors in the next chapter. Notice the connection string for the database. This tells the DriverManager to use JDBC to locate a MySQL database named *quoting* on the current machine listening to port 3306. Once you have a connection, you execute a query to retrieve all records from the customer table and store them in the ResultSet you declared earlier:

```
<%
  try {
    Class.forName("org.gjt.mm.mysql.Driver");
    Connection db = DriverManager.getConnection(
        "jdbc:mysql://localhost:3306/quoting");
    Statement s = db.createStatement();
    rs = s.executeQuery("select * from customer");
  }
  catch (Exception e) {
    // For now, just report the error to the system log
    System.out.println(e.toString());
  }
%>
```

Generating Rows of Customers

Now you need to replace those stubs you created during the page design with JSP expressions to retrieve the appropriate field from the query results. Each customer requires a row inside of an HTML table. You can loop through each customer and generate a new row by enclosing the row definition with a `while()` loop as follows:

```
<%
  try {
    while (rs.next()) {
%>
```

By separating the Java scriptlet from the HTML code, it's easy to generate the HTML layout with an editor or visual tool. You build the row using standard HTML code with JSP expressions providing necessary dynamic content. You then close the loop and handle the SQLException as you did previously:

```
<tr>
    <td width="20"><%= rs.getInt(1) %></td>
    <td width="70"><%= rs.getString(2) %></td>
    <td width="70"><%= rs.getString(3) %></td>
    <td width="40">
      <a href="custMaint.jsp?id=<%= rs.getString(1) %>&action=edit">
        edit
      </a>
    </td>
    <td width="40">
      <a href="custMaint.jsp?id=<%= rs.getString(1) %>&action=delete">
        delete
      </a>
    </td>
    <td width="40">
      <a href="custMaint.jsp?id=<%= rs.getString(1) %>&action=newQuote">
        new quote
      </a>
    </td>
  </tr>

<%
    }
  }
  catch (SQLException e) {
```

```
      // For now, just report the error to the system log
      System.out.println(e.toString());
   }
%>
```

Putting It All Together

Listing 1-1 shows the complete code for your simple application.
Underneath the \tomcat\webapps\jspBook directory, create a \ch1
subdirectory and store the file there as customers.jsp. Start the database
server and the application server. Open a browser window and type in
http://localhost:8080/jspBook/ch1/customers.jsp to view the results (see
Figure 1-8).

Listing 1-1. customers.jsp

```
<!-- JSP Directives -->
<%@ page import="java.sql.*" %>

<html>
<head>
   <title>Insurance Quoting System</title>
</head>

<body>

<basefont face="Arial">

<!-- JSP Declarations -->
<%! ResultSet rs = null; %>

<!-- JSP Scriptlet -->
<%
   try {
     Class.forName("org.gjt.mm.mysql.Driver");
     Connection db = DriverManager.getConnection(
         "jdbc:mysql://localhost:3306/quoting");
     Statement s = db.createStatement();
     rs = s.executeQuery("select * from customer");
   }
   catch (Exception e) {
     // For now, just report the error to the system log
     System.out.println(e.toString());
```

```
      }
%>


<!-- Template text -->
<table width="550" border="0" align="center">
  <tr>
    <td bgcolor="#006633">
      <div align="center">
            <font size="6" color="#FFFFFF">
               <b>Insurance Quoting System</b>
            </font>
      </div>
    </td>
  </tr>
  <tr>
    <td>
      <p> </p>
      <p> </p>
      <p align="center"><b>Customers</b></p>

      <table width="290" border="0" align="center">

<%
  try {
    while (rs.next()) {
%>

<!-- JSP Expressions used within template text -->
      <tr>
        <td width="20"><%= rs.getInt(1) %></td>
        <td width="70"><%= rs.getString(2) %></td>
        <td width="70"><%= rs.getString(3) %></td>
        <td width="40">
          <a href="custMaint.jsp?id=<%= rs.getString(1) %>&action=edit">
            edit
          </a>
        </td>
        <td width="40">
          <a href="custMaint.jsp?id=<%= rs.getString(1) %>&action=delete">
            delete
          </a>
        </td>
        <td width="40">
```

```
            <a href="custMaint.jsp?id=<%= rs.getString(1) %>&action=newQuote">
              new quote
            </a>
          </td>
        </tr>

<%
    }
  }
  catch (SQLException e) {
    // For now, just report the error to the system log
    System.out.println(e.toString());
  }
%>
      </table>
    </td>
  </tr>
  <tr>
    <td>
      <p> </p>
      <p align="center"><a href="custMaint.jsp?action=add">New Customer</a></p>
    </td>
  </tr>
</table>

</body>
</html>
```

Summary

This chapter provided the necessary foundation for developing JavaServer Pages.
Again, this chapter was not intended as a thorough examination of the JSP specification or as a beginner's tutorial. Although it's enough to help you as you
progress through the book, I recommend supplementing this book with a beginner's guide to JSP or at least a book covering the JSP syntax. You might also want
to print out or bookmark the JSP Quick Reference card available from Sun
(http://java.sun.com/products/jsp/technical.html).

   In the next chapter, you'll take a look at some more JSP features and
discuss a few techniques for session handling, page navigation, and improved
error handling.

CHAPTER 2

Using JSP

Now that you know the basic structure of JSP pages and have a general idea of how they operate within a web application, it's time to start building a foundation for handling some common development tasks. This foundation includes error handling, managing persistent data, modularization, page navigation, and form processing. You'll then build upon this foundation throughout the book as you learn to apply J2EE design patterns to handle common situations.

Handling Errors

As you saw in the last chapter, it's easy to wrap up your code into try-catch blocks and never do anything very meaningful when an exception is thrown. Ideally, if the exception can't be recovered from, the error should be reported to a system administrator and the user should be notified of the problem in a more elegant manner than simply displaying the exception message.

If you were to perform these actions every place in your code where an exception could occur, just think of all the code you'd have to write. Let's say that sometime in the future, a change is made to the error notification process. Now, you'll need to search through your entire code base and modify every try-catch block to accommodate the new process. Although you may have created a more robust system by adding sophisticated error handling, you also have created a maintenance nightmare.

Fortunately, JSP has an elegant solution for error handling built in. Many developers never take advantage of this feature and continue to code each exception handler individually. With JSP, you can create a single page that will handle every uncaught exception in your system. If your JSP code throws an exception not handled within a try-catch block, it'll forward the exception, and control, to a page you specify using a JSP page directive.

Creating an Error Page

As previously mentioned, an error page should take an exception, report it to a system administrator, and display a meaningful message to the user. The first thing you need to do, however, is declare that the page to be used is an error page. You do this using the isErrorPage page directive as follows:

```
<%@ page isErrorPage="true" %>
```

When reporting the error, it's sometimes helpful to pass in the name of the page in which the error occurred. As the error is being reported in a shared error page, without this information, the administrator would have a difficult time figuring out where the problem occurred. To retrieve the name of the page, you use the getParameter() method of the request object (more on this in the next section).

```
<% String from = (String) request.getParameter("from"); %>
```

The exception object is another implicit JSP object that does not need to be declared or instantiated. It's only available to those pages that have been designated as error pages. It'll report whatever the uncaught exception was that caused the error page to be called. For your purposes, you'll make use of the toString() method of the exception object. Remember, when using a JSP expression, the toString() method is called implicitly to convert the value of the object to a String. Listing 2-1 shows a simple error page named myError.jsp.

Listing 2-1. myError.jsp

```
<%@ page isErrorPage="true" %>

<html>
<head>
  <title>Error!</title>
</head>

<body>
<br>

<% String from = (String)request.getParameter("from"); %>

An error occurred on page <b><%= from %></b>.

<br><br>
```

```
The exception was:
<br>
<b><%= exception %></b>

<!-- Send exception report to administrator -->
<% System.out.println(exception.toString()); %>

</body>
</html>
```

Forwarding Errors

Now that you've created an error page, you need to code your pages to forward all uncaught exceptions to it. You do this by adding the JSP page directive errorPage. Each page you want to forward errors from needs this directive included. As you'll recall from the previous section, the error page is expecting a parameter named from to determine which page called the error page. Here's a look at the page directive:

```
<%@ page errorPage="myError.jsp?from=customers.jsp" %>
```

Add this directive to your customers.jsp file from Chapter 1 and remove all of the try-catch blocks surrounding the database code. To test it, change the port number from 3306 to 3307. This will trigger a SQLException and forward it to your error page (see Figure 2-1). Listing 2-2 shows what the new customers.jsp file looks like.

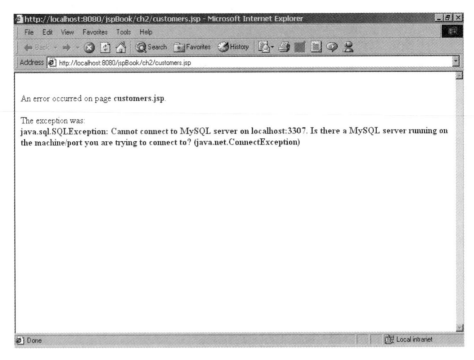

Figure 2-1. Results of customers.jsp *when an exception is thrown*

Listing 2-2. customers.jsp

```
<!-- JSP Directives -->
<%@ page import="java.sql.*"
        errorPage="myError.jsp?from=customers.jsp"
%>

<html>
<head>
    <title>Insurance Quoting System</title>
</head>

<body>

<basefont face="Arial">

<!-- JSP Declarations -->
<%! ResultSet rs = null;%>

<!-- JSP Scriptlet -->
<%
```

```
    Class.forName("org.gjt.mm.mysql.Driver");
    Connection db = DriverManager.getConnection(
        "jdbc:mysql://localhost:3307/quoting");
    Statement s = db.createStatement();
    rs = s.executeQuery("select * from customer");
%>


<!-- Template text -->
<table width="550" border="0" align="center">
    <tr>
        <td bgcolor="#006633">
        <div align="center">
            <font size="6" color="#FFFFFF"><b>Insurance Quoting System</b></font>
        </div>
        </td>
    </tr>
    <tr>
        <td>
            <p> </p>
            <p> </p>
            <p align="center"><b>Customers</b></p>

            <table width="290" border="0" align="center">

<%
    while (rs.next()) {
%>

<!-- JSP Expressions used within template text -->
        <tr>
            <td width="20"><%= rs.getInt(1) %></td>
            <td width="70"><%= rs.getString(2) %></td>
            <td width="70"><%= rs.getString(3) %></td>
            <td width="40">
             <a href="custMaint.jsp?id=<%= rs.getString(1) %>&action=edit">
                edit
             </a>
            </td>
            <td width="40">
             <a href="custMaint.jsp?id=<%= rs.getString(1) %>&action=delete">
                delete
             </a>
            </td>
```

```
          <td width="40">
            <a href="custMaint.jsp?id=<%= rs.getString(1) %>&action=newQuote">
              new quote
            </a>
          </td>
        </tr>

<%
    }
%>
      </table>
    </td>
  </tr>
  <tr>
    <td>
      <p> </p>
      <p align="center"><a href="custMaint.jsp?action=add">New Customer</a></p>
    </td>
  </tr>
</table>

</body>
</html>
```

Including Other Files

In many applications, there are usually at least a few common page elements duplicated in many places. These elements are typically page headers and footers, but they could also include elements such as menus or even a piece of static or dynamic content presented in multiple pages. A problem arises when these common elements are coded separately in multiple places. Not only is this a maintenance nightmare, it also presents the possibility of errors or stale content (if one page gets updated while another does not).

With JSP, you can organize your code so that common elements are stored in single files pulled in to multiple JSP pages. It's a good design practice to put headers, menu bars, and footers in separate files. It helps to standardize the look-and-feel of an application. It also makes it easy to build new pages. The page designer can concentrate on the body of the page without regard to these common elements.

There are two choices for including files inside of a JSP page. You can include a page at compile-time or at runtime. When including a file at compile-time, the file's contents are inserted into the JSP code before it's compiled into a servlet.

When including a file at runtime, the JSP page will not include the file until it has been compiled and receives a request. When the servlet engine reaches the point of the page where the included file is supposed to be, it'll execute the included page (or servlet) and insert the results in the original page (see Figure 2-2).

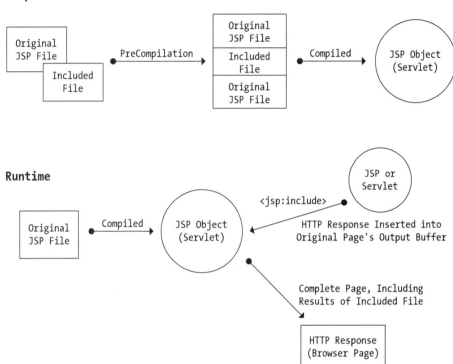

Figure 2-2. Including a file at compile-time vs. runtime

Including Files at Compile-Time

If you want to include a file at compile-time, then you need to use the JSP include directive. This method of including files is generally more efficient and should be used whenever the included file is relatively static and does not change much. Here's what the include directive looks like:

```
<%@ include file="myFile.html" %>
```

As an example, let's build a standard header and footer for the insurance quoting system you started in Chapter 1. The header will consist of a single graphic and some simple HTML content. The footer will simply be a copyright tagline. Listing 2-3 and Listing 2-4 show the code for each of the included files.

Listing 2-3. `myHeader.html`

```
<table border="0" bgcolor="#006600" align=center>
  <tr>
    <td><img src="images/logo.gif"></td>
    <td>
      <font color="#FFFFFF" face="Arial " size="5">
        <b>Insurance Quoting System</b>
      </font>
    </td>
  </tr>
</table>
```

Listing 2-4. `myFooter.html`

```
<center>
    <font face="Arial" size="2">Copyright 2001, AP Enterprises</font>
</center>
```

To use these HTML fragments, you'll modify your previous `customers.jsp` file to now include the standard header and footer (and rename it to `customerList.jsp`). Listing 2-5 shows the code (only the sections that have changed). See Figure 2-3 for a look at the new page.

Listing 2-5. `customerList.jsp`

```
.
.
.

<%@ include file="myHeader.html" %>

<!-- Template text -->
<br><br>
<table width="550" border="0" align="center">
  <tr>
    <td>
      <p align="center"><b>Customers</b></p>
.
.
.

</table>
```

```
<br><br>
<%@ include file="myFooter.html" %>
    .
    .
    .
```

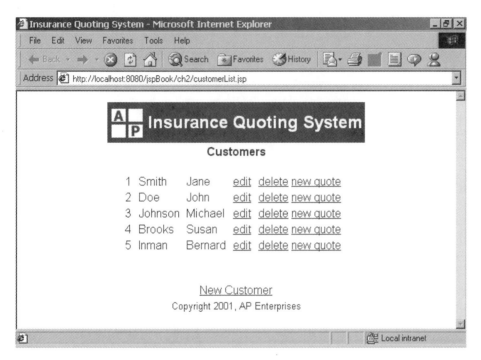

Figure 2-3. Results of customerList.jsp *using included header and footer*

Including Files at Runtime

Sometimes, you may want to include some content that may change more frequently than a static page header. One problem with using the include directive to include frequently changing files is that some servlet engines will fail to recognize when an included file has been modified and will not recompile the JSP. The solution to this problem is to include the file at runtime instead. Here's an example of including a file at runtime:

```
<jsp:include page="myContent.jsp" flush="true"/>
```

The flush attribute tells the servlet engine to flush the output buffer before including the file. Another benefit of including files in this manner is that you can pass parameters to the included page. Here's an example of including a file with parameters:

```
<jsp:include page="conversion.jsp" flush="true">
  <jsp:param name="temperature" value="76"/>
  <jsp:param name="scale" value="celsius"/>
</jsp:include>
```

This will call the conversion.jsp file with the temperature and scale parameters. The output from this page will be inserted in the output from the original JSP page. The only real restriction on including files in this manner is that the included file can't change any of the HTTP headers. This makes sense because the included file is really treated as a separate HTTP request and response, with only the output being inserted into the original JSP.

Processing Form Data

Perhaps the most common trait among web applications is the ability to collect data from the user. You typically do this using an HTML form to collect the data and a server-side program to process the data. In a J2EE web application, the HTML form can be submitted to either a JSP page or a Java servlet. In many cases, it makes sense to combine the HTML form with the JSP page for a single page that both displays the input form and processes the inputted data (see Figure 2-4). One benefit of this approach is that any data validation errors can be displayed and highlighted along with the original form data.

HTML Form to JSP/Servlet Handler

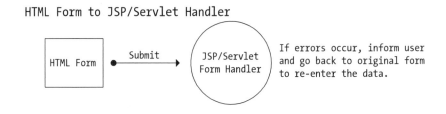

Single JSP to Collect and Process Data

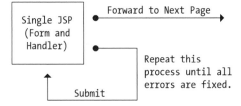

Figure 2-4. Patterns for form handling

Once the user has submitted the form, the JSP that will process the form data needs to first retrieve the data that was entered by the user. You do this through methods on the request object. The request object is an implicit object. It does not need to be declared, obtained, or instantiated. It's the equivalent of the HttpServletRequest object found in servlets. To use methods on the request object, simply call the desired method. As you might have guessed, the methods of the request object are the same as those for the HttpServletRequest object.

The most basic, and most used, method of the request object is the getParameter method. This method takes a single String value as an argument and returns a String containing the value of the requested parameter. For example, if a form contained an input field named last_name, then the code to retrieve the contents of that field would be as follows:

```
<% String lname = request.getParameter("last_name"); %>
```

Some forms contain fields that may have multiple values associated with them. The request object provides the getParameterValues method to return an array of values associated with a single parameter. For instance, a list box containing states in which an insurance agent is licensed could have multiple values returned. This is what that code might look like:

```
<% String states[] = request.getParameterValues("states_licensed_in");
    for (int n = 0; n < states.length; n++) {
        out.println("State: " + states[n]);
    }
%>
```

In some cases, it might not be possible to know all of the field names until runtime. The request object gives us the getParameterNames method. This method will return an enumeration of all of the parameter names that have been passed in to the page through the request object. Here's an example of how to use this method:

```
<% java.util.enumeration pNames = request.getParameterNames();
    while (pNames.hasMoreElements()) {
        String pName = (String) pNames.nextElement();
        out.println(pName + " : " + request.getParameter(pName));
    }
%>
```

It might be helpful at this point to see a complete example using these methods on the request object. Chapter 3 will go through form processing in much greater detail and cover areas such as field validation and the separation of form logic from the presentation of the data. For now, a simple form will illustrate the basic concepts (see Listing 2-6). Figure 2-5 shows what the input form looks like.

Listing 2-6. `simpleForm.html`

```html
<html>
<head>
    <title>Simple Form Example</title>
</head>

<body>

<center>
<form action="simpleForm.jsp">
<table>
    <tr>
        <td>Name: </td>
        <td><input type="Text" name="name"/></td>
    </tr>
    <tr>
        <td>Occupation: </td>
        <td><input type="Text" name="job"/></td>
    </tr>
    <tr>
        <td>Hobbies: </td>
        <td>
            <select name="hobbies" multiple size="5">
                <option value="Sports">Sports</option>
                <option value="Cooking">Cooking</option>
                <option value="Camping">Camping</option>
                <option value="Reading">Reading</option>
                <option value="Music">Music</option>
            </select>
        </td>
    </tr>
</table>

<input type="submit" value="submit"/>

</form>
</center>

</body>
</html>
```

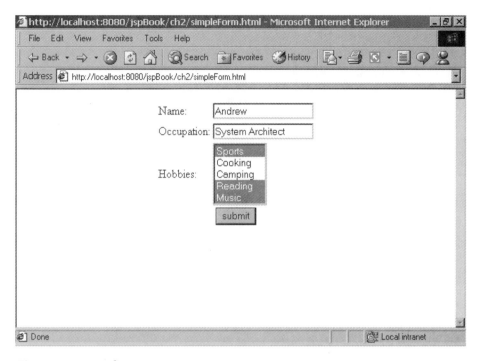

Figure 2-5. Input form

Listing 2-7 retrieves the value of the job field as well as all of the values that have been selected in the hobbies list field. Figure 2-6 shows the results of the form processing.

Listing 2-7. simpleForm.jsp

```
<html>
<head>
    <title>Simple Form Example</title>
</head>

<body>

Hello <%= request.getParameter("name") %>.<br><br>

It must be very interesting being employed as a
  <%= request.getParameter("job") %>.<br><br>

I see you enjoy the following hobbies: <br><br>
<%
    String hobbies[] = request.getParameterValues("hobbies");
```

```
    for (int n = 0; n < hobbies.length; n++) {
%>
    <%= hobbies[n] %> <br>
<%
    }
%>


</body>
</html>
```

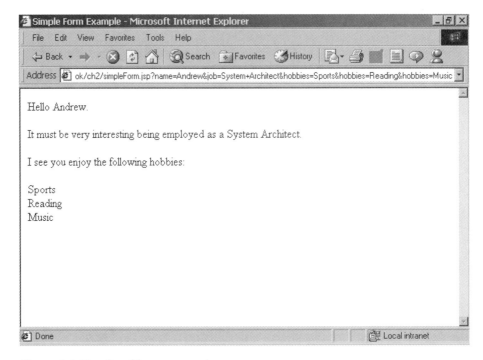

Figure 2-6. Results of form processing

Controlling Page Navigation with JSP

Later in the book, you'll learn about using a controller to examine page requests, assemble the required data, and forward it on to the appropriate JSP page to display the desired content. Chapter 1 first introduced this idea when discussing the JSP Model 2 architecture. This is commonly referred to as a Model-View-Controller architecture (MVC). For now you'll see how you can forward requests from one page to another.

You've seen with the `<jsp:include>` tag that it's possible to interrogate the request object, pass it on to another page for processing, and insert the results inside of your original JSP. A similar tag is the `<jsp:forward>` tag (see Figure 2-7). The big difference between the two is that the forward tag never returns to the original page. It simply enables you to perform some processing with the request object and pass it on to another page. These tags are the JSP equivalent of the `RequestDispatcher` interface used in servlets to pass control from one servlet to another.

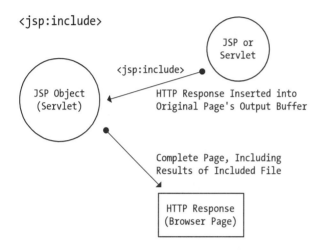

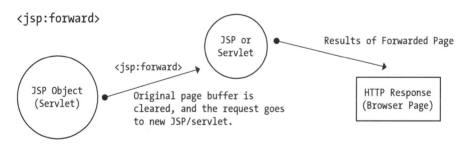

Figure 2-7. Forward vs. include tags

One thing to consider when using the forward tag is that when a request is forwarded to another JSP or servlet, the current output buffer is cleared. Whatever may have been written to the output stream prior to the forward tag will be ignored. Here's an example of how the forward tag might look:

```
<jsp:forward page="finalPage.jsp">
    <jsp:param name="param1" value="10"/>
</jsp:forward>
```

Maintaining State

Chapter 1 discussed how HTTP is a static protocol. It has no built-in functionality to persist data from one request to another. Once one request has been processed, the server picks up the next request with no prior knowledge of the first request. Although this may provide performance benefits, it also presents a problem with most web applications. Specifically, how can one part of the application make use of previously entered data?

Well, the obvious answer to this question is to store the data in a database at the time it's collected and simply retrieve it as necessary. This solution is not practical, however. It makes sense to store application data in a database but not presentation data. Presentation data is the kind of information required throughout a user session to properly configure the user interface. This data includes information such as user preferences, security information, and temporary data used to build a set of continuous screens. If this kind of information were stored in a database, each page would be required to retrieve the data through a database connection. This could be costly to the overall performance of the application.

JSP technology provides access to a session object for you to store and retrieve keyed values at any given time a user is interacting with the application. This session object is unique to each specific user and is managed by the servlet container within the application server. The first time a user requests a JSP page, the session is created on the server. This session has a session ID associated with it. This ID is passed back and forth between the server and the user through an HTTP cookie. Each time the user requests a JSP page, the session ID is passed along and therefore the appropriate session is associated with the user (see Figure 2-8).

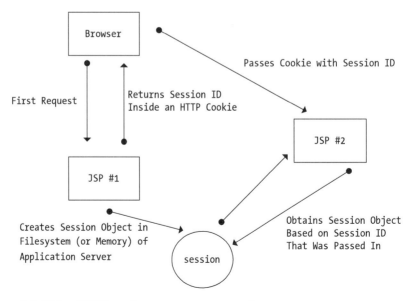

Figure 2-8. Using HTTP sessions to manage user data

The session object is analogous to the HttpSession object used by servlets. The only real difference is that the session object in a JSP is typically implicitly obtained and prepared for use. However, some JSP environments might not automatically create the session for you. In that case, you need to obtain the session by calling the getSession method of the request object. This will return an instance of HttpSession. The only argument to this method is a boolean value indicating whether to create a new session if one doesn't already exist. This is an example of getting the session manually:

```
<% HttpSession session = request.getSession(true); %>
```

Once you have a session (in most cases it'll be an implicit object), it's possible to write, retrieve, and remove attributes from the session object. These attributes are stored in much the same fashion as a hashtable. Each value is associated with a named key. To write an attribute to the session, you would use the setAttribute method as follows:

```
<% session.setAttribute("firstName", "Christina"); %>
```

The first argument is the attribute name. The second argument is the value of the attribute. This can be any valid Java object. In this case it's a String object. To retrieve this value, you would use the getAttribute method.

```
<% String fName = (String) session.getAttribute("firstName"); %>
```

Notice how you cast the result of this method to String. This is necessary because the session only stores an object and returns an object without regard to the type of object it's storing. To remove this attribute, you would use the removeAttribute method.

```
<% session.removeAttribute("firstName"); %>
```

Each of these methods can throw an IllegalStateException. This will occur if any of these methods are called on an invalid session. A session will become invalid if the servlet has timed it out. The session timeout property is configurable inside the servlet engine.

As an example, let's build a simple form that accepts a single field containing a person's name. You'll submit this form to a JSP page that will store the name in the session and then present the user with two simple hyperlinks to other JSP pages. Once the user goes to one of these pages, the name will be retrieved from the session and a personalized message will appear. Listing 2-8 shows the HTML form.

Listing 2-8. `sessionExample.html`

```
<html>
<head>
    <title>Session Example</title>
</head>

<body>

<center>
<h1>Session Example</h1>
<form action="sessionExample.jsp">
    What is your name? <input type="Text" name="name"/><br><br>
    <input type="Submit" value="submit"/>
</form>
</center>

</body>
</html>
```

Next, code the page that will write the session attribute and display the hyperlinks (see Listing 2-9).

Listing 2-9. `sessionExample.jsp`

```
<html>
<head>
    <title>Session Example</title>
</head>

<body>

<%
    String val = request.getParameter("name");
    if (val != null)
        session.setAttribute("name", val);
%>

<center>
<h1>Session Example</h1>

Where would you like to go?<br><br>

<a href="sessionExamplePage1.jsp">Page 1</a>
<a href="sessionExamplePage2.jsp">Page 2</a>
```

```
</body>
</html>
```

Listing 2-10 and Listing 2-11 show the two pages referenced in the sessionExample.jsp file.

Listing 2-10. sessionExamplePage1.jsp

```
<html>
<head>
    <title>Session Example</title>
</head>

<body>

<center>
<h1>Session Example</h1>

Hello, <%= session.getAttribute("name") %>. Welcome to Page 1!

</body>
</html>
```

Listing 2-11. sessionExamplePage2.jsp

```
<html>
<head>
    <title>Session Example</title>
</head>

<body>

<center>
<h1>Session Example</h1>

Hello, <%= session.getAttribute("name") %>. Welcome to Page 2!

</body>
</html>
```

Figure 2-9 shows the session in action as it's used to retrieve the username entered in a previous screen.

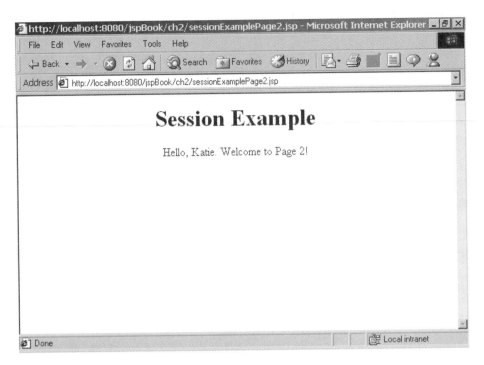

Figure 2-9. Session example

Summary

A major problem with most JSP applications is that they tend to start out as small projects, or research and development efforts, and eventually grow out of control until they're extremely difficult to maintain. This may improve, with time, as developers mature and JSP becomes a more mainstream technology. The most important step anyone can take right now to improve their JSP development projects is to focus on building a solid framework with an emphasis on good design.

This chapter presented a few concepts required to build a good foundation for most JSP applications. Error handling, session management, form processing, modularization, and navigation are fundamental components of any web application. These will help to form the building blocks of a good framework. The next chapter begins the discussion of role separation. You'll learn how to use JavaBeans and custom tag extensions to organize your code as well as hide the complexities of Java from the web page designer.

CHAPTER 3

Role Separation
with JavaBeans

As PROGRAMMERS, DESIGNING WEB PAGES is not our forte. Although some of us may have modest design skills, web pages are much better left to those who make a living out of designing eye-popping, user-friendly, browser-independent websites. On the other hand, most good web designers have little, if any, programming skills. Therefore, how can you expect to build good web applications that not only function well but have an appealing interface, too?

The answer is to separate the layers between content generation (programmer) and content presentation (page designer). The idea is to be able to provide a page designer with a clean interface to the application, enabling them to design the pages separately from the application code. They would then plug in the necessary hooks to provide dynamic content to their beautifully designed pages. I know that this sounds too ideal to be practical, but it's possible to take steps toward this *role separation*. The more the programmer can hide the application code from the page itself, the better chance there is of producing a clean presentation layer.

This chapter will present the use of JavaBeans within JSP. This approach does a good job of hiding a lot of application code inside of a JavaBean and then exposing it through a predefined set of JSP tags. You'll not only learn how to use JavaBeans inside your JSP pages, but you'll also see how to use JavaBeans to solve some common application problems. Using JavaBeans to organize your code is a very good idea, and it takes us one step closer to achieving role separation. The next chapter will present the use of custom tag extensions to achieve role separation. You'll see in later chapters how you apply each of these techniques to various design patterns.

Introducing JavaBeans

JavaBeans are simple Java classes that provide a set of properties and accessor methods for those properties. They implement the Serializable interface so they can be serialized by their container. This makes it possible for the servlet container to capture the current state of the bean and then reconstruct it at some point in the future. JavaBeans may also include a set of custom methods to perform operations on the data they contain. Initially, JavaBeans were introduced to provide IDEs with a standard set of visual components that could simply be dropped onto a page. Now, developers use them mostly as non-visual components that hide application data and the operations performed on that data.

JSP provides a set of useful tags for dealing with JavaBeans. Although you can use JavaBeans from within an ordinary scriptlet, these tags enable the page designer to access bean properties without messing around with Java code. JavaBeans play an important role in a Model-View-Controller (MVC) architecture. They typically store the model, or data, of an application. While the controller is responsible for updating the model, the page only needs to read the data out of the model to present the view (see Figure 3-1). You can accomplish this through JavaBeans and the JSP tags used to access JavaBeans.

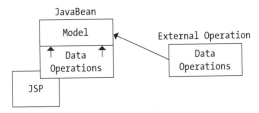

The JSP page presents the data contained in the model. The model is updated either by its own bean or an external operation.

Figure 3-1. JavaBeans and JSP

Building a JavaBean

Later in the chapter, you'll build some useful beans that employ the technology to handle some common development tasks. For the purposes of illustrating the mechanics of building a bean and using it in a JSP page, for now you'll build a simple bean with two properties and a single method. Our bean will contain properties for first and last name, accessor methods for those properties, and a method to display a personalized welcome message. Listing 3-1 shows the code for our simple bean.

Listing 3-1. `SimpleBean.java`

```java
package jspbook.ch3;

public class SimpleBean implements java.io.Serializable {

  /* Member Variables */
  private String lname;
  private String fname;

  public SimpleBean() {
    /* Initialize bean properties */
    setLname("");
    setFname("");
  }

  /* Accessor Methods */
  public String getLname() {
    return lname;
  }
  public void setLname(String _lname) {
    lname = _lname;
  }
  public String getFname() {
    return fname;
  }
  public void setFname(String _fname) {
    fname = _fname;
  }

  /* Display personalized message */
  public String welcomeMsg() {
    return "Hello " + fname + " " + lname +
      ", welcome to the wonderful world of JavaBeans!";
  }
}
```

Using a JavaBean in a JSP Page

You can access a JavaBean within a JSP page either through a scriptlet or by using a special set of JSP tags. Either way, before using a JavaBean you must first declare it and initialize it for use. You do this through the <jsp:usebean> tag. Here's how this tag might look for our simple bean:

```
<jsp:useBean id="simpleBean" scope="page" class="jspbook.ch3.SimpleBean"/>
```

The id attribute gives the bean a name that you can use to reference the bean throughout the JSP page. The class attribute specifies the actual name of the bean class. In this case, it's jspbook.ch3.SimpleBean. The web container will look for this package structure and class in either the respective application's \WEB-INF\classes directory or in a JAR file located in the \WEB-INF\lib directory.

The scope attribute defines the life of this bean. Valid options for this attribute are page, session, request, and application. The page scope attribute tells the web container that this bean will remain for the life of this particular page. As soon as the page is done executing, the bean disappears. If the bean has a scope of request, and then it gets stored in the request object and passed along through the life of the request. In other words, if the page is forwarded to another page, then the bean can be obtained through the request object. The session scope attribute tells the web container to store the bean in the user's session object. It'll remain available throughout the life of that specific session. To make a bean available to other JSP pages or Servlets, use the application scope attribute. This will store the bean in the ServletContext object.

Accessing Bean Properties

You can set and retrieve the properties of a JavaBean using the <jsp:setProperty> and <jsp:getProperty> tags, respectively. This will only work if your JavaBean has a set of accessor methods (getXxx and setXxx) for each property. For more information about JavaBeans and naming conventions, see the documentation at Sun's Java website (http://java.sun.com/docs/index.html). To set a property you could do it either of two ways. You'll use the simpleBean as an example:

```
<jsp:setProperty name="simpleBean" property="fname" value="Andrew"/>
<jsp:setProperty name="simpleBean" property="fname" param="fname"/>
```

The first tag sets the value of the fname property of the simpleBean JavaBean class. It does this by explicitly setting the value within the tag. Another option, as seen in the second tag, is to have the property set automatically from the request parameters. The `param` attribute tells the bean which request parameter populates the respective property. You can only use either the `param` attribute or the `value` attribute. They cannot coexist within a single tag.

To get a bean property, you would use the `<jsp:getProperty>` tag like this:

```
<jsp:getProperty name="simpleBean" property="fname"/>
```

When setting and getting properties from a JavaBean, type conversions are automatically performed for all of the Java primitive datatypes and their corresponding wrapper classes (see Table 3-1). This makes it possible to set numeric properties directly from String variables. It also enables the `<jsp:getProperty>` to return a valid String to be inserted into the HTML content.

Table 3-1. Conversion of Datatypes within JavaBeans

PROPERTY	CONVERTED USING THIS METHOD
boolean, Boolean	java.lang.Boolean.valueOf(String)
byte, Byte	java.lang.Byte.valueOf(String)
char, Character	java.lang.String.charAt(0)
double, Double	java.lang.Double.valueOf(String)
integer, Integer	java.lang.Integer.valueOf(String)
float, Float	java.lang.Float.valueOf(String)
long, Long	java.lang.Long.valueOf(String)
short, Short	java.lang.Short.valueOf(String)

Listing 3-2 contains a simple example illustrating the use of our `SimpleBean` class.

Listing 3-2. `hello.jsp`

```
<!-- JSP Directives -->
<%@ page
    errorPage="myError.jsp?from=hello.jsp"
%>

<html>
<head>
  <title>Hello</title>
</head>

<body>
```

```
<basefont face="Arial">

<jsp:useBean id="simpleBean" scope="session" class="jspbook.ch3.SimpleBean"/>

<!-- Set bean properties -->
<jsp:setProperty name="simpleBean" property="fname" value="Andrew"/>
<jsp:setProperty name="simpleBean" property="lname" value="Patzer"/>

<!-- Display welcome message -->
<center>
  <b><%= simpleBean.welcomeMsg() %></b>
</center>
</body>
</html>
```

Figure 3-2 shows the results of using the SimpleBean class to retrieve a welcome message and display it in a JSP page.

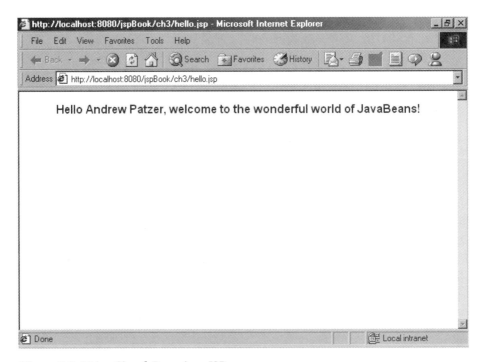

Figure 3-2. Using SimpleBean in a JSP page

Dealing with Large Sets of Data

Now that you know the basics of using JavaBeans in JSP, it's time to tackle some common web application issues with JavaBeans. Remember, the goal of using JavaBeans in our JSP page is to hide cumbersome application code and provide a clean interface for the page designer to use. The first issue you're going to deal with is that of handling large sets of data within a single page. This problem arises when a user displays a list of items that contains a large set of database records. It's not a good design practice to display 200 records on a single page and expect the user to scroll down the page to view all the records.

A few obvious solutions to this problem include setting limits on search parameters or even truncating the result list. A more ideal solution would be to initially retrieve all of the records into some sort of cache (see Figure 3-3). Each page would then consist of a small set of records along with navigational controls to move the user backward and forward through the results. Each subsequent page request would grab the appropriate set of records from the cache and display them along with links to view the previous set of records or the next set of records.

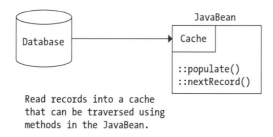

Figure 3-3. Handling large sets of data

Creating the Solution

Our solution to this problem is to create a JavaBean that will maintain a cache of records and provide the methods necessary to move through the records and update the model (individual record represented by the bean) as needed (see Figure 3-4). To illustrate this solution, you'll build a JavaBean that represents a row of data from a product table in a database we'll call catalog.

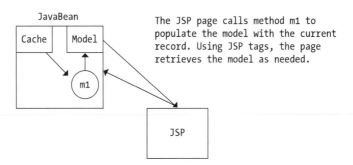

The JSP page calls method m1 to populate the model with the current record. Using JSP tags, the page retrieves the model as needed.

Figure 3-4. Caching data with a JavaBean

Setting Up the Database

To set up the database, first create the catalog database and then run the script in Listing 3-3 to add the records using this:

```
c:\mysql catalog <  createProducts.sql
```

Listing 3-3. createProducts.sql

```
DROP TABLE IF EXISTS product;
CREATE TABLE product (id varchar(10) not null, description varchar(30),
                      manuf varchar(30), price float);
INSERT INTO product VALUES
    ('p001', 'Product 1', 'ABC Manufacturing Co.', 75.00);
INSERT INTO product VALUES
    ('p002', 'Product 2', 'ABC Manufacturing Co.', 33.00);
INSERT INTO product VALUES
    ('p003', 'Product 3', 'ABC Manufacturing Co.', 26.00);
.
. {repeat this to create around 30 unique records}
.
INSERT INTO product VALUES
    ('p033', 'Product 33', 'ABC Manufacturing Co.', 25.00);
```

Creating the Bean and Its Properties

You'll create a JavaBean called ProductBean that'll hold a cache of product records and provide navigational controls to scroll back and forth through the record cache. The first thing you need to do is declare the class and be sure it implements the Serializable interface:

```
public class ProductBean implements java.io.Serializable
```

The bean properties will consist of each of the fields in the product table. The product table contains a product ID, product description, manufacturer, and price. These fields need to be declared like this:

```
private String prodID;
private String prodDesc;
private String prodManuf;
private float prodPrice;
```

The next step is to provide accessor methods for each of these. These are the getter and setter methods that make it possible to access bean properties through the <jsp:getProperty> and <jsp:setProperty> tags. Here's what one set of accessor methods looks like:

```
public String getProdID() {
  return prodID;
}

public void setProdID(String _prodID) {
  prodID = _prodID;
}
```

The final step is to initialize these properties. You do this in the constructor by calling the setter method for each individual property. In this case, you just initialize each property to either blank or zero. Here's what this looks like inside of our constructor:

```
setProdID("");
setProdDesc("");
setProdManuf("");
setProdPrice(0.00f);
```

Connecting to the Database

You'd like to hide the details of interacting with the database inside of the bean itself. A more sophisticated solution would obtain a connection from a pool of database connections, rather than create a new connection for every instance of the bean. For the purposes of our example, however, you'll just create a connection for the life of bean. As you'll see later on, the bean will remain in memory for the entire session, so our database operations will be minimal. Here's the code for connecting to the database, which is called once in the constructor for the bean:

```
private void dbConnect() {
  if (db == null) {
    try {
      Class.forName("org.gjt.mm.mysql.Driver");
      db = DriverManager.getConnection("jdbc:mysql://localhost:3306/catalog");
    }
    catch (Exception e) {
      System.out.println("Error Connecting to catalog DB: " + e.toString());
    }
  }
}
```

Populating the Cache

You can implement a data cache within your bean in a few different ways. You'll use an ArrayList object for each of the bean properties that you'll be populating. Once you execute the query, the results are looped through and each column value is added to the appropriate ArrayList. You also want to be sure this is only done once, so before doing anything you check if one of the ArrayLists has already been populated:

```
public boolean populate() {
  /* If prodIDList is empty, then execute the query to populate it */
  if (prodIDList.isEmpty()) {
    try {
      /* Execute Query */
      Statement s = db.createStatement();
      ResultSet rs = s.executeQuery("select * from product");

      prodIDList.clear();
      prodDescList.clear();
      prodManufList.clear();
      prodPriceList.clear();

      rowCount = 0;
      while (rs.next()) {
```

```
            prodIDList.add(rs.getString("id"));
            prodDescList.add(rs.getString("description"));
            prodManufList.add(rs.getString("manuf"));
            prodPriceList.add((new Float(rs.getFloat("price"))));
            rowCount++;
        }
    }
    catch (Exception e) {
        System.out.println("Error populating ProductBean: "
          + e.toString());
        return false;
    }
}


    /* Return status of operation (assume success if it made it this far) */
    return true;
}
```

Refreshing the Model

In our JSP page, to advance to the next record you simply need to call the following method and retrieve the current set of bean properties. This method checks if the current row pointer is valid (not past the end of the record set), calls the setter methods for each of the properties using the ArrayLists to populate them, and finally increments the row pointer and returns it to the calling JSP:

```
public int nextRow() {

    if (currentRow == rowCount) {
      currentRow = 0; // Reset for next page request
      return 0; // return 0 to indicate end of recordset
    }

    /* Populate bean properties with current row */
    setProdID((String)prodIDList.get(currentRow));
    setProdDesc((String)prodDescList.get(currentRow));
    setProdManuf((String)prodManufList.get(currentRow));
    Float price = (Float)prodPriceList.get(currentRow);
    setProdPrice(price.floatValue());

    currentRow++;
```

```
      /* return currentRow*/
      return currentRow;
  }
```

Listing 3-4 shows the complete code for ProductBean.java.

Listing 3-4. ProductBean.java

```
package jspbook.ch3;

import java.util.*;
import java.sql.*;

public class ProductBean implements java.io.Serializable {

  /* Member Variables */
  private String prodID;
  private String prodDesc;
  private String prodManuf;
  private float prodPrice;

  /* ArrayLists to hold recordsets */
  private List prodIDList, prodDescList, prodManufList, prodPriceList;

  /* Helper Variables */
  private int currentRow;
  private int rowCount;

  private Connection db = null;

  /* Constructor */
  public ProductBean() {

    /* Initialize bean properties */
    setProdID("");
    setProdDesc("");
    setProdManuf("");
    setProdPrice(0.00f);

    /* Initialize arrayLists to hold recordsets */
    prodIDList = new ArrayList();
    prodDescList = new ArrayList();
    prodManufList = new ArrayList();
    prodPriceList = new ArrayList();
```

```java
    /* Initialize helper variables */
    currentRow = 0;
    rowCount = 0;

    /* Get database connection */
    dbConnect();

}

/* Get Database Connection */
private void dbConnect() {

    if (db == null) {
        try {
            Class.forName("org.gjt.mm.mysql.Driver");
            db = DriverManager.getConnection("jdbc:mysql://localhost:3306/catalog");
        }
        catch (Exception e) {
            System.out.println("Error Connecting to catalog DB: " + e.toString());
        }
    }

}

/* Accessor Methods */
public String getProdID() {
    return prodID;
}

public void setProdID(String _prodID) {
    prodID = _prodID;
}

public String getProdDesc() {
    return prodDesc;
}

public void setProdDesc(String _prodDesc) {
    prodDesc = _prodDesc;
}

public String getProdManuf() {
    return prodManuf;
}
```

```
public void setProdManuf(String _prodManuf) {
  prodManuf = _prodManuf;
}


public float getProdPrice() {
  return prodPrice;
}


public void setProdPrice(float _prodPrice) {
  prodPrice = _prodPrice;
}


/* Read-only attribute */
public int getCurrentRow() {
  return currentRow;
}


/* Populate Record List */
public boolean populate() {

  /* If prodIDList is empty, then execute the query to populate it */
  if (prodIDList.isEmpty()) {
    try {
      /* Execute Query */
      Statement s = db.createStatement();
      ResultSet rs = s.executeQuery("select * from product");

      prodIDList.clear();
      prodDescList.clear();
      prodManufList.clear();
      prodPriceList.clear();

      rowCount = 0;
      while (rs.next()) {
        prodIDList.add(rs.getString("id"));
        prodDescList.add(rs.getString("description"));
        prodManufList.add(rs.getString("manuf"));
        prodPriceList.add((new Float(rs.getFloat("price"))));
        rowCount++;
      }
    }
```

```
      catch (Exception e) {
        System.out.println("Error populating productBean: " + e.toString());
        return false;
      }
    }

    /* Return status of operation (assume success if it made it this far) */
    return true;
  }

  /* Reset current row */
  public void setStartRow(int _start) {
    if (_start < rowCount) {
      currentRow = _start;
    }
  }

  /* Move to next row */
  public int nextRow() {

    if (currentRow == rowCount) {
      currentRow = 0; // Reset for next page request
      return 0; // return 0 to indicate end of recordset
    }

    /* Populate bean properties with current row */
    setProdID((String)prodIDList.get(currentRow));

    setProdDesc((String)prodDescList.get(currentRow));

    setProdManuf((String)prodManufList.get(currentRow));

    Float price = (Float)prodPriceList.get(currentRow);
    setProdPrice(price.floatValue());

    currentRow++;

    /* return currentRow*/
    return currentRow;
  }

}
```

Showing an Example

To use the ProductBean, the page designer will need to have an interface definition with some instructions of how to use it. In this case, the page designer will need to do some programming to cycle through the records, but it's still far less programming than would be required without the bean. In the next chapter, you'll revisit this example and attempt to further separate roles through custom tag extensions. For now, though, let's put together a JSP page that uses the bean.

Declaring the Bean

Our first step is to declare and initialize the bean for use within the page as follows:

```
<jsp:useBean id="pBean" scope="session" class="jspbook.ch3.ProductBean"/>
```

The important thing to point out here is the scope of the bean. You'll be reloading this page numerous times to cycle through the record cache, so you'd like the bean to remain throughout our session. Therefore, you set the scope to be session.

Populating the Cache

Before cycling through the records, the record cache needs to be populated. You do this through a call to the populate method of the bean. Next, the starting position is set. This is grabbed from the request parameters and set using the setStartRow method of the bean. If the start parameter does not exist, then the bean will assume zero and start at the beginning of the record cache:

```
if (pBean.populate()) {

    String start = (String) request.getParameter("start");
    if (start != null) {
        startRow = new Integer(start).intValue();
        pBean.setStartRow(startRow);
    }
```

Building the Table

To build the table, you create a loop that will advance the record pointer and refresh the bean properties for a given number of times (in this case, ten times). You obtain the bean properties using the `<jsp:getProperty>` tag and present them inside of a table column:

```
    while (rowCount < 10 && pBean.nextRow() > 0) {
        rowCount++;
%>

    <tr>
        <td width="20%"><jsp:getProperty name="pBean" property="prodID"/></td>
        <td width="30%"><jsp:getProperty name="pBean" property="prodDesc"/></td>
        <td width="30%"><jsp:getProperty name="pBean" property="prodManuf"/></td>
        <td width="20%"><jsp:getProperty name="pBean" property="prodPrice"/></td>
    </tr>

<%
    }
```

Creating Navigational Links

Finally, you create and display the Back and Next links below the set of records. You create a link to the same page and set the start parameter to either the current row (for the Next link), or ten rows back to display the previous ten records:

```
    <tr>
        <td colspan="2" align="center">
            <br><a href="?start=<%= (startRow > 9) ? startRow - 10 : 0%>">Back</a>
        </td>
        <td colspan="2" align="center">
            <br><a href="?start=<%= pBean.getCurrentRow() %>">Next</a>
        </td>
    </tr>
```

Listing 3-5 shows a complete code listing for `productList.jsp`.

Listing 3-5. `productList.jsp`

```
<!-- JSP Directives -->
<%@ page
        errorPage="myError.jsp?from=productList.jsp"
%>

<html>
<head>
    <title>Product List</title>
</head>

<body>

<basefont face="Arial">

<jsp:useBean id="pBean" scope="session" class="jspbook.ch3.ProductBean"/>

<!-- Build table of products -->

<table align="center" width="600">

    <tr>
        <td width="20%"><b>Product ID</b></td>
        <td width="30%"><b>Description</b></td>
        <td width="30%"><b>Manufacturer</b></td>
        <td width="20%"><b>Price</b></td>
    </tr>

<%
    int rowCount = 0;
    int startRow = 0;

    if (pBean.populate()) {

        String start = (String) request.getParameter("start");
        if (start != null) {
            startRow = new Integer(start).intValue();
            pBean.setStartRow(startRow);
        }
```

```
        while (rowCount < 10 && pBean.nextRow() > 0) {
            rowCount++;
%>


    <tr>
        <td width="20%"><jsp:getProperty name="pBean" property="prodID"/></td>
        <td width="30%"><jsp:getProperty name="pBean" property="prodDesc"/></td>
        <td width="30%"><jsp:getProperty name="pBean" property="prodManuf"/></td>
        <td width="20%"><jsp:getProperty name="pBean" property="prodPrice"/></td>
    </tr>

<%

        }
    }
%>


    <!-- Display the back and next links -->
    <tr>
        <td colspan="2" align="center">
            <br><a href="?start=<%= (startRow > 9) ? startRow - 10 : 0%>">Back</a>
        </td>
        <td colspan="2" align="center">
            <br><a href="?start=<%= pBean.getCurrentRow() %>">Next</a>
        </td>
    </tr>

</table>

</body>
</html>
```

To run this example, place the ProductBean class inside the
\WEB-INF\classes directory and the productList.jsp file in the application root
folder under a \ch3 subdirectory. Figure 3-5 shows the results of paging through
a set of records from the product table using the ProductBean class.

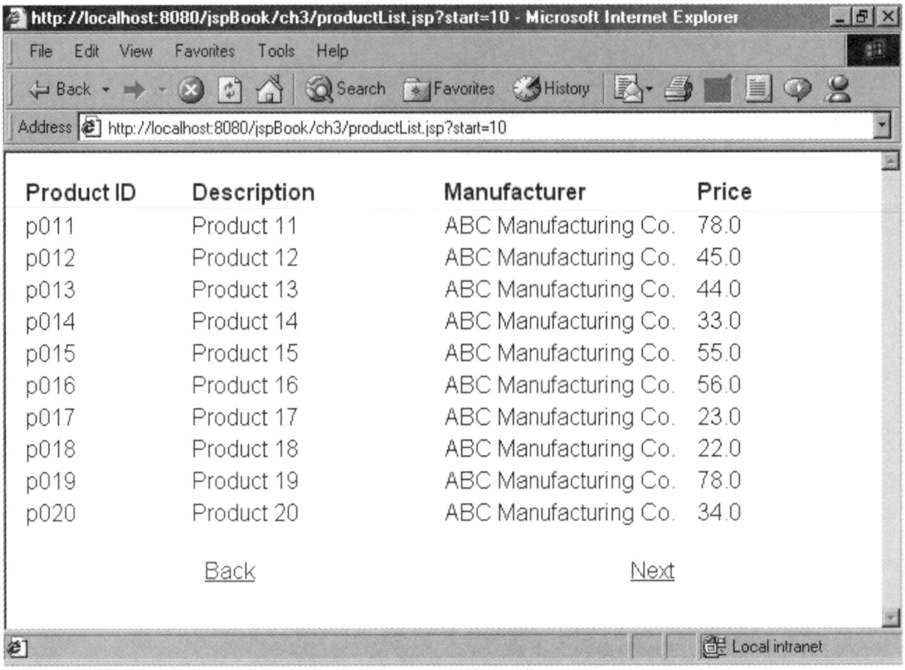

Figure 3-5. Paging large sets of data

Standardizing Form Handling

Perhaps the biggest pitfall of most web applications is their inability to provide a consistent and clean process for accepting form data and reporting errors in the contents of the form back to the user. Most developers begin their efforts with good intentions, but without a standard piece of framework code, it becomes difficult to accept and validate the data in a manner consistent with the rest of the application.

As you may have guessed, you're going to assemble a JavaBean that provides data validation and error reporting. This solution is more of a way to standardize a common task rather than an attempt at role separation, although it does provide somewhat of a clean break between page designer and programmer. As with the previous example, the page designer will need to insert some basic JSP code to make proper use of the JavaBean.

Creating the Solution

You can accomplish a good form-handling solution by separating the data (model) from the page (view). The page is responsible for interacting with the model to validate and submit the page data and then present the results to the user. The page, in our case, is a JSP page. You implement the model as a JavaBean. Overall, the interactions between the page and the bean are responsible for the following:

- Persisting the form data in a temporary model

- Validating the model

- Returning errors to the user

- Highlighting individual fields that are in error

- Upon successful validation, committing the data to the database

- Returning the status of the operation to the user

Figure 3-6 shows a flow chart of these activities.

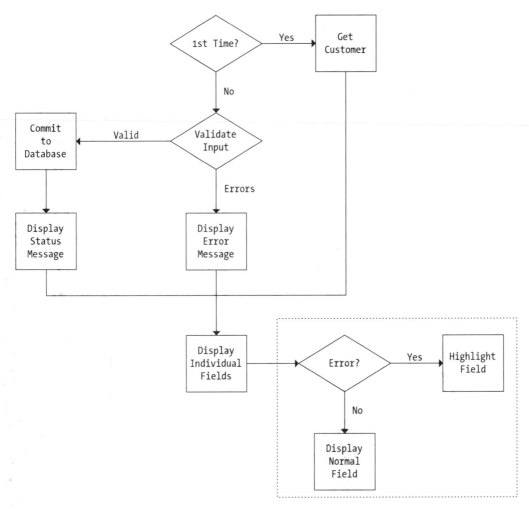

Figure 3-6. Steps required to process form data

Implementing a Form-Handling Solution

The example you'll build involves editing customer records from our quoting database (built in Chapter 1). From the customer list, the Edit link will take us directly to an edit form containing the customer data. You'll need to make a slight modification to your customerList.jsp file from the last chapter. Change the edit link from this:

```
<a href="custMaint.jsp?id=<%= rs.getString(1) %>&action=edit">
```

to this:

```
<a href="customerDetail.jsp?id=<%= rs.getString(1) %>">
```

The JavaBean will contain most of the functionality. The only real logic included within the page determines if the page has been submitted or if it's loading for the first time. It then directs the bean to perform its validations and commits the data if successful. The validations you're performing in this example are somewhat trivial; they merely illustrate the overall process. Obviously, you can do these kinds of validation better within the browser using a scripting language. Validation on the client-side will help to eliminate common errors on a form and reduce traffic between the client and the server. However, you should also use server-side validation to identify any uncaught errors and to prepare the submission for further processing.

Building the Bean

The JavaBean you'll create provides three main functions. It persists the inputted data (model), validates the data, and eventually commits the data to the database. Refer to Listing 3-6 for the entire source code used to build the bean. Remember to compile this bean and place it in your application server's \jspBook\WEB-INF\classes\jspbook\ch3 directory.

The data is persisted as properties of the bean. As with all JavaBean properties, you provide a set of accessor methods for each of them (getter and setter). These properties are initialized in the constructor of the bean. You'll notice that some of these properties are non-String data. The <jsp:getProperty> and <jsp:setProperty> tags will automatically convert these values accordingly.

Data validation occurs in the validate method and makes use of a hashtable called errors to store each individual error. You do this so that our page can display a list of all the errors on the page rather than simply one at a time. For instance, if the user had invalid data in three different fields, rather than going through them one at a time, they have the chance to correct all three errors in one screen. Once again, the validations you perform here are trivial and for the purpose of illustrating the validation process. You would typically do more complex validations to validate data against databases and even remote objects.

Another component of data validation has to do with displaying the field names and field values in the JSP page. By using the getField method of the bean, you have the opportunity to check if the field was in error and, if so, to highlight the field for the user. You simply look up the field in the errors Hashtable and wrap a special `<font>` tag around the field name.

Committing the data to the database is a simple task. You've presumably already validated the data and can be fairly confident the database will accept the data with no problems. You accomplish this inside of the submit method by assembling an update SQL statement and executing it against the database.

Listing 3-6. `CustomerBean.java`

```
package jspbook.ch3;

import java.util.*;
import java.sql.*;

public class CustomerBean implements java.io.Serializable {

  /* Member Variables */
  private String id, lname, fname, sex;
  private int age, children;
  private boolean spouse, smoker;

  /* Helper Variables */
  private Connection db = null;
  private String status;

  /* Error collection */
  Hashtable errors = new Hashtable();

  /* Constants */
  public static final int FIELD_NAME = 0;
  public static final int FIELD_VALUE = 1;

  /* Constructor */
  public CustomerBean() {
    /* Initialize properties */
    setLname("");
    setFname("");
    setSex("");
    setAge(0);
    setChildren(0);
    setSpouse(false);
    setSmoker(false);
    setStatus("");
```

```
    id = "";   // Not really a property, so no accessor method

  /* Get database connection */
  dbConnect();
}

/* Get Database Connection */
private void dbConnect() {
  if (db == null) {
    try {
      Class.forName("org.gjt.mm.mysql.Driver");
      db = DriverManager.getConnection("jdbc:mysql://localhost:3306/quoting");
    }
    catch (Exception e) {
      System.out.println("Error Connecting to quoting DB: " + e.toString());
    }
  }
}

/* Accessor Methods */

/* Last Name */
public void setLname(String _lname) {
  lname = _lname;
}
public String getLname() {
  return lname;
}

/* First Name */
public void setFname(String _fname) {
  fname = _fname;
}
public String getFname() {
  return fname;
}

/* Sex */
public void setSex(String _sex) {
  sex = _sex;
}
public String getSex() {
  return sex;
}
```

```
/* Age */
public void setAge(int _age) {
  age = _age;
}
public int getAge() {
  return age;
}

/* Number of Children */
public void setChildren(int _children) {
  children = _children;
}
public int getChildren() {
  return children;
}

/* Spouse ? */
public void setSpouse(boolean _spouse) {
  spouse = _spouse;
}
public boolean getSpouse() {
  return spouse;
}

/* Smoker ? */
public void setSmoker(boolean _smoker) {
  smoker = _smoker;
}
public boolean getSmoker() {
  return smoker;
}

/* Status ("Customer saved . . . ") */
public void setStatus(String _msg) {
  status = _msg;
}
public String getStatus() {
  return "<br><center><font color=red>" + status + "</font></center>";
}

public void loadCustomer(String _id) {
  try {
    String sql = "select * from customer where id='" + _id + "'";
```

```
      Statement s = db.createStatement();
      ResultSet rs = s.executeQuery(sql);

      if (rs.next()) {
        setLname(rs.getString("lname"));
        setFname(rs.getString("fname"));
        setSex(rs.getString("sex"));
        setAge(rs.getInt("age"));
        setChildren(rs.getInt("children"));
        setSpouse((rs.getString("married") == "Y") ? true : false);
        setSmoker((rs.getString("smoker") == "Y") ? true : false);
        id = _id;
      }
      else {
        setStatus("Customer Does Not Exist.");
      }
    }
    catch (SQLException e) {
      System.out.println("Error loading customer: " +
        _id + " : " + e.toString());
    }
  }

  public boolean validateString(String _input) {
    char[] chars = _input.toCharArray();
    for(int i = 0; i < chars.length; i++) {
      if(Character.isDigit(chars[i]))
        return false;
    }
    return true;
  }

  public boolean validateAge(int _age) {
    if (age < 1 || age > 100) {
      return false;
    }
    else {
      return true;
    }
  }
  public boolean validate() {
    errors.clear(); // Reset the errors hashtable
```

```java
    if (!validateString(lname))
      errors.put("lname", "Last name must be all letters.");
    if (!validateString(fname))
      errors.put("fname", "First name must be all letters.");
    if (!validateAge(age))
      errors.put("age", "Age must be a numeric value between 1 and 100.");

    return (errors.isEmpty()) ? true : false;
  }

  public String getErrors() {

    StringBuffer errTable = new StringBuffer();
    if (!errors.isEmpty())
      errTable.append("<br><center><table border='1'>");

    Enumeration errs = errors.elements();
    while (errs.hasMoreElements()) {
      errTable.append("<tr><td><font color=red>");
      errTable.append(errs.nextElement());
      errTable.append("</font></td></tr>");
    }

    if (!errors.isEmpty())
      errTable.append("</table></center>");

    return errTable.toString();
  }

  public String getField(String _field, int _part) {

    String err = null;
    String pre = "<font color=red>*";
    String post = "</font>";

    if (_part == FIELD_NAME) {
      if (_field.equals("lname")) {
        err = (String) errors.get("lname");
        if (err != null) {
          return pre + "Last Name: " + post;
        }
        else {
          return "Last Name: ";
```

```
        }
      }
      if (_field.equals("fname")) {
        err = (String) errors.get("fname");
        if (err != null) {
          return pre + "First Name: " + post;
        }
        else {
          return "First Name: ";
        }
      }
      if (_field.equals("sex")) {
        err = (String) errors.get("sex");
        if (err != null) {
          return pre + "Sex: " + post;
        }
        else {
          return "Sex: ";
        }
      }

      if (_field.equals("age")) return "Age: ";
      if (_field.equals("children")) return "Children: ";
      if (_field.equals("spouse")) return "Spouse ? ";
      if (_field.equals("smoker")) return "Smoker ? ";
    }

    if (_part == FIELD_VALUE) {
      if (_field.equals("lname")) return getLname();
      if (_field.equals("fname")) return getFname();
      if (_field.equals("sex")) return getSex();
      if (_field.equals("age")) return (Integer.toString(getAge()));
      if (_field.equals("children")) return (Integer.toString(getChildren()));
      if (_field.equals("spouse")) return ((getSpouse()) ? "true" : "false");
      if (_field.equals("smoker")) return ((getSmoker()) ? "true" : "false");
    }

    return "";
  }

  public void submit() {
    try {
      StringBuffer sql = new StringBuffer(256);
```

```
    sql.append("UPDATE customer SET ");
    sql.append("lname='").append(lname).append("', ");
    sql.append("fname='").append(fname).append("', ");
    sql.append("age=").append(age).append(", ");
    sql.append("sex='").append(sex).append("', ");
    sql.append("married='").append(spouse).append("', ");
    sql.append("children=").append(children).append(", ");
    sql.append("smoker='").append(smoker).append("'");
    sql.append("where id='").append(id).append("'");

    Statement s = db.createStatement();
    s.executeUpdate(sql.toString());
  }
  catch (SQLException e) {
    System.out.println("Error saving customer: " + id + " : " + e.toString());
  }
 }

}
```

Building the JSP Page

The JSP page is responsible for directing the JavaBean to load the customer record (if it's the first time through), populate the model, validate the fields, and display the form. Refer to Listing 3-7 for the entire JSP code. As you can see, you're implementing our form handler within the form itself. You do this intentionally. When a user is entering data into a form, it's helpful to keep them within the context of the form as they correct errors. It would also be difficult for us to highlight individual fields in error.

Because you're sharing the form with the handler, you need to do a few things first to determine what processing should take place. (For a high-level view of these tasks, refer to Figure 3-6.) First, the JSP page looks for a request parameter to determine if it has been submitted. If this is the first time through, then that parameter will not exist. If it has been submitted, it continues to set the properties directly from the request parameters and then attempts to validate and commit the data. If this is the first time through, then it loads the customer data into the model.

Prior to displaying the form, the getErrors method is called to return an HTML table of errors. This will display directly above the form and will correspond to individually highlighted fields. To display the form fields, the JSP page relies on the getField method of the bean to display both the field name and the field value. It does this to enable the bean to highlight field names that have invalid data associated with them.

Listing 3-7. `customerDetail.jsp`

```
<!-- JSP Directives -->
<%@ page
        errorPage="myError.jsp?from=customerDetail.jsp"
%>


<html>
<head>
  <title>Customer Detail</title>
</head>

<body>

<basefont face="Arial">

<jsp:useBean id="custBean" scope="session" class="jspbook.ch3.CustomerBean"/>

<%@ include file="myHeader.html" %>

<!-- Static constants -->
<%! public static final int FIELD_NAME = 0; %>
<%! public static final int FIELD_VALUE = 1; %>

<!-- Reset status message -->
<jsp:setProperty name="custBean" property="status" value=""/>

<!-- Check if the form has been submitted -->
<%
  String submitted = (String) request.getParameter("submit");
  if (submitted != null) {
%>

<!-- Set bean properties from request parameters -->
  <jsp:setProperty name="custBean" property="lname" param="lname"/>
  <jsp:setProperty name="custBean" property="fname" param="fname"/>
  <jsp:setProperty name="custBean" property="age" param="age"/>
  <jsp:setProperty name="custBean" property="sex" param="sex"/>
  <jsp:setProperty name="custBean" property="spouse" param="spouse"/>
  <jsp:setProperty name="custBean" property="children" param="children"/>
  <jsp:setProperty name="custBean" property="smoker" param="smoker"/>

<!-- Validate the fields and submit -->
<%
```

```
      if (custBean.validate()) {
        custBean.submit();
        custBean.setStatus("Customer record has been saved.");
      }
    }

    /* If first time through (not submitted), load existing customer record --> */

    else {
      String id = (String) request.getParameter("id");
      if (id != null) {
        custBean.loadCustomer(id);
      }
    }
%>

<!-- Retrieve a list of any errors and a status message -->
<%= custBean.getErrors() %>
<jsp:getProperty name="custBean" property="status"/>

<form action="customerDetail.jsp">

<input type="Hidden" name="submit" value="true"/>

<center>

<table>
  <tr>
    <td><%= custBean.getField("fname", FIELD_NAME) %></td>
    <td><input type="Text" name="fname" value="
      <%= custBean.getField("fname", FIELD_VALUE) %>"/></td>
  </tr>
  <tr>
    <td><%= custBean.getField("lname", FIELD_NAME) %></td>
    <td><input type="Text" name="lname" value="
      <%= custBean.getField("lname", FIELD_VALUE) %>"/></td>
  </tr>
  <tr>
    <td><%= custBean.getField("age", FIELD_NAME) %></td>
    <td><input type="Text" name="age" value="
      <%= custBean.getField("age", FIELD_VALUE) %>"/></td>
  </tr>
  <tr>
```

```
    <td><%= custBean.getField("sex", FIELD_NAME) %></td>
    <td>
      <select name="sex">
        <option value="M" <%= (custBean.getField("sex",
          FIELD_VALUE).equals("M")) ? "selected" : "" %>M</option>
        <option value="F" <%= (custBean.getField("sex",
          FIELD_VALUE).equals("F")) ? "selected" : "" %>F</option>
      </select>
    </td>
  </tr>
  <tr>
    <td><%= custBean.getField("spouse", FIELD_NAME) %></td>
    <td>
      <select name="spouse">
        <option value="true" <%= (custBean.getField("spouse",
          FIELD_VALUE).equals("true")) ? "selected" : "" %>Y</option>
        <option value="false" <%= (custBean.getField("spouse",
          FIELD_VALUE).equals("false")) ? "selected" : "" %>N</option>
      </select>
    </td>
  </tr>
  <tr>
    <td><%= custBean.getField("children", FIELD_NAME) %></td>
    <td><input type="Text" name="children" value="
      <%= custBean.getField("children", FIELD_VALUE) %>"/></td>
  </tr>
  <tr>
    <td><%= custBean.getField("smoker", FIELD_NAME) %></td>
    <td>
      <select name="smoker">
        <option value="true" <%= (custBean.getField("smoker",
          FIELD_VALUE).equals("true")) ? "selected" : "" %>Y</option>
        <option value="false" <%= (custBean.getField("smoker",
          FIELD_VALUE).equals("false")) ? "selected" : "" %>N</option>
      </select>
    </td>
  </tr>
  <tr>
    <td colspan="2" align="center"><input type="Submit" value="Submit"/></td>
  </tr>
  <tr>
    <td colspan="2" align="center">
      <br><br><a href="customerList.jsp">Return to Customer List</a>
```

```
        </td>
      </tr>
    </table>

  </center>

  </form>

  <%@ include file="myFooter.html" %>

  </body>
  </html>
```

Using the Form-Handling Solution

The first validation you'll test is the First Name and Last Name fields. Each field must contain a string of valid non-numeric characters. The bean's validate method triggers this validation. This method calls separate methods for each of the validations to be performed on the form data. In the case of both the First Name and Last Name fields, the validate method calls the validateString method, which tests whether each character is numeric. If any character in the first or last name fields is numeric, an error will be added to the errors hashtable. When the page is displayed, the getErrors method of the bean will insert a table of errors at the top of the form. In addition to the list of errors, when the fields are displayed, the First Name and Last Name fields will be displayed in red to highlight the error. See Figure 3-7 for an example of entering a numeric value in the First Name field.

Figure 3-7. Inputting an invalid name

The other validation included in the CustomerBean is for the Age field. The bean's validate method calls the validateAge method to verify that the age is between the values of 1 and 100. You assume the inputted value is numeric because the bean will make the conversion when it sets the value. If it's not numeric, the application server will throw an exception when it attempts to convert the value from a String to an integer. This is a good place for some client-side validation using a scripting language such as JavaScript. See Figure 3-8 for an example of typing an age that falls outside of the defined limits.

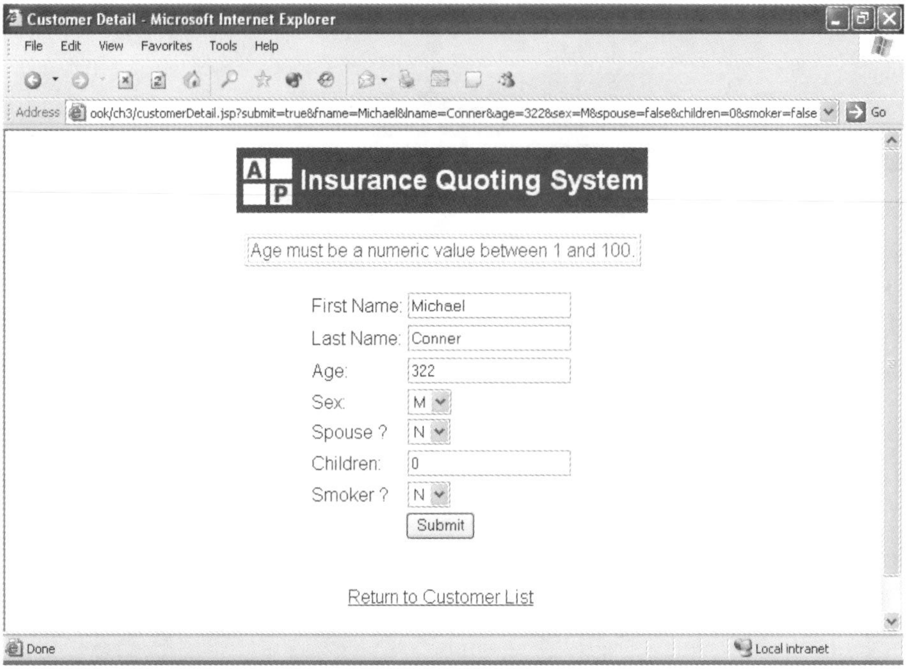

Figure 3-8. Inputting an invalid age

Summary

This chapter has presented one method in which you can hide complex Java code from the page designer. Obviously, the page designer needs a rudimentary knowledge of JSP and Java to incorporate these beans within the presentation code, but using JavaBeans does make for much cleaner, more readable JSP pages.

You can adapt this chapter's examples to just about any specific domain. By modifying the bean properties and some of the validation and database code, you implement these beans rather quickly into whichever application you choose. However, with a little bit of work, it's possible to abstract the domain-specific code out of the bean and make it more generic. You could then configure the bean through some additional properties in your JSP code.

Chapter 4 will take role separation a step further by introducing the concept of custom tag extensions. These custom tags hide Java code inside of standard JSP-like tags. You can group tags by functionality and then package and deploy them as tag libraries. You'll see some useful techniques to accomplish common tasks through the use of custom tags. After that, you'll take a look at some enterprise development patterns that make use of JSP, Servlets, JavaBeans, and custom tags to build elegant and efficient web applications.

CHAPTER 4

Role Separation
with Custom Tags

THE LAST CHAPTER INTRODUCED THE USE of JavaBeans within your JSP pages to help separate Java code from the presentation template (the HTML page). Now, you're going to take this idea a step further and see how you can encapsulate your Java code inside custom tags. These tags are similar to the set of JSP tags you've been using. The only difference is that you get to define their behavior by attaching special tag handlers to them.

I'll begin with a discussion of custom tags and how they work. Then, I'll walk you through a simple tag and show how to develop the tag handler and deploy it in your JSP application. You'll also see how custom tags can process content contained within the start and end tags and how to nest tags within each other. Once armed with these tools, along with those discussed in earlier chapters, you can begin applying these techniques to real-world enterprise problems as I discuss some patterns for development that use custom tags, JavaBeans, and Java servlets.

Using Custom Tags

A nice feature of JSP is that it gives you the ability to define your own set of HTML-like tags, allowing the page designer to simply select from a set of custom tags to include dynamic content wherever it's needed within the page. When you expose your Java code through these custom tags, you make it easier on the page designer by giving them a familiar coding paradigm.

To learn how to create custom tags, it helps to first understand how the servlet container handles custom tags. First, when a custom tag is encountered as the page is processed, the page will pass control to a tag handler that will perform the necessary processing and then return control to the page. This tag handler is a Java class that extends, or implements, the appropriate class within the `javax.servlet.jsp.tagext` package. The servlet container instantiates these tag handlers, and then a pool of other tag handlers maintains them. Many application servers will optimize the use of custom tags by placing multiple instances of a tag handler into a pool and distributing them as needed by the application.

You can locate the tag handler using the taglib directive in your JSP. This taglib directive points to a URI in the web.xml file. The web.xml file matches the given URI with a specific descriptor file known as a Tag Library Descriptor (tld) file. This tld file contains information about the tag handler such as the location of the class file that will perform the processing as well as any attributes that can be passed into it. See Figure 4-1 for a summary of this interaction. You can use multiple tag libraries within a single web application to further differentiate the processing or capabilities of a given tag library.

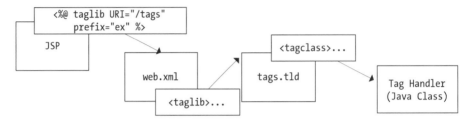

Figure 4-1. Locating a tag handler

The tag handler itself is a Java class that will implement either the Tag interface or the BodyTag interface located in the javax.servlet.jsp.tagext package. The Tag interface is used when creating an empty tag that will not process any content contained within its start and end tags. It can, however, determine whether to display the content contained within its start and end tags. The Tag interface can be rather cumbersome to implement, so it's often better to simply extend the TagSupport class, which provides a default implementation of the Tag interface.

The BodyTag interface is similar to the Tag interface, except that it's capable of processing the content contained within its start and end tags. This would be useful if you were to write a tag that formats a block of content or maybe needs to sort a list in a specialized manner. Just like the Tag interface, the BodyTag interface comes with a default implementation, called BodyTagSupport. These support classes implement all the methods necessary to respond to lifecycle events generated by the servlet container.

Depending on which type of tag you're implementing, you'll need to override one of the lifecycle methods of the supporting class to include specialized code to perform the necessary processing. Once the processing is complete, this method will return an integer value that lets the servlet container know how to proceed with processing the rest of the page. Table 4-1 lists the various lifecycle methods and the return values for the Tag interface and the BodyTag interface.

Table 4-1. Lifecycle Methods of Tag and BodyTag Interfaces

INTERFACE	METHOD	RETURN VALUE	EFFECT
Tag	doStartTag	EVAL_BODY_INCLUDE	Content contained within the tag is included in the page's output.
		SKIP_BODY	Content contained within the tag is ignored.
	doEndTag	EVAL_PAGE	Content after the tag is processed normally.
		SKIP_PAGE	Content after the tag is skipped.
BodyTag	doAfterBody	EVAL_BODY_TAG	Content contained within the tag is evaluated by the doAfterBody method again, presumably until a specific condition is met.
		SKIP_BODY	Processing of the tag is complete.

Figure 4-2 shows how a tag implementing the Tag interface is evaluated at runtime.

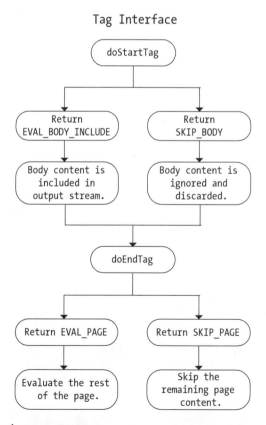

Figure 4-2. Processing a custom tag

These interfaces will be described in greater detail as you examine their use in the following examples. Let's start with a simple tag to illustrate how to create a tag and describe it to the JSP container.

Looking at a Simple Tag Example

For your first attempt at creating a custom tag, you'll build a tag handler that does not process its body content and therefore extends the TagSupport class. The next section will deal with the BodyTag interface and its corresponding support class. This example will simply take a message and output it in a specific color. The message and the color will be passed into the tag as attributes. First, you'll build the tag handler, then the tag descriptor (the tld file), after which you'll add an entry to the web.xml file, and finally, you'll declare it in your JSP page and demonstrate its use. Let's get started!

Implementing the Tag Handler Class

The tag handler extends the TagSupport class, which, in turn, implements the Tag interface. To perform the processing required by this tag, you'll override the doStartTag and doEndTag methods. In addition to these methods, you'll need to provide a set of accessor methods for each attribute that your tag will be using. These methods are similar to those used in the JavaBeans from Chapter 3.

Let's start with defining the two attributes that the tag will be using: color and message. You can provide default values for each of these attributes, therefore optimizing them for the page designer. Again, the accessor methods you need to provide for each of these attributes are identical to those you would use for the properties of a JavaBean.

In the doStartTag method, you obtain a JspWriter and output the given message with the appropriate HTML formatting instructions. The return value that you'll be using is SKIP_BODY. This value is returned because this tag will be an empty tag with no content within its start and end tags. If, however, this tag was to include content and you wanted to display it conditionally, you would return the EVAL_BODY_INCLUDE value.

Finally, the doEndTag method is overridden. Again, you can choose to conditionally display content by returning the appropriate value. In this case, however, the return value determines whether the remainder of the page will be processed. To display the current output buffer and halt processing of the page, you could return SKIP_PAGE from this method. In this case, though, you want to continue processing so you return EVAL_PAGE instead. See Listing 4-1 for a complete class definition.

Listing 4-1. `SimpleTag.java`

```java
package jspbook.ch4;

import javax.servlet.http.*;
import javax.servlet.jsp.*;
import javax.servlet.jsp.tagext.*;
import java.io.IOException;

public class SimpleTag extends TagSupport {

  /* Tag Attributes */
  protected String color = "#000000";
  protected String message = "Hello World!";

  /* Process Start Tag */
  public int doStartTag() throws JspTagException {
    try {
      JspWriter out = pageContext.getOut();
      out.println("<font color=\"" + color + "\">");
      out.println(message);
      out.println("</font>");
    }
    catch (IOException e) {
      throw new JspTagException(e.toString());
    }
    return SKIP_BODY;
  }

  /* Process End Tag */
  public int doEndTag() throws JspTagException {
    return EVAL_PAGE;
  }

  /* Attribute Accessor Methods */
  public String getColor() {
    return color;
  }

  public void setColor(String _color) {
    color = _color;
  }
```

```
  public String getMessage() {
    return message;
  }

  public void setMessage(String _message) {
    message = _message;
  }
}
```

Creating the Tag Library Descriptor

To describe your tag to the JSP container, you need to provide a descriptor file. This descriptor file, or tld, is an XML file that contains a single <taglib> element, which itself contains several elements that describe the tag library in question. The two elements you'll use for this tag library are <tlib-version> and <jsp-version>. You can version your tag library using a <tlib-version> element. The <jsp-version> element specifies the minimum version of JSP required by your tag. Other elements you could define are <short-name>, <uri>, and <info>—all used to provide information to a JSP authoring tool.

A tag library can describe several tags using <tag> elements. Each <tag> element contains several subelements used to describe each individual tag. The elements we'll be using are <name>, <tag-class>, <body-content>, and <attribute>. The <name> element specifies the name that will be used within the JSP to invoke this specific tag handler. The <tag-class> element points to the fully qualified Java class implementing the given tag. You can use the <body-content> element to declare the tag as a body tag or an empty tag. Finally, because your tag supports two attributes, you'll need to add an <attribute> element for each of them. See Listing 4-2 for a complete tld file, located in the \WEB-INF\tlds folder of the web application.

Listing 4-2. `simple.tld`

```
<?xml version="1.0" encoding="ISO-8859-1" ?>
<!DOCTYPE taglib
        PUBLIC "-//Sun Microsystems, Inc.//DTD JSP Tag Library 1.2//EN"
            "http://java.sun.com/j2ee/dtd/web-jsptaglibrary_1_2.dtd">

<taglib>
  <tlib-version>1.0</tlib-version>
  <jsp-version>1.2</jsp-version>
  <short-name>simpleTag</short-name>
  <description>
    Tag library to support the examples in Chapter 4
```

```
    </description>
    <tag>
      <name>simpleTag</name>
      <tag-class>jspbook.ch4.SimpleTag</tag-class>
      <body-content>empty</body-content>
      <attribute>
        <name>color</name>
        <required>no</required>
      </attribute>
      <attribute>
        <name>message</name>
        <required>no</required>
      </attribute>
    </tag>
</taglib>
```

Declaring the Tag Library

Now that you have a descriptor file for your tag library, you need to make your web application aware of its existence. You do this by adding a `<taglib>` element to the web.xml file. This element defines the location of the descriptor file using the `<taglib-location>` tag. It also declares a URI for the tag library that will be used within the JSP to locate this entry in the web.xml file. Listing 4-3 shows what your web.xml might look like after adding the appropriate taglib element.

Listing 4-3. web.xml

```
<?xml version="1.0" encoding="ISO-8859-1"?>

<!DOCTYPE web-app
    PUBLIC "-//Sun Microsystems, Inc.//DTD Web Application 2.2//EN"
    "http://java.sun.com/j2ee/dtds/web-app_2_2.dtd">

<web-app>
    <taglib>
        <taglib-uri>/simple</taglib-uri>
        <taglib-location>/WEB-INF/tlds/simple.tld</taglib-location>
    </taglib>
</web-app>
```

Using Your Tag Library in a JSP Page

Now let's look at using your custom tag, starting with the JSP page. At the top of your page, you use a taglib directive to identify the tag library and match it to the entry you made in the web.xml file using the URI attribute. The tag library descriptor file is then located through this entry in the web.xml file. The tag handler is then instantiated using the information contained in the tag library descriptor file.

The taglib directive also defines a prefix you can use to invoke custom tags contained within the tag library. In this example, you choose to select the prefix ex. When you invoke the custom tag, you refer to it as <ex:simpleTag>. The ex points back to the taglib directive, which in turn points you to the web.xml file and eventually the tag library descriptor file where it locates the simpleTag entry and loads the appropriate handler. See Listing 4-4 for a complete JSP example using the simpleTag custom tag.

Listing 4-4. simpleTagExample.jsp

```
<!-- JSP Directives -->
<%@ page errorPage="myError.jsp?from=simpleTagExample.jsp" %>
<%@ taglib uri="/simple" prefix="ex" %>

<html>
<head>
    <title>Simple Tag Example</title>
</head>

<body>

<basefont face="Arial">

<!-- Display message -->
<center>
    <ex:simpleTag
        color="#008000"
        message="This is a very, very, very simple tag!"
    />
</center>

</body>
</html>
```

Figure 4-3 shows the simple tag example in action. The message is passed to the tag handler as an attribute and then displayed in green.

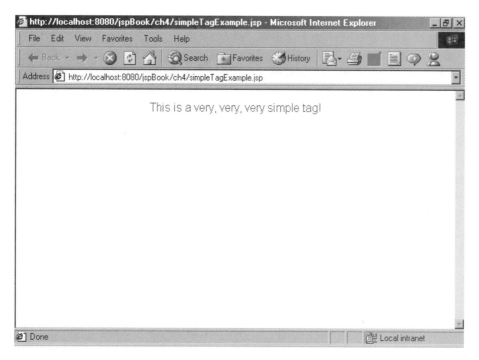

Figure 4-3. Simple tag example

Processing Body Content

Extending the TagSupport class, as you did in the previous example, enables you to perform some processing, generate some output, and even dictate whether the content included within the start and end tags should be included in the JSP output. If you'd like to actually manipulate any included content, however, you need to extend a different class. The BodyTagSupport class implements the BodyTag interface and provides a standard tag implementation in much the same way as the TagSupport class does. Here's an example of a custom JSP tag using a BodyTag:

```
<util:formatTable>
    123,Widget A,300.00,48
    234,Widget B,250.00,64
    345 Widget C,325.00,13
</util:formatTable>
```

This example uses a tag called formatTable to take the included content and output it as an HTML formatted table. The BodyTagSupport class makes this content available through the setBodyContent method. There's no need to override this method; it just takes the included content and creates a BodyContent object for you to use later.

When processing an empty tag, you extended the TagSupport class, overrode the doStartTag method, and sent the appropriate return value. When processing a body tag, you extend the BodyTagSupport class, override the doAfterBody method, obtain the BodyContent object, process the content, and return the appropriate value. Another difference between these methods is the use of JspWriter. The doStartTag method has a JspWriter available to it through the PageContext object. Because the doAfterBody method does not, you need to obtain a JspWriter through the BodyContent object using its getEnclosingWriter method, like this:

```
BodyContent body = getBodyContent();
JspWriter out = body.getEnclosingWriter();
```

Getting at the content is fairly easy; you can do it in one of two ways. The easiest way is to call the getString method of the BodyContent object and store the results in a String object. In most instances, this will work just fine. There may be some circumstances, however, that will require you to process the content line by line, or perhaps apply a filter to the content as it is read in. In these cases, you can get the content returned as a Reader using the getReader method. This is an example of how to read the content using a Reader:

```
BufferedReader contentReader = new BufferedReader(body.getReader());
while ((String record = contentReader.readLine()) != null) {
    ...
}
```

When you're done processing the body content and outputting your results, you need to return the appropriate value from the doAfterBody() method (refer to Table 4-1). Valid options are SKIP_BODY and EVAL_BODY_TAG. The SKIP_BODY return value tells the JSP container that you're done processing the body of this tag and that you'd like to flush the output buffer and continue processing the rest of the page (after the current tag). The EVAL_BODY_TAG return value will cause the container to re-evaluate the body content. In other words, this enables you to loop through the body content repeatedly until a particular condition has been met. Be careful to avoid infinite loops when using this approach!

Seeing a Body Tag in Action

This example will evaluate the included content and output an HTML-formatted table. The included content needs to be in the form of comma-delimited values, with each row on its own line. This kind of tag might be useful when used as a decorating filter as part of a standard utility library. I'll discuss the idea of filtering content in future chapters that deal with enterprise design patterns.

Modifying web.xml and Tag Library Descriptor Files

First, you modify the application deployment descriptor, web.xml, to include a <taglib> entry for the tag library, which describes the HtmlUtils tag that you'll be using for this example. The web.xml file is located in the \WEB-INF directory of your web application. Listing 4-5 shows what the web.xml file should look like.

Listing 4-5. web.xml

```
<?xml version="1.0" encoding="ISO-8859-1"?>

<!DOCTYPE web-app
    PUBLIC "-//Sun Microsystems, Inc.//DTD Web Application 2.2//EN"
    "http://java.sun.com/j2ee/dtds/web-app_2_2.dtd">

<web-app>
  <taglib>
    <taglib-uri>/tableUtils</taglib-uri>
    <taglib-location>/WEB-INF/tlds/utils.tld</taglib-location>
  </taglib>
</web-app>
```

Next, you create the tag library descriptor file. This particular file describes a single tag, tableFormat, that is associated with the HtmlUtils tag handler. This file should be stored in the \WEB-INF\tlds directory of your web application. Listing 4-6 shows what the utils.tld file should look like.

Listing 4-6. utils.tld

```
<?xml version="1.0" encoding="ISO-8859-1" ?>
<!DOCTYPE taglib
        PUBLIC "-//Sun Microsystems, Inc.//DTD JSP Tag Library 1.2//EN"
          "http://java.sun.com/j2ee/dtd/web-jsptaglibrary_1_2.dtd">
```

```
<taglib>
  <tlib-version>1.0</tlib-version>
  <jsp-version>1.2</jsp-version>
  <short-name>utilTag</short-name>
  <description>
    Tag library to support the examples in Chapter 4
  </description>
  <tag>
    <name>tableFormat</name>
    <tag-class>jspbook.ch4.HtmlUtils</tag-class>
    <body-content>tagdependent</body-content>
  </tag>
</taglib>
```

Writing the Tag Handler

The HtmlUtils tag handler simply takes each line of comma-delimited text, contained within its start and end tags, and parses it into individual table elements. The end result is a formatted HTML table in place of the original tag. Each row is processed inside of a while loop until there's no more content to process. The actual parsing uses a StringTokenizer object to break the row of data into individual fields. Once the data has been written out as an HTML table, the SKIP_BODY value is returned and the remainder of the JSP page is processed. Listing 4-7 contains the complete code for the HtmlUtils tag.

Listing 4-7. HtmlUtils.java

```
package jspbook.ch4;

import javax.servlet.http.*;
import javax.servlet.jsp.*;
import javax.servlet.jsp.tagext.*;
import java.util.*;
import java.io.*;

public class HtmlUtils extends BodyTagSupport{

  public int doAfterBody()
    throws JspException
  {
    try {
      boolean altRow = false;
      String record = "";
```

```
/* Get Body Content and Enclosing JSP Writer */
BodyContent body = getBodyContent();
JspWriter out = body.getEnclosingWriter();

out.println("<center>");
out.println("<table>");

/* Get body content as a reader and process each line individually */
BufferedReader contentReader = new BufferedReader(body.getReader());
while ((record = contentReader.readLine()) != null) {
    /* Alternate row colors */
                            " : "#c0c0c0") + "'>");
                          y */
                        okenizer(record, ",");




                        g());




        return SKIP_BODY;
    }

}
```

Writing the JSP

The JSP page that uses the HtmlUtils tag handler begins with a taglib directive associating the util prefix with the taglib described by the /tableUtils URI. The tag wraps several rows of input data and displays them as an HTML table. Remember that the HtmlUtils tag handler is associated with the tableFormat tag in the tag library descriptor file. Therefore, the `<util:tableFormat>` tag really invokes the HtmlUtils tag handler class. See Listing 4-8 and Figure 4-4.

Listing 4-8. bodyTagExample.jsp

```
<!-- JSP Directives -->
<%@ page errorPage="myError.jsp?from=bodyTagExample.jsp" %>
<%@ taglib uri="/tableUtils" prefix="util" %>

<html>
<head>
  <title>Body Tag Example</title>
</head>

<body>

<basefont face="Arial">

<br><br>

<util:tableFormat>
   100,Lorrain Davies,$500.00
   200,Christina Inman,$450.34
   300,Lori Peterson,$475.23
   400,Sandy Andre,$423.00
   500,Lani Tobias,$445.34
</util:tableFormat>

</body>
</html>
```

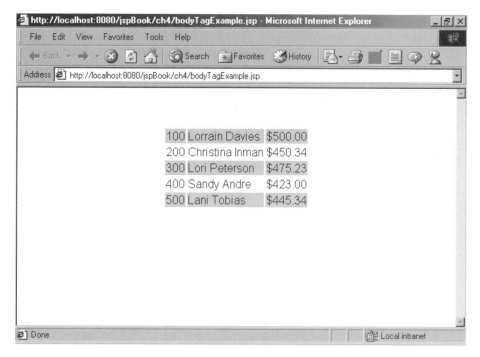

Figure 4-4. Body tag example

Nesting Tags

A nice benefit of using custom tags is that you can actually nest the tags within some kind of hierarchy with the ability to have child tags invoke methods of parent tags. Nesting tags is similar to the way you'd nest standard HTML tags. For instance, the `<td>` tag must exist within a `<tr>` tag, which itself must exist within a `<table>` tag. All of these tags work together to render a group of data in tabular format.

When nesting a tag within another tag, it's important to note that the child tag can obtain an instance of the parent tag, but the parent tag has no knowledge of its child tags. The child tag can traverse up the tag hierarchy until it finds the specific tag for which it's looking. You do this with the `findAncestorWithClass` method. This method will look at the parent tag (set in one of the `BodyTagSupport` or `TagSupport` lifecycle methods) and determine if it's an instance of a particular class. For instance, if you're looking for a tag of type `outlineTag`, then this is an example of how you'd access that tag:

```
outlineTag parent = (outlineTag) findAncestorWithClass(this, outlineTag.class);
parent.updateCount();
```

There's another method for obtaining an instance of the parent tag. This method is called getParent and will simply return the parent immediately above the current tag. This may be okay in some circumstances, but what if the page designer decides to insert another tag between the current tag and the desired parent tag? Instead of getting an instance of the appropriate parent tag, you might end up with some kind of formatting tag instead. For this reason, I recommend always using the findAncestorWithClass method to look up parent tags.

To illustrate the use of nested tags, let's build a set of tags that, when used together inside of a JSP, displays a grocery order with line item totals and a grand total at the bottom. A GroceryItem tag will represent each line item. A single GroceryOrder tag will contain these GroceryItem tags. Each GroceryItem tag will be responsible for calculating a line total and updating the grand total in the GroceryOrder tag. The GroceryOrder tag will then display the items in a table as well as the grand total for the order. This is what the web.xml entry looks like:

```
<taglib>
  <taglib-uri>/groceries</taglib-uri>
  <taglib-location>/WEB-INF/tlds/groceries.tld</taglib-location>
</taglib>
```

The tag library descriptor file will contain <tag> entries for each of these tags. These tags each manipulate their body content, so the <body-content> element is set to tagdependent. This is what the <tag> entries look like:

```
<tag>
  <name>Order</name>
  <tag-class>jspbook.ch4.GroceryOrder</tag-class>
  <body-content>tagdependent</body-content>
</tag>
<tag>
  <name>LineItem</name>
  <tag-class>jspbook.ch4.GroceryItem</tag-class>
  <body-content>tagdependent</body-content>
</tag>
```

The tag handler for the line items is responsible for reading in a line of body content, calculating the line item total, updating the grand total (in the GroceryOrder tag), and finally outputting a new line of comma-delimited content that includes the line item total. To update the grand total, you obtain an instance of the GroceryOrder tag and invoke the updateTotal method to add the line item total to the grand total stored inside of the GroceryOrder tag. Listing 4-9 shows the code for the GroceryItem tag handler.

Listing 4-9. `GroceryItem.java`

```
package jspbook.ch4;

import javax.servlet.http.*;
import javax.servlet.jsp.*;
import javax.servlet.jsp.tagext.*;
import java.util.*;
import java.io.*;
import java.text.*;

public class GroceryItem extends BodyTagSupport {

  public int doAfterBody()
    throws JspException
  {
    int qty = 0;
    String desc = "";
    float price = 0.00f;
    float lineTotal = 0.00f;

    /* Get Body Content and Enclosing JSP Writer */
    BodyContent body = getBodyContent();
    JspWriter out = body.getEnclosingWriter();

    // Parse line into data fields
    String line = body.getString();
    StringTokenizer st = new StringTokenizer(line, ",");

    qty = Integer.parseInt(st.nextToken());
    desc = st.nextToken();
    price = Float.parseFloat(st.nextToken());

    // Calculate line item total
    lineTotal = qty * price;

    // Get parent tag and invoke method to update order total
    GroceryOrder order =
      (GroceryOrder) findAncestorWithClass(this, GroceryOrder.class);
    order.updateTotal(lineTotal);

    // Output line as CSV row including lineTotal
    try {
      String priceFmt = NumberFormat.getCurrencyInstance().format(
```

```
            Double.parseDouble(String.valueOf(price)));
        String totalFmt = NumberFormat.getCurrencyInstance().format(
            Double.parseDouble(String.valueOf(lineTotal)));
        out.println(qty + "," + desc + "," + priceFmt + "," + totalFmt);
      }
      catch (IOException e) {
        throw new JspTagException(e.toString());
      }

      return SKIP_BODY;
    }

}
```

The tag handler for the grocery order is responsible for maintaining a grand total as well as outputting the grocery items as an HTML-formatted table. This is not much different than the previous BodyTag examples, with one notable exception. Because you're maintaining a total, you'd like to be sure that this number does not carry over to new invocations of this tag. So, you make use of the release method of BodyTagSupport to reset the value of the grand total. This method is called just before the instance of the tag handler is returned to the pool of handlers managed by the server. Listing 4-10 shows the code for the GroceryOrder tag handler.

Listing 4-10. GroceryOrder.java

```java
package jspbook.ch4;

import javax.servlet.http.*;
import javax.servlet.jsp.*;
import javax.servlet.jsp.tagext.*;
import java.util.*;
import java.io.*;
import java.text.*;

public class GroceryOrder extends BodyTagSupport {

    float orderTotal = 0.00f;

    public int doAfterBody()
      throws JspException
    {
      try {
        BodyContent body = getBodyContent();
        JspWriter out = body.getEnclosingWriter();
```

```java
      out.println("<table>");

      out.println("<tr>");
      out.println("<td><b>Quantity</b></td>");
      out.println("<td><b>Description</b></td>");
      out.println("<td><b>Item Price</b></td>");
      out.println("<td><b>Item Total</b></td>");
      out.println("</tr>");

      // Parse records and output as HTML table
      BufferedReader contentReader = new BufferedReader(body.getReader());
      String record = "";
      while ((record = contentReader.readLine()) != null) {
        out.println("<tr>");
        StringTokenizer st = new StringTokenizer(record, ",");
        while (st.hasMoreTokens()) {
          out.println("<td>");
          out.println(st.nextToken());
          out.println("</td>");
        }
        out.println("</tr>");
      }

      out.println("</table>");

      // Display order total
      out.println("<br>");
      out.println("<b>Order Total: ");
      out.println(NumberFormat.getCurrencyInstance().format(
        Double.parseDouble(String.valueOf(orderTotal))));
      out.println("</b>");
    }
    catch (IOException e) {
      throw new JspTagException(e.toString());
    }

    return SKIP_BODY;
}

public void updateTotal(float lineTotal)
{
    orderTotal += lineTotal;
}
```

```
public void release()
{
  super.release();
  orderTotal = 0.00f;
}
```

```
}
```

Now that you've coded your tag handlers and updated your descriptors, it's time to make use of them. The JSP is really quite simple. It contains a taglib directive that declares the tag library and sets a prefix for it. It then wraps a series of LineItem tags inside of an Order tag. Listing 4-11 shows the code for the JSP (see Figure 4-5 for the results).

Listing 4-11. groceryList.jsp

```jsp
<!-- JSP Directives -->
<%@ page errorPage="myError.jsp?from=groceryList.jsp" %>
<%@ taglib uri="/groceries" prefix="grocery" %>

<html>
<head>
  <title>Grocery List</title>
</head>

<body>

<basefont face="Arial">

<h1>Grocery Bill:</h1>
<br>
<grocery:Order>
  <grocery:LineItem>1,Milk,2.56</grocery:LineItem>
  <grocery:LineItem>5,Canned Carrots,0.33</grocery:LineItem>
  <grocery:LineItem>1,Paper Towel,1.26</grocery:LineItem>
  <grocery:LineItem>1,Magazine,4.50</grocery:LineItem>
  <grocery:LineItem>3,Donut,0.33</grocery:LineItem>
  <grocery:LineItem>9,Peanut Butter,3.99</grocery:LineItem>
</grocery:Order>

</body>
</html>
```

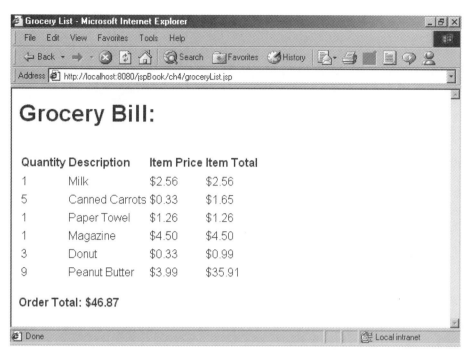

Figure 4-5. Nesting tags

Summary

This chapter concludes the introductory section of the book. Before moving on, you should have a good understanding of JSP fundamentals as well as how to use JavaBeans and custom tags with your JSP pages to separate Java code from page design. The next part of the book will look at ways to apply enterprise patterns to real-world development problems. Each pattern will employ the use of one or more of the techniques discussed to this point.

CHAPTER 5

Development Using Patterns

A KEY ADVANTAGE TO USING JAVA TECHNOLOGY is that it's an Object-Oriented (OO) language. This enables you to write code that is reusable and highly scalable. As you become more accustomed to OO development, you might recognize a few *best practices* that you follow when developing solutions of a particular class. For instance, you may find that for every data-entry application you work on, you tend to code the data validation routines in a similar way. If you were to formalize this best practice and abstract away some of the implementation details, it's conceivable that others could use it as a roadmap to jumpstart their own development efforts by implementing an already proven technique for data validation. This eliminates a lot of design effort as well as numerous testing iterations.

Published best practices have come to be known as *design patterns*. These originated in the OO world and have been published in various forms specific to their implementations in C++ and Java, as well as several general studies. In particular, the book *Design Patterns* by Erich Gamma, Richard Helm, Ralph Johnson, and John Vlissides (Addison-Wesley, 1995) has become the definitive guide to OO design patterns. Recently, the concept of design patterns has influenced the J2EE developer community, prompting Sun to publish a *J2EE Patterns Catalog* (http://developer.java.sun.com/developer/technicalArticles/J2EE/patterns/). These patterns address typical design issues and how you can apply the various J2EE technologies to solve such issues.

This chapter is the first of several that will deal with enterprise design patterns. I'll discuss the merits of using patterns, review the *J2EE Patterns Catalog*, highlight the patterns relevant to the presentation tier (and therefore the subject matter of this book), and finish with a discussion of the Model-View-Controller (MVC) pattern upon which most of the J2EE patterns are based.

Why Use Patterns?

I'll begin the patterns coverage by answering this question: Why should you look to design patterns for help with your own development efforts? The answer to this question is simple. Design patterns are proven techniques that can be reused and applied to many similar problems. They also provide you with a common vocabulary when discussing application design.

They're Proven Techniques

When designing an application, many problems need to be solved. In most cases, these problems are not unique to the specific application you're designing. If you were to design and implement a custom solution to the problem, then that piece of code will need to undergo perhaps several iterations of testing and subsequent coding until it's exactly what you need for your particular application.

If you were to take the previous scenario and use a design pattern instead of a custom solution, then you would greatly reduce development and testing time. The design pattern has already undergone many iterations of testing and development to produce an industry-wide best practice. Obviously, you'll still need to do some custom development to implement the pattern, but now you only need to test the implementation-specific code and not the entire piece of functionality.

They're Reusable

In the spirit of OO design, enterprise design patterns are intended to be reused across projects. Each pattern provides a proven solution for a specific class of problems. These problems tend to exist in many different applications. Rather than reinvent the wheel each time, it makes more sense to apply a design pattern requiring minimal modifications.

It's a Common Vocabulary

When speaking of application design, it helps to have a common vocabulary to communicate your options to the rest of the development team. For instance, a common OO design pattern is the factory pattern. This pattern is useful when an object needs to be instantiated at runtime, but the class of that object is not known at compile-time. So, when discussing design options, you might say something such as, "Well, if we implement a factory pattern in the reporting module, we can add new reports in the future without modifying the application framework." If everyone on the team understands the factory pattern, they can all envision the solution based on the given statement.

Introducing the *J2EE Patterns Catalog*

The architects at Sun have compiled a series of design patterns and published them as the *J2EE Patterns Catalog* available at the Java Developer Connection website (http://developer.java.sun.com). These patterns address common application problems through the application of J2EE technologies. The patterns catalog groups the various patterns into the following tiers:

- **Presentation tier**: Whatever is required to present application data and user interface elements to the user is inside of the presentation tier of the application. Key technologies in use are JavaServer Pages (JSP) and Java Servlets.

- **Business tier**: The business tier is where all the business processing takes place. The primary J2EE technologies in use for this tier are Enterprise JavaBeans (EJBs).

- **Integration tier**: The integration tier provides connections to the resource tier. The resource tier includes things such as message queues, databases, and legacy systems. The J2EE technologies in use at the integration tier are the Java Message Service (JMS), Java Database Connectivity (JDBC), and the Java Connector Architecture (JCA).

Because this is a JSP book, I'll mostly present those patterns that deal with the presentation tier. I won't attempt to describe each pattern in detail; the patterns catalog does a fine job of that. The goal of this book is to provide best practices and examples. To that end, I'll provide enough definition to enable you to apply these patterns to common development tasks using JSP pages and Java servlets.

Looking at Presentation Design Patterns

The patterns I'll discuss in this book are commonly known as the Decorating Filter, Front Controller, Dispatcher View, and View Helper patterns. There are a few more presentation patterns in the J2EE catalog that I won't discuss. These four patterns are sufficient to illustrate the examples and best practices that I'll cover.

These patterns each cover a different *layer* of the presentation logic. As the request comes in, it can pass through a filter prior to the actual processing of the request (Decorating Filter pattern). It could then go to a centralized servlet to be processed (Front Controller Pattern). Once it has been processed, the servlet could then dispatch the results to a specific JSP page (Dispatch View Pattern). Finally, the JSP page could make use of custom tags or JavaBeans to help include the data in the HTML output (View Helper Pattern). Figure 5-1 illustrates the relationship between these patterns.

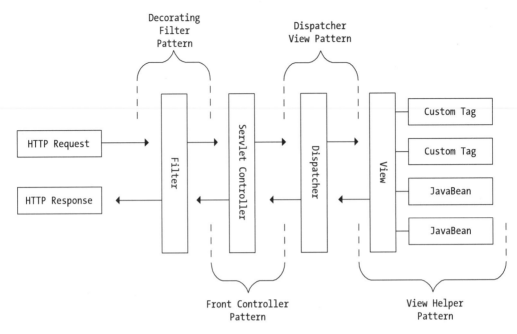

Figure 5-1. Presentation patterns

Here's a preview of each pattern I'll be discussing:

- **Decorating filter**: This pattern applies a kind of filter to either the request or response object as it passes in and out of the web container. You can use filters as a common place to log transactions, authenticate users, and even format data.

- **Front Controller pattern**: The Front Controller pattern is built upon the concept of the MVC pattern (see the next section). This pattern suggests the use of a single servlet to handle each and every request as opposed to embedding controller code inside of each JSP page.

- **Dispatcher view**: Inside of the controller, a piece of code exists that determines where the processed request should go to be displayed. In other words, it applies some kind of strategy to figure out which view, or JSP page, to use to display the current data.

- **View helper**: Once the specific view has been chosen, the JSP makes use of several "helpers" to adapt the data to the final outputted content. These helpers consist of either custom tags or JavaBeans.

Understanding Model-View-Controller (MVC)

The presentation patterns in the J2EE catalog are all based upon the MVC architecture. MVC is applied to software development projects in an effort to separate
the application data from the presentation of the data. This separation enables the
interface, or view, to take many different forms with little modification to
the application code. For instance, using an MVC pattern, a user interface can be
presented as both an HTML page (for web browsers) and a WML page (for mobile
devices), depending on the device requesting the page. The controller would recognize the source of the request and apply the application data to the
appropriate view (see Figure 5-2).

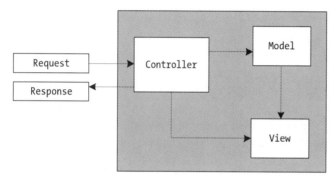

Figure 5-2. MVC architecture

The idea of separating presentation logic from the data and managing it with
a controller has its roots in graphical user interface (GUI) development. Take, for
instance, a user interface consisting of many different user controls. These controls contain the data, the formatting instructions, and the code that fires an
event when the control is activated. This makes the user interface platform-
specific and coupled with the application code itself. By applying an MVC
pattern and separating each of these components, the user interface becomes
lightweight, pluggable, and transportable across platforms. The Java Swing API
illustrates this best.

You can apply the MVC pattern to other areas of software development
besides client/server GUIs. Web development has benefited from this idea by
clearly separating presentation code from the application data and the controller
code that ties the two together. Let's take, for example, a simple web application
that displays catalog pages. Typically, this would consist of a search page,
a results page, and an item detail page. Each page has the responsibility of
authenticating the user, retrieving user preferences, retrieving the requested
data, and managing page navigation (see Figure 5-3).

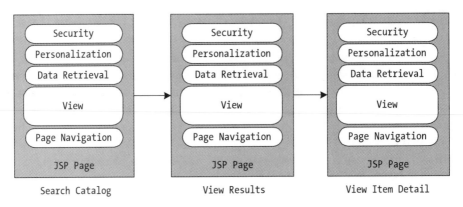

Figure 5-3. Simple catalog application (without MVC)

Looking at this application, it's easy to see that a lot of redundant code is being used to display each page. Not only does this introduce the potential for errors, but it also ties the application to the presentation by including many non-presentation functions inside of the presentation code. When you apply an MVC pattern to this application, the common functions move to a controller on the server. The presentation code is now only responsible for rendering the application data in a format that's appropriate for a particular device (typically a web browser). See Figure 5-4 for an MVC approach to this application.

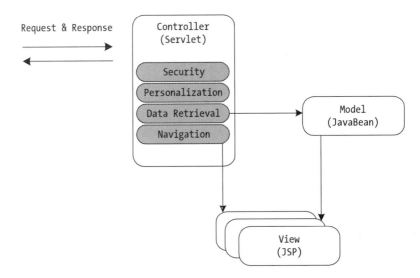

Figure 5-4. Simple catalog application (with MVC)

Seeing MVC in Action

To illustrate the MVC pattern, you're going to build a simple web application that collects data and stores it in a database. The data you'll be collecting is health information that will be stored in the customer table of our quoting database. In addition to collecting the data, the application will require the user to login to the system before accessing any of the pages.

This example is a simple one, but it illustrates some of the benefits of using an MVC architecture. You'll see how to centralize application security by giving the user a single access point into the application. You'll also standardize and share the database connection using a connection pooling mechanism built into the application server. In the next few chapters, I'll use this example (among others) to introduce new patterns. With that in mind, this example is basic at this point. You'll add features such as field validation and improved error handling later.

The application starts with a login page and then moves to a main servlet that will act as the controller (see Figure 5-5). The servlet will determine whether to proceed to the next page based upon the success of the login procedure. Once the user has logged in, they'll go to a survey page where they'll enter their information and submit it. Once again, the servlet will interrogate the request and move the user to the next page. If the data is successfully recorded, the user is taken to a confirmation page.

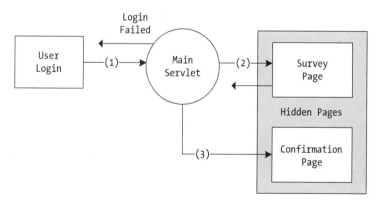

Figure 5-5. Simple survey application

Another benefit of using a servlet as a single entry point is that it enables you to hide your JSP pages from the outside world. This helps to secure the system by not allowing direct access to your application. The only page the user can access directly is the login page. If they were to type in the name of another page, the server would return a 404 error ("not found"). You accomplish this by "hiding" your JSP pages inside of the \WEB-INF directory. By definition, everything underneath this directory is inaccessible by direct access from the user. However, the servlet that acts as our controller can access this directory and therefore is allowed to forward requests to pages that reside there. Here's what your directory structure will look like when you're done with this example:

```
webapps\jspBook\ch5\login.jsp
webapps\jspBook\ch5\myError.jsp
webapps\jspBook\ch5\myHeader.htm
webapps\jspBook\ch5\myFooter.htm
webapps\jspBook\ch5\images\logo.gif
webapps\jspBook\WEB-INF\jsp\ch5\census.jsp
webapps\jspBook\WEB-INF\jsp\ch5\thankyou.jsp
```

Setting Up the Application

Before you begin coding, you need to add a table to the database and then modify your application server configuration to accommodate the use of DataSources. The table you need to add is a user table containing the user ID, password, and a customer ID. The customer ID creates a customer record that corresponds to the user. Ideally, this field would be dynamically generated, but for these purposes you're just going to hard-code this value. Here's the script to update the database:

```
createUsers.sql (c:\mysql quoting < createUsers.sql)

DROP TABLE IF EXISTS user;
CREATE TABLE user (id varchar(10) not null, pwd varchar(10), cust_id int);
INSERT INTO user VALUES ('apatzer', 'apress', 6);
```

The next task you need to do is modify your configuration to use DataSources. The J2EE specification allows a DataSource to be defined inside of the application server itself. Servlets and JSP pages can locate and use these DataSources using Java Naming and Directory Interface (JNDI). A key advantage to accessing a database this way is that the connection information is stored in one place outside of the application code. Also, most application servers have a built-in connection pooling mechanism you can take advantage of by accessing your database using a DataSource. To set this up, you'll need to be sure your application server supports this capability. Before modifying the appropriate configuration files, be sure to add your database drivers to a directory accessible to the application server (for Tomcat 4.0.1, put the drivers in the \common\lib directory). To create a DataSource in your application server, you'll need to add a description of it to the server.xml file. This description goes inside of your context definition like the one seen in Listing 5-1 (see the J2EE specification for more details).

Listing 5-1. server.xml

```
<Context path="/jspBook"
  docBase="jspBook"
  crossContext="false"
  debug="0"
  reloadable="true" >

  <Logger className="org.apache.catalina.logger.FileLogger"
            prefix="localhost_jspBook_log." suffix=".txt"
          timestamp="true"/>

  <Resource name="jdbc/QuotingDB" auth="SERVLET"
            type="javax.sql.DataSource"/>

    <ResourceParams name="jdbc/QuotingDB">
      <parameter>
        <name>driverClassName</name>
        <value>org.gjt.mm.mysql.Driver</value>
      </parameter>
      <parameter>
        <name>driverName</name>
        <value>jdbc:mysql://localhost:3306/quoting</value>
      </parameter>
    </ResourceParams>

</Context>
```

Now that you've described the DataSource to the application server, you need to tell your application about it. You do this by adding a resource entry into your web.xml file. Listing 5-2 shows what should go into this file (inside of your <web-app> tags).

Listing 5-2. web.xml

```
<resource-ref>
  <description>
    Resource reference to a factory for java.sql.Connection
    instances that may be used for talking to a particular
    database that is configured in the server.xml file.
  </description>
  <res-ref-name>
    jdbc/QuotingDB
  </res-ref-name>
  <res-type>
    javax.sql.DataSource
  </res-type>
  <res-auth>
    SERVLET
  </res-auth>
</resource-ref>
```

Finally, to use the DataSource, you need to replace any code that gets a database connection with the following piece of code (in this example's servlet you execute this code once inside of your init method):

```
try {
  Context initCtx = new InitialContext();
  Context envCtx = (Context) initCtx.lookup("java:comp/env");
  DataSource ds = (DataSource) envCtx.lookup("jdbc/QuotingDB");
  dbCon = ds.getConnection();
}
catch (javax.naming.NamingException e) {
  System.out.println("A problem occurred retrieving a DataSource object");
  System.out.println(e.toString());
}
catch (java.sql.SQLException e) {
  System.out.println("A problem occurred connecting to the database.");
  System.out.println(e.toString());
}
```

Defining the Model

Before walking through the controller or the views, you need to define the model. The model is responsible for storing data that will be displayed by one or more views. Typically, a model exists as an Enterprise JavaBean (EJB) or simply a regular JavaBean. For this example, you'll just use a JavaBean. You might recall from Chapter 3 that you used a JavaBean to model the customer data. You'll reuse some of that and add a few additional methods to suit these purposes.

Aside from removing some unnecessary code, you'll need to add two new methods to the CustomerBean you built back in Chapter 3. The first method you'll add is the populateFromParameters method. This method takes an HttpServletRequest object as a parameter. The method is responsible for reading the input fields from the request object and populating the bean properties with their values. Also, the user ID is pulled out of the user's session and stored in the bean for later use. The other new method you'll be adding to this bean is the submit method. This method takes a Connection object as a parameter and is responsible for updating the database with the stored data residing in the properties (fields) of the bean. Listing 5-3 shows the updated code for the CustomerBean.

Listing 5-3. CustomerBean.java

```java
package jspbook.ch5;

import java.util.*;
import java.sql.*;
import javax.servlet.http.*;

public class CustomerBean implements java.io.Serializable {

  /* Member Variables */
  private String lname, fname, sex;
  private int age, children;
  private boolean spouse, smoker;

  /* Helper Variables */;
  private String uid ;

  /* Constructor */
  public CustomerBean() {
    /* Initialize properties */
    setLname("");
    setFname("");
    setSex("");
    setAge(0);
    setChildren(0);
    setSpouse(false);
    setSmoker(false);
  }
```

```
public void populateFromParms(HttpServletRequest _req) {
  // Populate bean properties from request parameters
  setLname(_req.getParameter("lname"));
  setFname(_req.getParameter("fname"));
  setSex(_req.getParameter("sex"));
  setAge(Integer.parseInt(_req.getParameter("age")));
  setChildren(Integer.parseInt(_req.getParameter("children")));
  setSpouse((_req.getParameter("married").equals("Y")) ? true : false);
  setSmoker((_req.getParameter("smoker").equals("Y")) ? true : false);
  // Get session and populate uid
  HttpSession session = _req.getSession();
  uid = (String) session.getAttribute("uid");
}

/* Accessor Methods */

/* Last Name */
public void setLname(String _lname) {lname = _lname;}
public String getLname() {return lname;}

/* First Name */
public void setFname(String _fname) {fname = _fname;}
public String getFname() {return fname;}

/* Sex */
public void setSex(String _sex) {sex = _sex;}
public String getSex() {return sex;}

/* Age */
public void setAge(int _age) {age = _age;}
public int getAge() {return age;}

/* Number of Children */
public void setChildren(int _children) {children = _children;}
public int getChildren() {return children;}

/* Spouse ? */
public void setSpouse(boolean _spouse) {spouse = _spouse;}
public boolean getSpouse() {return spouse;}

/* Smoker ? */
public void setSmoker(boolean _smoker) {smoker = _smoker;}
public boolean getSmoker() {return smoker;}
```

```
                                      {

********************************

GET A $20 GIFT CARD

                              (256);

                      se uid to get custID)

                    * from user where id = '" + uid + "'");

              st_id");

                  ect * from customer where id = " + custId);

                  customer SET ");
    sql.append("lname='").append(lname).append("', ");
    sql.append("fname='").append(fname).append("', ");
    sql.append("age=").append(age).append(", ");
    sql.append("sex='").append(sex).append("', ");
    sql.append("married='").append((spouse) ? "Y" : "N").append("', ");
    sql.append("children=").append(children).append(", ");
    sql.append("smoker='").append((smoker) ? "Y" : "N").append("'");
    sql.append("where id='").append(custId).append("'");
  }
  else {
    // Insert record
    sql.append("INSERT INTO customer VALUES(");
    sql.append(custId).append(",'");
    sql.append(lname).append("', '");
    sql.append(fname).append("', ");
    sql.append(age).append(", '");
    sql.append(sex).append("', '");
    sql.append((spouse) ? "Y" : "N").append("', ");
    sql.append(children).append(", '");
    sql.append((smoker) ? "Y" : "N").append("')");
  }
  s.executeUpdate(sql.toString());
}
```

```
    catch (SQLException e) {
      System.out.println("Error saving customer: "
                              + custId + " : " + e.toString());

      return false;
    }
    return true;
  }


}
```

Setting the View

The presentation logic of the application is stored in three JSP files. The first one, login.jsp, is accessible to the public, and the other two are only accessible from the controller servlet. The login page is a simple user and password entry screen that submits its data to the Main servlet. You'll notice that you add a parameter to the servlet called action. This tells the servlet what it needs to do. In this case, the action is login. If there's an error while attempting to log in, the servlet will add an attribute to the session indicating a problem and then return the user to the login page. Because of this, the login page checks the session for the appropriate attribute and displays corresponding error message if it finds it. Listing 5-4 shows the complete listing of the login page.

Listing 5-4. login.jsp *(\webapps\jspBook\ch5\login.jsp)*

```
<%@ page
       errorPage="myError.jsp?from=login.jsp"
%>

<html>
<head>
  <title>Quoting System Login</title>
</head>

<body bgcolor="#FFFF99">

<%@ include file="myHeader.html" %>

<form method="post" action="Main?action=login">
```

```
<p align="center">
  <font face="Arial, Helvetica, sans-serif" size="6" color="#003300">
    <b><i>Login to Quoting System</i></b>
  </font>
</p>

<p> </p>

<%  String loginError = (String) session.getAttribute("loginError");
    if (loginError != null && loginError.equals("y")) {
%>
<center>
  <font color="#ff0000">Invalid login, please try again.</font>
</center>
<%  }
%>

<table width="199" border="0" align="center" cellpadding="5">
  <tr>
    <td>
      <font face="Arial, Helvetica, sans-serif" size="2">User ID:</font>
    </td>
    <td><input type="text" name="UID"></td>
  </tr>
  <tr>
    <td><font face="Arial, Helvetica, sans-serif" size="2">Password:</font></td>
    <td><input type="password" name="PWD"></td>
  </tr>
  <tr align="center">
    <td colspan="2"><input type="submit" name="Submit" value="Login"></td>
  </tr>
</table>

</form>

<%@ include file="myFooter.html" %>

</body>
</html>
```

Figure 5-6 shows the login page.

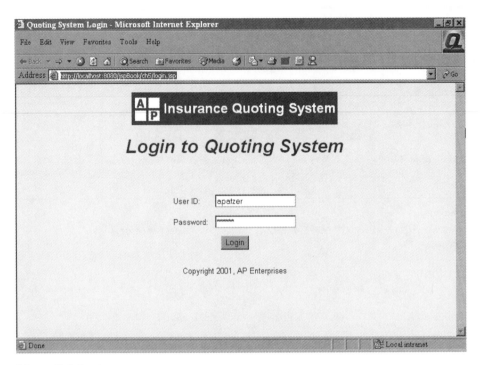

Figure 5-6. Login page

The survey page (census.jsp) collects data from the user and submits it to the Main servlet. The action parameter is set to submit to indicate to the servlet that you want to submit data to the database. This page is a good example of one that needs to be enhanced to include field validation and error handling. You'll do this in future chapters as you explore other presentation patterns. See Listing 5-5 for the complete code of the simple data collection page.

Listing 5-5. census.jsp *(\WEB-INF\jsp\ch5\census.jsp)*

```
<!-- JSP Directives -->
<%@ page
      errorPage="myError.jsp?from=census.jsp"
%>

<html>
<head>
  <title>Insurance Quoting System</title>
</head>

<body bgcolor="#FFFF99">

<basefont face="Arial">
```

```
<%@ include file="/ch5/myHeader.html" %>

<form action="Main?action=submit" method="post">

<br><br>

<%  String submitError = (String) session.getAttribute("submitError");
    if (submitError != null && submitError.equals("y")) {
%>
<center>
  <font color="#ff0000">Error recording survey data, please try again.</font>
</center>
<br><br>
<%  }
%>

<center><b>Enter personal information:</b></center>
<br><br>
<table cellspacing="2" cellpadding="2" border="0" align="center">
<tr>
    <td align="right">First Name:</td>
    <td><input type="Text" name="fname" size="10"></td>
</tr>
<tr>
    <td align="right">Last Name:</td>
    <td><input type="Text" name="lname" size="10"></td>
</tr>
<tr>
    <td align="right">Age:</td>
    <td><input type="Text" name="age" size="2"></td>
</tr>
<tr>
    <td align="right">Sex:</td>
    <td>
      <input type="radio" name="sex" value="M" checked>Male</input>
      <input type="radio" name="sex" value="F">Female</input>
    </td>
</tr>
<tr>
    <td align="right">Married:</td>
    <td><input type="Text" name="married" size="2"></td>
</tr>
<tr>
```

```
        <td align="right">Children:</td>
        <td><input type="Text" name="children" size="2"></td>
</tr>
<tr>
        <td align="right">Smoker:</td>
        <td><input type="Text" name="smoker" size="2"></td>
</tr>
<tr>
        <td colspan="2" align="center"><input type="Submit" value="Submit"></td>
</tr>
</table>

<br><br>

</form>
<%@ include file="/ch5/myFooter.html" %>

</body>
</html>
```

Figure 5-7 shows the survey page.

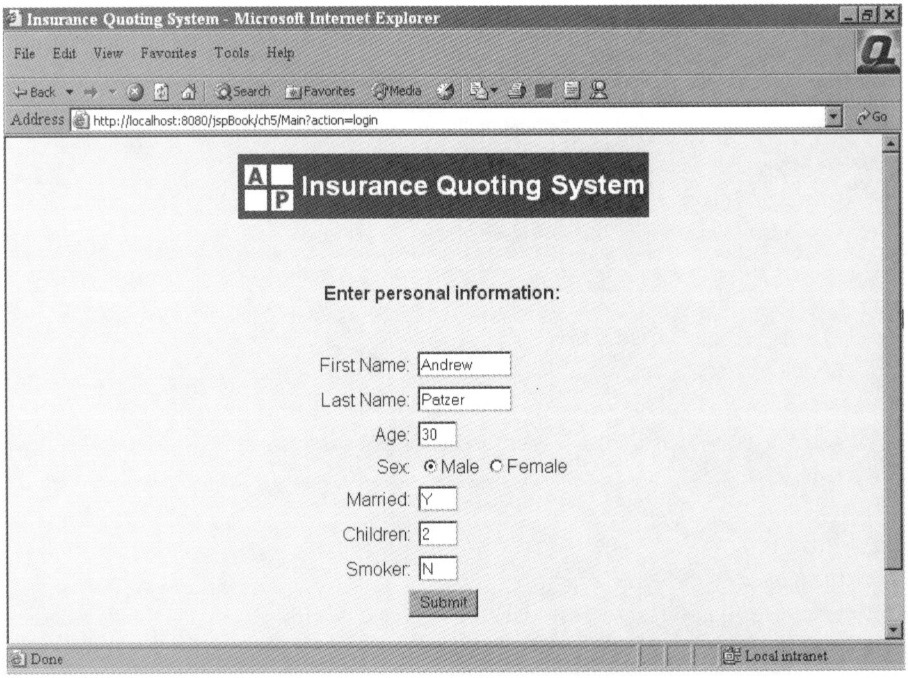

Figure 5-7. Survey page

Finally, once the data has been submitted, the request is forwarded to a confirmation page (thankyou.jsp). This is a simple page confirming that the data has been accepted. If there were an error trying to submit the data, control would return to the survey page (census.jsp) and an error message would appear at the top (similar to what you did with the login page). See Listing 5-6 for the confirmation page.

Listing 5-6. thankyou.jsp *(\WEB-INF\jsp\ch5\thankyou.jsp)*

```
<!-- JSP Directives -->
<%@ page
        errorPage="myError.jsp?from=thankyou.jsp"
%>

<html>
<head>
  <title>Insurance Quoting System</title>
</head>

<body bgcolor="#FFFF99">

<basefont face="Arial">

<%@ include file="/ch5/myHeader.html" %>

<br><br>

<center>
Your survey answers have been recorded.
Thank you for participating in this survey.
</center>

<br><br>

<%@ include file="/ch5/myFooter.html" %>

</body>
</html>
```

See Figure 5-8 for the confirmation page that's displayed upon successfully recording the survey data.

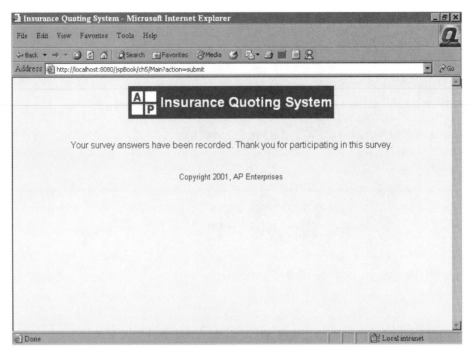

Figure 5-8. Confirmation page

Building the Controller

You'll be using a servlet as your controller (`Main`). To make this accessible, add the following entry to your `web.xml` file (inside of the `<web-app>` tags):

```
<servlet>
    <servlet-name>
        Main
    </servlet-name>
    <servlet-class>
        jspbook.ch5.Main
    </servlet-class>
</servlet>
<servlet-mapping>
    <servlet-name>
        Main
    </servlet-name>
    <url-pattern>
        /ch5/Main
    </url-pattern>
</servlet-mapping>
```

The init method obtains your database connection using the DataSource you created earlier. This database connection is closed in the destroy method at the end of the servlet's lifecycle. Each request is serviced by the doPost method. Inside of there, the action is determined by checking the parameter action. The first time through, the login action directs the servlet to the authenticate method. If the login is successful, the user is taken to the census.jsp page.

The important thing to point out is that all security, database connectivity, and navigational control is centralized inside of this one servlet. You reuse code in several places. For instance, the navigational code goes into the gotoPage method. If you need to change this functionality, you only need to do it in one place. You'll see as you explore other patterns how useful this architecture really is. The goal of this example is simply to illustrate the basic idea of an MVC pattern. See Listing 5-7 for the controller servlet.

Listing 5-7. Main.java

```java
package jspbook.ch5;

import javax.servlet.*;
import javax.servlet.http.*;
import java.io.*;
import java.sql.*;
import javax.naming.*;
import javax.sql.*;

import jspbook.ch5.CustomerBean;

public class Main extends HttpServlet {


  DataSource ds;
  HttpSession session;

  /* Initialize servlet. Use JNDI to look up a DataSource */

  public void init() {

    try {
      Context initCtx = new InitialContext();
      Context envCtx = (Context) initCtx.lookup("java:comp/env");
      ds = (DataSource) envCtx.lookup("jdbc/QuotingDB");
    }
    catch (javax.naming.NamingException e) {
      System.out.println(
```

```
                        "A problem occurred while retrieving a DataSource object");
                    System.out.println(e.toString());
                }


    }

    public void doPost (HttpServletRequest _req, HttpServletResponse _res)
        throws ServletException, IOException {

        /* Refresh session attributes */
        session = _req.getSession();
        session.removeAttribute("loginError");
        session.removeAttribute("submitError");

        String action = _req.getParameter("action");

        /* Authenticate user if request comes from login page */
        if (action.equals("login")) {
            String uid = _req.getParameter("UID");
            String pwd = _req.getParameter("PWD");
            if (authenticate(uid, pwd)) {
                session.setAttribute("validUser", "y");
                session.setAttribute("loginError", "n");
                session.setAttribute("uid", uid);
                gotoPage("/WEB-INF/jsp/ch5/census.jsp", _req, _res);
            }
            /* If the user login fails, then return them to the login page to retry */
            else {
                loginError(_req, _res);
            }
        }

        /* Record the survey data if the request comes from the survey form */
        else if (action.equals("submit")) {
            /* Make sure the user has logged in before recording the data */
            String validUser = (String) session.getAttribute("validUser");
            if (validUser.equals("y")) {
                if (recordSurvey(_req)) {
                    /* Reset validUser flag and forward to ThankYou page */
                    session.removeAttribute("validUser");
                    gotoPage("/WEB-INF/jsp/ch5/thankyou.jsp", _req, _res);
                }
```

```
      else {
        session.setAttribute("submitError", "y");
        gotoPage("/ch5/login.jsp", _req, _res);
      }
    }
    /* If the user did not login, then send them to the login page */
    else {
      loginError(_req, _res);
    }
  }

}


/* Send request to a different page */
private void gotoPage(String _page, HttpServletRequest _req,
  HttpServletResponse _res)
  throws IOException, ServletException {

  RequestDispatcher dispatcher = _req.getRequestDispatcher(_page);
  if (dispatcher != null)
    dispatcher.forward(_req, _res);

}


/* Set error attributes in session and return to Login page */
private void loginError(HttpServletRequest _req, HttpServletResponse _res)
  throws IOException, ServletException {

  session.setAttribute("validUser", "n");
  session.setAttribute("loginError", "y");
  gotoPage("/ch5/login.jsp", _req, _res);

}

/* Check if the user is valid */
private boolean authenticate(String _uid, String _pwd) {

  Connection dbCon = null;
  ResultSet rs = null;
  try {
    dbCon = ds.getConnection();
    Statement s = dbCon.createStatement();
    rs = s.executeQuery("select * from user where id = '"
```

```
            + _uid + "' and pwd = '" + _pwd + "'");
      return (rs.next());
    }
    catch (java.sql.SQLException e) {
      System.out.println("A problem occurred while accessing the database.");
      System.out.println(e.toString());
    }
    finally {
      try {
        dbCon.close();
      }
      catch (SQLException e) {
        System.out.println("A problem occurred while closing the database.");
        System.out.println(e.toString());
      }
    }

    return false;

  }

  /* Using the CustomerBean, record the data */
  public boolean recordSurvey(HttpServletRequest _req) {

    Connection dbCon = null;
    try {
      dbCon = ds.getConnection();
      CustomerBean cBean = new CustomerBean();
      cBean.populateFromParms(_req);
      return cBean.submit(dbCon);
    }
    catch (java.sql.SQLException e) {
      System.out.println("A problem occurred while accessing the database.");
      System.out.println(e.toString());
    }
    finally {
      try {
        dbCon.close();
      }
      catch (SQLException e) {
        System.out.println("A problem occurred while closing the database.");
        System.out.println(e.toString());
      }
    }
```

```
    return false;

  }


  public void destroy() {
  }

}
```

Summary

This chapter introduced you to the idea of using patterns to design your applications. Patterns are industry-wide best practices that have been tested and proven by many different developers. The *J2EE Patterns Catalog* contains several design patterns for enterprise Java development. This book covers four specific presentation-tier patterns that help to describe several best practices for JSP development.

Each of these patterns assumes an MVC architecture, which organizes your web application into three logical pieces. The model stores the application data, the view displays the application data, and the controller manages requests and handles navigation through the application. The next few chapters will explore J2EE patterns that extend each of these areas and applies strategies to maximize the efficiency of developing MVC-based web applications.

CHAPTER 6

The Decorating Filter Pattern

THE FIRST PATTERN I'LL DISCUSS in this book enables you to manipulate the HTTP request and response objects both before and after they're processed by either a Java servlet or a JSP page. This gives you a great amount of flexibility to customize a base application without requiring modifications to the application code itself. For instance, let's say you have two different applications, each with their own security model. You'd like to avoid making users log in to both systems and maintain multiple login IDs. Although there are many complicated solutions to this problem, filters provide a way to intercept each request and perform the necessary security negotiation between the different systems (see Figure 6-1).

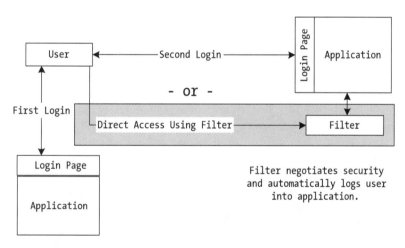

Figure 6-1. Using filters for integrated security

This chapter will show you how to create filters and some useful ways to apply them to your JSP and servlet development projects. I'll start each of the pattern chapters with a general definition of the pattern itself.

For more detailed pattern definitions, please refer to the *J2EE Patterns Catalog* at the Java Developer Connection (`http://developer.java.sun.com/developer/technicalArticles/J2EE/patterns/`).

Next, I'll discuss various strategies for applying the pattern. Finally, you'll apply these strategies to some common functionality you'd like to build into a web application.

Defining the Pattern

The Decorating Filter pattern (also referred to as the Intercepting Filter pattern) involves setting up a series of *filters* that intercept an HTTP request (or an HTTP response), perform a series of operations on the object, and then pass it along to its intended target. This allows for pre-processing and post-processing of the request and response objects without affecting the core application. Here are some potential uses for filters:

- Log important information about each request

- Authenticate users

- Transform input data prior to processing

- Transform response data for a specific device

- Validate form data and interrupt processing if necessary

The general idea behind using filters is that the request passes through a filter manager. This filter manager would associate the request with a specific filter chain and pass the request to the first filter in the chain. Each filter would perform its processing and pass the request on to the next filter in the chain. This would continue until the last filter in the chain is finished processing the request (see Figure 6-2). The *filtered* request is then forwarded onto its intended target.

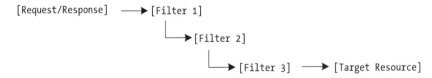

Figure 6-2. Using filters to pre-process a request

Applying Strategies

There are two main strategies for applying the Decorating Filter pattern. The first strategy is to develop a custom filter manager and individual filters. The second strategy is to make use of the filtering capabilities built into the 2.3 version of the Java Servlet API. It's pretty obvious that you should use the standard filtering whenever possible, but there may however be a situation where a custom filtering mechanism is necessary. For instance, your application may need to run in an environment that doesn't support the 2.3 servlet API.

Developing a Custom Filter Strategy

To implement your own filtering mechanism, you could wrap the core request processing logic with any number of custom filters. These filters would each execute in turn before finally executing the core processing code. Once this filter chain has been completed, the servlet controller would then dispatch the request to the appropriate view. Custom filters are simply Java classes that make up a sort of linked list. Each filter executes the processing logic of the next filter until each filter in the chain has been executed (see Figure 6-3).

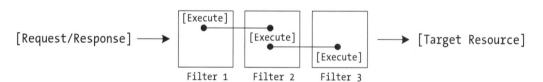

Figure 6-3. Custom filter strategy

The problem with using a custom filter strategy is that it must be hard-coded into the servlet controller. This means you must make any changes to the filter chain inside the servlet and then recompile it. Another disadvantage to this approach is that you can't modify the request and response objects within the filters because they'll be dispatched upon completion. Although it may sometimes be necessary to build custom filters, the preferred approach is to use a standard filter strategy, as discussed in the following section.

Using a Standard Filter Strategy

It would be nice to be able to declaratively add and remove filters from a filter chain and then associate the filter chain with a specific URL pattern. With the release of version 2.3 of the servlet API, it's now possible to create standard filters and then declare and associate them inside of the web.xml file. Generically speaking, though, the standard filter strategy involves invoking a filter manager with each request, which in turn would invoke each of the filters associated with the request URL pattern (see Figure 6-4). Each filter would be a completely autonomous "black box" capable of receiving standard request and response objects, processing them, and returning control to the filter manager. The filter manager would then invoke the next filter in the chain. This would continue until the end of the filter chain is reached and the request is passed on to its intended target.

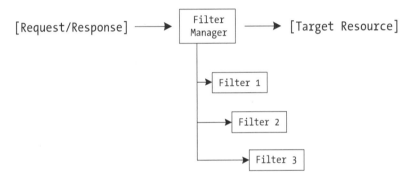

Figure 6-4. Standard filter strategy

A key advantage to using a standard filter mechanism is that you can add and remove modifiers to the HTTP Request and Response without affecting the application code. It also makes it possible to modify the request object as well as the output stream because it happens outside of the servlet controller. Next, you'll see exactly how to implement a standard filter chain using the filtering mechanism built in to the Tomcat 4.0 servlet container (and therefore any J2EE application server supporting the 2.3 version of the servlet API).

Applying the Decorating Filter Pattern

The servlet API includes a standard mechanism for applying the standard filter strategy. Therefore, any application server (or servlet container) that supports the 2.3 version of the servlet API has this mechanism already built in. To use filters with your application, simply create the filter classes, declare them in your web.xml file, and map them to a specific URL or URL pattern (see Figure 6-5).

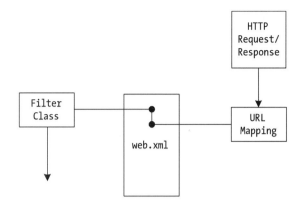

Figure 6-5. Filtering with J2EE

Creating the Filter Class

All filters are Java classes that implement the `javax.servlet.Filter` interface. This interface defines the following three methods that must be implemented:

- **void init(FilterConfig) throws ServletException**: Called when the filter is first put into service. The important thing that happens is that the `FilterConfig` is copied locally within the filter.

- **void doFilter(ServletRequest, ServletResponse, FilterChain) throws IOException, ServletException**: This method is the equivalent of a `doPost` or `doGet` in a servlet. Whenever the filter is executed, the `doFilter` method is called. Upon completion of any filter-specific processing, a call to the `doFilter` method of the `FilterChain` object will continue processing any remaining filters.

- **void destroy()**: Called just before the filter is taken out of service. This is where any cleanup tasks would be performed.

It's important to point out that a Java filter operates on Servlet objects and not HTTPServlet objects. Remember that, although uncommon, a servlet can exist in a non-HTTP environment. With that in mind, to use the request or response objects, they must be cast to their HTTP equivalents like so:

```
if (request instanceOf HttpServletRequest) {
    HttpServletRequest httpReq = (HttpServletRequest) request;
}
```

Here's a basic template of a Java filter object:

```java
import java.io.*;
import javax.servlet.*;
import javax.servlet.http.*;

public class TestFilter implements Filter {

  private FilterConfig config =  null;

  public void init(FilterConfig _config)
    throws ServletException
  {
    this.config = _config;
    // Perform initialization tasks here
  }

  public void doFilter(ServletRequest _req, ServletResponse _res,
    FilterChain _chain) throws IOException, ServletException
  {
    HttpServletRequest httpReq;

    // Cast request object to HttpServletRequest
    if (_req instanceof HttpServletRequest) {
      httpReq = (HttpServletRequest) _req;
    }

    // Perform filter-specific processing here

    // Continue with filter chain
    _chain.doFilter(_req, _res);
  }

  public void destroy()
  {
    config = null;

    // Perform any cleanup tasks here
  }

}
```

Declaring the Filter

The first thing you need to do to add a filter to your web application is declare it inside of the web.xml file. Inside of the <web-app> tag, add a <filter> tag to describe your filter. This will simply associate a common name with the filter class you've written. This name will be used later to map the filter to a specific URL pattern. Inside of the <filter> tag, add a <filter-name> and a <filter-class> element like this:

```
<filter>
  <filter-name>sampleFilter</filter-name>
  <filter-class>jspbook.filters.SampleFilter</filter-name>
</filter>
```

Mapping the Filter to a URL

Now that you have a filter declared, the next thing you need to do is associate the filter with a specific resource. You do this by adding a <filter-mapping> tag inside of the <web-app> tag in your web.xml file. You can map a filter to either a URL pattern or a specific servlet. Here's an example of each type of mapping:

```
<filter-mapping>
  <filter-name>sampleFilter</filter-name>
  <url-pattern>/*</url-pattern>
</filter-mapping>

<filter-mapping>
  <filter-name>testFilter</filter-name>
  <servlet-name>MainServlet</servlet-name>
</filter-mapping>
```

Using Filters to Log HTTP Requests

There have been many times in the past when I needed to examine the HTTP request and response objects as they pass back and forth with each request. For instance, while I was debugging a problem the browser was having while trying to render a dynamically generated PDF document, I needed to obtain an HTTP *sniffer* to examine the contents and headers of the response object. Although this solution worked, it required locating the software, setting it up, and modifying my application to use this sniffer as a proxy server. It would have been much easier if I had been able to create a simple filter that dumped out the contents of the HTTP response without having to install and use a third-party application to do so.

You're going to build a simple filter that logs the HTTP parameters before they reach their intended target. The example will extend this to display the contents of the HTTP response, as well. Here's what the output of this filter might look like after you log in to an application and then submit some form data (from the example in Chapter 5):

```
HTTP Request: Wed Oct 24 11:00:20 CDT 2001:

Remote Address: 127.0.0.1
Remote Host: 127.0.0.1

UID = apatzer
PWD = apress
Submit = Login
action = login

HTTP Request: Wed Oct 24 11:00:32 CDT 2001:

Remote Address: 127.0.0.1
Remote Host: 127.0.0.1

age = 30
lname = Patzer
children = 2
married = Y
sex = M
action = submit
smoker = N
fname = Andrew
```

To implement this filter, you need to declare it and then map it to a URL pattern. In this case, just map it to every request for your particular web application (jspBook). Listing 6-1 shows the updated web.xml file that describes and maps the RequestLoggingFilter.

Listing 6-1. web.xml
```
<?xml version="1.0" encoding="ISO-8859-1"?>

<!DOCTYPE web-app
    PUBLIC "-//Sun Microsystems, Inc.//DTD Web Application 2.3//EN"
    "http://java.sun.com/dtd/web-app_2_3.dtd">
```

```
<web-app>

  <!-- Define filters -->
  <filter>
    <filter-name>requestLoggingFilter</filter-name>
    <filter-class>jspbook.ch6.RequestLoggingFilter</filter-class>
  </filter>
  <filter-mapping>
    <filter-name>requestLoggingFilter</filter-name>
    <url-pattern>/*</url-pattern>
  </filter-mapping>

  <!-- Servlet mappings -->
  <servlet>
    <servlet-name>
      Main
    </servlet-name>
    <servlet-class>
      jspbook.ch5.Main
    </servlet-class>
  </servlet>
  <servlet-mapping>
    <servlet-name>
      Main
    </servlet-name>
    <url-pattern>
      /ch5/Main
    </url-pattern>
  </servlet-mapping>

  <!-- Describe a DataSource -->
  <resource-ref>
    <description>
      Resource reference to a factory for java.sql.Connection
      instances that may be used for talking to a particular
      database that is configured in the server.xml file.
    </description>
    <res-ref-name>
      jdbc/QuotingDB
    </res-ref-name>
    <res-type>
      javax.sql.DataSource
    </res-type>
```

```
        <res-auth>
          SERVLET
        </res-auth>
      </resource-ref>

  </web-app>
```

To write a filter class, you need to implement the `javax.servlet.Filter` interface. You then need to implement the `init`, `destroy`, and `doFilter` methods. This filter will first open up a log file with a unique timestamp in the filename. You do this in the `init` method so the file can remain open as long as the filter remains in service. You make the file accessible to the rest of the filter by declaring the `FileOutputStream` at the class level, rather than inside the `init` method.

```java
private FileOutputStream fos;

public void init(FilterConfig _config)
  throws ServletException
{
  this.config = _config;
  try {
    /* Timestamp log file */
    File f = new File("c:\\development\\tomcat_"
      + new Date().getTime() + ".log");
    fos = new FileOutputStream(f);
  }
  catch (FileNotFoundException e) {
    System.out.println("Error opening log file.");
    System.out.println(e.toString());
  }
}
```

This file is eventually closed in the `destroy` method by closing the `FileOutputStream` object. Inside of the `doFilter` method, which executes on each request, the `ServletRequest` object is cast to an `HttpServletRequest` object and passed to a custom method to assemble a log entry containing the HTTP parameters included inside of the request. After the log file is written to, the `doFilter` method of the `FilterChain` is executed to continue processing any remaining filters.

```java
  public void doFilter(ServletRequest _req, ServletResponse _res,
    FilterChain _chain) throws IOException, ServletException
  {
    /* Log HTTP form parameters */
    if (_req instanceof HttpServletRequest) {
      String log = getParms((HttpServletRequest)_req);
      fos.write(log.getBytes());
    }

    /* Continue with filter chain */
    _chain.doFilter(_req, _res);
  }
```

For a complete listing of the RequestLoggingFilter class, see Listing 6-2.

Listing 6-2. RequestLoggingFilter.java

```java
package jspbook.ch6;

import java.io.*;
import java.util.*;
import javax.servlet.*;
import javax.servlet.http.*;

public class RequestLoggingFilter implements Filter {

  private FilterConfig config =  null;
  private FileOutputStream fos;

  public void init(FilterConfig _config)
    throws ServletException
  {
    this.config = _config;
    try {
      /* Timestamp log file */
      File f = new File("c:\\development\\tomcat_"
        + new Date().getTime() + ".log");
      fos = new FileOutputStream(f);
    }
    catch (FileNotFoundException e) {
      System.out.println("Error opening log file.");
      System.out.println(e.toString());
    }
  }
```

```java
public void doFilter(ServletRequest _req, ServletResponse _res,
  FilterChain _chain) throws IOException, ServletException
{
  /* Log HTTP form parameters */
  if (_req instanceof HttpServletRequest) {
    String log = getParms((HttpServletRequest)_req);
    fos.write(log.getBytes());
  }

  /* Continue with filter chain */
  _chain.doFilter(_req, _res);
}

public void destroy()
{
  config = null;
  try {
    fos.close();
  }
  catch (IOException e) {
    System.out.println("Error closing log file.");
    System.out.println(e.toString());
  }
}

private String getParms(HttpServletRequest _req)
  throws ServletException
{
  StringBuffer log = new StringBuffer();

  /* Get Http Parms */
  log.append("HTTP Request: ");
  log.append(new Date());
  log.append(":\n\n");

  log.append("Remote Address: " + _req.getRemoteAddr() + "\n");
  log.append("Remote Host: " + _req.getRemoteHost() + "\n\n");

  Enumeration e = _req.getParameterNames();
  while (e.hasMoreElements()) {
    String key = (String)e.nextElement();
    String[] values = _req.getParameterValues(key);
    log.append(key + " = ");
```

```
        for(int i = 0; i < values.length; i++) {
            log.append(values[i] + " ");
        }
        log.append("\n");
    }

    return log.toString();
  }

}
```

Using Filters to Log HTTP Responses

Filters can also be useful for manipulating content after it has been generated, just before it has been rendered by the browser. To illustrate this, you're going to modify the previous example to write the response content, rather than the request parameters, to your log file. To manipulate the HTTP response, the response object is first wrapped inside of a custom wrapper object, the doFilter method is called with the wrapped response rather than the original response, and finally the response content is obtained and manipulated as necessary (see Figure 6-6).

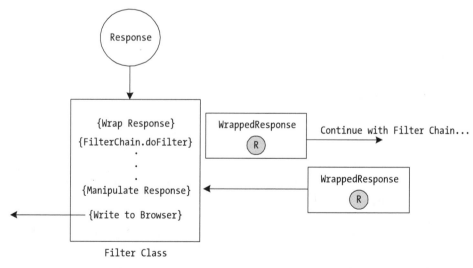

Figure 6-6. Manipulating response content

The reason you wrap the response object is that you need to store the response output and be able to reference it locally within your filter. The servlet API gives you a standard wrapper to extend called HttpServletResponseWrapper. To make use of it, you extend it and override the getWriter and getOutputStream methods to return references to local objects within the filter. The writer and stream you return are enclosed within a custom class called ByteArrayPrintWriter (see Listing 6-2). Here's how you wrap the response inside of the doFilter method:

```
final ByteArrayPrintWriter b = new ByteArrayPrintWriter();
final HttpServletResponse HttpResp = (HttpServletResponse) _res;
HttpServletResponse wrappedRes = new HttpServletResponseWrapper(HttpResp) {
  public PrintWriter getWriter() {
    return b.getWriter();
  }
  public ServletOutputStream getOutputStream() {
    return b.getStream();
  }
  public void setContentType(String type) {
    HttpResp.setContentType(type);
  }
};

/* Continue Processing */
_chain.doFilter(_req, wrappedRes);
```

The remainder of the doFilter method retrieves the contents as a String object, writes it to the log file, and continues to write the content to the original response object. This is necessary because you passed a wrapped object through the filter chain rather than the original response. Here's the code that executes after the filter chain returns from its processing:

```
/* Log the response content */
StringBuffer log = new StringBuffer();
log.append("*** HTTP Response: ").append(new Date()).append("***\n\n");
String output = b.getStream().toString();
log.append(output).append("\n\n");
fos.write(log.toString().getBytes());

/* Write content to browser */
_res.setContentLength(output.length());
_res.getWriter().print(output);
_res.getWriter().close();
```

To deploy this filter, add the appropriate entries to your web.xml file like you did in the previous example (just replace RequestLoggingFilter with ResponseLoggingFilter). For a complete listing of the filter code see Listing 6-3.

Listing 6-3. ResponseLoggingFilter.java

```
package jspbook.ch6;

import java.io.*;
import java.util.*;
import javax.servlet.*;
import javax.servlet.http.*;

public class ResponseLoggingFilter implements Filter {

  private FilterConfig config =  null;
  private FileOutputStream fos;

  private static class ByteArrayServletStream extends ServletOutputStream
  {
    ByteArrayOutputStream baos;
    ByteArrayServletStream(ByteArrayOutputStream baos) {
      this.baos = baos;
    }
    public void write(int param) throws java.io.IOException {
      baos.write(param);
    }
    public String toString() {
      return baos.toString();
    }
  }

  private static class ByteArrayPrintWriter
  {
    private ByteArrayOutputStream baos = new ByteArrayOutputStream();
    private PrintWriter pw = new PrintWriter(baos);
    private ServletOutputStream sos = new ByteArrayServletStream(baos);

    public PrintWriter getWriter() {
      return pw;
    }
    public ServletOutputStream getStream() {
      return sos;
    }
```

```
      byte[] toByteArray() {
        return baos.toByteArray();
      }
    }

    public void init(FilterConfig _config)
      throws ServletException
    {
      this.config = _config;
      try {
        /* Timestamp log file */
        File f = new File("c:\\development\\tomcat_"
          + new Date().getTime() + ".log");
        fos = new FileOutputStream(f);
      }\
      catch (FileNotFoundException e) {
        System.out.println("Error opening log file.");
        System.out.println(e.toString());
      }
    }

    public void doFilter(ServletRequest _req, ServletResponse _res,
      FilterChain _chain) throws IOException, ServletException
    {

      /* Wrap the response object */
      final ByteArrayPrintWriter b = new ByteArrayPrintWriter();
      final HttpServletResponse HttpResp = (HttpServletResponse) _res;
      HttpServletResponse wrappedRes = new HttpServletResponseWrapper(HttpResp) {
        public PrintWriter getWriter() {
          return b.getWriter();
        }
        public ServletOutputStream getOutputStream() {
          return b.getStream();
        }
        public void setContentType(String type) {
          HttpResp.setContentType(type);
        }
      };
```

```
    /* Continue Processing */
    _chain.doFilter(_req, wrappedRes);

    /* Log the response content */
    StringBuffer log = new StringBuffer();
    log.append("*** HTTP Response: ").append(new Date()).append("***\n\n");
    String output = b.getStream().toString();
    log.append(output).append("\n\n");
    fos.write(log.toString().getBytes());

    /* Write content to browser */
    _res.setContentLength(output.length());
    _res.getWriter().print(output);
    _res.getWriter().close();
  }

  public void destroy()
  {
    config = null;
    try {
      fos.close();
    }
    catch (IOException e) {
      System.out.println("Error closing log file.");
      System.out.println(e.toString());
    }
  }

}
```

Using the RequestLoggingFilter and the ResponseLoggingFilter, each and every HTTP request made to the server is written to a log file. Each response is written to a different log file. To see this in action, open up the MVC example from Chapter 5. Access the login.jsp page and enter a valid username and password. Enter a set of data into the next page (see Figure 6-7 for an example). Click the submit button to complete the survey.

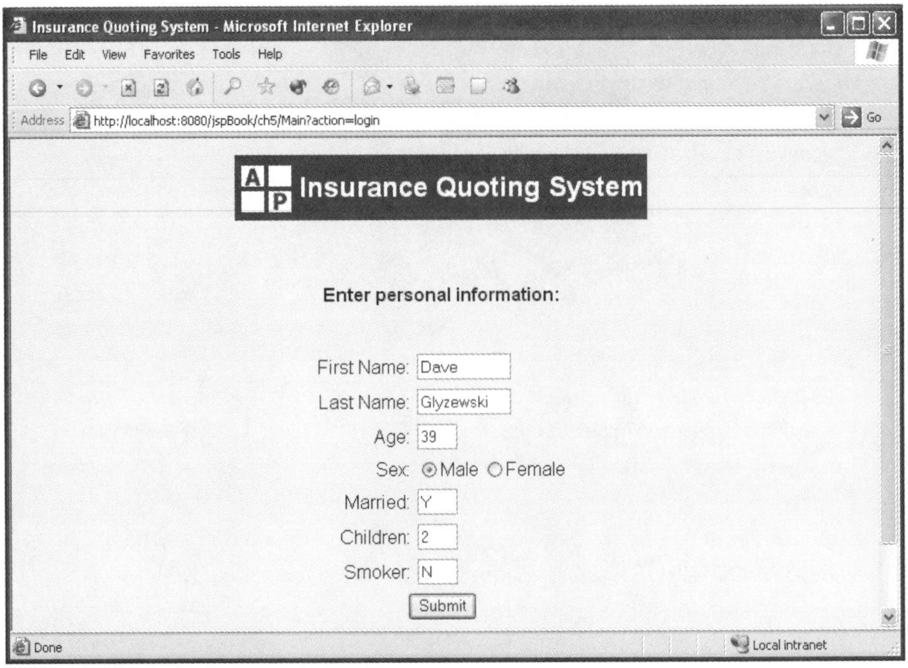

Figure 6-7. Entering form data to test filters

The previous set of actions produced three HTTP requests. The first request was to display the login.jsp page. The second request was to submit the login data and display the survey form. The final request was to submit the survey data and display a confirmation page. Listing 6-4 shows the log file for the request filter.

Listing 6-4. Log File for Request Filter

```
HTTP Request: Mon Feb 25 20:37:45 CST 2002:

Remote Address: 127.0.0.1
Remote Host: localhost

HTTP Request: Mon Feb 25 20:37:53 CST 2002:

Remote Address: 127.0.0.1
Remote Host: localhost

UID = apatzer
PWD = apress
Submit = Login
action = login
```

```
HTTP Request: Mon Feb 25 20:40:54 CST 2002:

Remote Address: 127.0.0.1
Remote Host: localhost

age = 39
lname = Glyzewski
children = 2
married = Y
sex = M
action = submit
smoker = N
fname = Dave
```

The ResponseLoggingFilter logged three separate responses to go along with the three requests logged by the RequestLoggingFilter. The first response generated was the HTML to display the login page. The second response was the HTML to display the survey form. The final response was the HTML to display the confirmation page. Listing 6-5 shows an abbreviated log file containing these three responses.

Listing 6-5. Abbreviated Log File for Response Filter

```
*** HTTP Response: Mon Feb 25 20:37:44 CST 2002***

<html>
<head>
    <title>Quoting System Login</title>
</head>

<body bgcolor="#FFFF99">

==> HTML code to display login page (omitted)

</body>
</html>

*** HTTP Response: Mon Feb 25 20:37:55 CST 2002***

<!-- JSP Directives -->

<html>
<head>
    <title>Insurance Quoting System</title>
</head>
```

```
<body bgcolor="#FFFF99">

==> HTML code to display survey page (omitted)

</body>
</html>


*** HTTP Response: Mon Feb 25 20:40:55 CST 2002***

<!-- JSP Directives -->

<html>
<head>
    <title>Insurance Quoting System</title>
</head>

<body bgcolor="#FFFF99">

==> HTML code to display confirmation page (omitted)

</body>
</html>
```

Summary

This chapter showed a great way to perform pre-processing and post-processing of an HTTP request and response using the Decorating Filter pattern from the *J2EE Patterns Catalog*. Fortunately, the servlet API provides a standard filtering mechanism that enables you to create filters and declaratively add and remove them from filter chains associated with specific URL patterns. As you learn about the remaining presentation patterns, you'll begin to see how filters can play a big part in the design of your web applications. In the last section of this book, you'll use filters again as you put everything together into a web application framework.

CHAPTER 7

The Front Controller Pattern

BACK IN CHAPTER 5, I INTRODUCED THE IDEA of a Model-View-Controller (MVC) architecture. This chapter will take that a few steps further as I introduce the various ways to centralize processing within your web applications. As with the last chapter, I'll start by defining the pattern, then move to the various strategies for implementing the pattern, and finish with some concrete examples of the pattern in use. This chapter's goal is to build a solid request-handling framework using the Front Controller pattern.

Defining the Pattern

Most web applications begin as a simple set of pages performing simple data collection and reporting functionality. One page performs some processing and then displays the next page. This page performs some more processing and then displays another page with some kind of results. Each page contains the necessary security authorization, request handling code, business logic, presentation logic, and navigation code. Much of this code is duplicated across each page, but for a simple application that will never change, this shouldn't be a problem, right? Unfortunately, these simple applications will typically evolve into fairly sophisticated systems that the business relies upon heavily. The result of this is either a set of JSP pages, or Java servlets, with navigational logic hard-coded inside each page, duplicate code embedded within each page, and no easy way to integrate other services into the application.

The Front Controller pattern defines how to implement an MVC pattern within your applications using JSP pages and Java servlets. Perhaps even more important, the Front Controller pattern encourages a standard framework for handling requests. This will allow for the easier integration of new functionality as the application grows beyond its original scope. The Front Controller pattern consists of a central controller, either a servlet or JSP, that serves as a single point of entry into your application (see Figure 7-1). This controller can manage shared resources such as database connections and HTTP sessions. It also can handle code that's typically executed across multiple requests such as user authentication. Another benefit of defining a single point of entry is that you can plug in common services as filters in a filter chain as described in the last chapter.

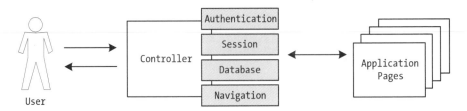

Figure 7-1. The Front Controller pattern

Developing Strategies

The Front Controller pattern by itself is nothing more than the MVC pattern applied to JSP pages and servlets. The real fun exists in the various strategies used to build a solid request-handling framework within the Front Controller pattern. Once this framework is built, not only does it make your current application more efficient and extensible, but it can also be reused on other applications. Remember, the point of using design patterns is to give you a jumpstart on development. A reusable request-handling framework can be a proven piece of the application that does not require further testing and modification, enabling you to focus your efforts on application-specific code rather than figuring out how to handle incoming requests and route them appropriately.

A good request-handling framework defines a standard path for the request to follow as it moves through the application. For these purposes, I'll define the lifecycle of a request to consist of the following:

- The user issues a request to the application controller (servlet or JSP page).

- The request is parsed into form parameters.

- The request is authenticated.

- The request action is mapped to a specific resource.

- A command object is built to process the request.

- The request is forwarded to the appropriate page.

- The output of the request action is displayed to the user.

This lifecycle provides a good basis for defining the framework. There are several strategies for implementing the Front Controller pattern that address each step in this lifecycle. This chapter's goal is to use these strategies to build a solid request-handling framework that can be reused across projects. You'll build upon each strategy until you arrive at the final framework. When you're done, you'll have a standard mechanism for accepting a request, parsing it, processing it, and forwarding it to an appropriate resource for displaying its results (see Figure 7-2). Within this framework, you can insert common tasks at appropriate points within the request lifecycle. For instance, user authentication can happen using the request helper object before the command object is built.

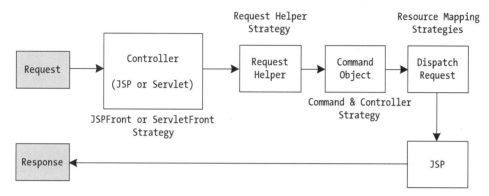

Figure 7-2. Request-handling framework within the Front Controller pattern

JSP Front vs. Servlet Front Strategy

You can embed the controller as either a JSP page or a Java servlet. Implementing a controller as a JSP page is a viable option; however, it's not preferable to using a servlet as your controller. Creating a controller as a JSP page is a bit counterintuitive. Controller code has nothing to do with the display of content and is more suited to a servlet rather than a markup page. Most programmers would prefer to work with a servlet rather than a JSP page when dealing with controller code. JSP pages are more suited for the adaptation and presentation of data. Here's a basic idea of how a controller servlet might look (minus the necessary exception handling):

```
public class ControllerServlet extends HttpServlet {

  public void init ()
  {
    /* Perform first-time initialization of shared
       resources like database connections. */
  }
```

```
public void doGet(HttpServletRequest _req, HttpServletResponse _res)
  throws ServletException, IOException
{
  /* Forward to doPost method */
  doPost(_req, _res);
}

public void doPost(HttpServletRequest _req, HttpServletResponse _res)
  throws ServletException, IOException
{
  /* Create request helper object */
  ReqUtil reqUtil = new ReqUtil(_req);

  /* Create action object (command) */
  Action action = reqUtil.getAction();

  /* Execute action */
  String view = action.execute(_req, _res);

  /* Dispatch to appropriate view */
  RequestDispatcher dispatcher = _req.getRequestDispatcher(view);
  dispatcher.forward(_req, _res);
}

public void destroy()
{
  /* Perform cleanup operations here
     like closing databases. */
}

}
```

The servlet controller provides the opportunity to initialize shared resources prior to the first request and close them before the servlet is taken out of service. These shared resources are usually database connections, but they could also be things like message queues or Enterprise JavaBeans (EJBs). There are typically two different ways a request will access your controller. A request can come in via the doGet or doPost method. In most cases, you can defer one method to the other by overriding one method and telling it to call the other method, passing it the request and response objects. You could also create a separate method to process the request and have both the doGet and doPost methods defer processing to the new method.

Inside of the request processing method (or doGet/doPost), you create a helper object that wraps the original request object. This helper object parses the request parameters and extracts the requested action from the request object. This action tells the controller what it should do with the request. A command object is then created by the request helper object, which then executes its business logic. Any data generated as a result of the action is typically stored as an EJB or simply a JavaBean. The view corresponding to the action receives the request and will use the EJB or JavaBean to adapt the data to the appropriate presentation code. The following sections discuss the details of this set of operations.

Request Helper Strategy

To implement a request-handling framework, it's important to build a standard mechanism that wraps the request with additional functionality that may be needed to process the request such as parsing the request parameters or determining the action the servlet should take. The request helper strategy has you create a helper object that accepts the request object in its constructor. This helper object, along with its added functionality, is then available to the rest of the method. Here's how this object might be used inside of the doPost method you saw earlier:

```
/* Wrap request object with helper */
ReqUtility reqUtil = new ReqUtility(_req);

/* Create an Action object based on request parameters */
Action action = reqUtil.getAction();
```

The helper object itself can contain as much additional functionality as your application requires. At a minimum, it should wrap the request object inside of its constructor and provide a method to generate an action for the servlet to take based on the parameters given to the request. Here's what a minimal request helper looks like:

```
public class ReqUtility
{
  HttpServletRequest request;

  public ReqUtility(HttpServletRequest _req)
    throws ServletException, IOException
  {
    request = _req;
  }
```

```
public Action getAction()
{
  /* Use factory to create action based on request parms */
  String action = (String) request.getParameter("action");
  return ActionFactory.createAction(action);
}
}
```

The request helper strategy provides you with a wrapped request object, but to process the request you need to provide command objects, or actions, to execute the business logic and provide you with the model and view to complete the request. In the next few sections, you'll complete the picture and look at the remainder of the request-handling framework.

Command and Controller Strategy

A good request-handling framework makes it easy to extend the application without interfering with the controller or the request-handling code itself. To achieve this level of separation, you need a flexible mechanism for adding new behavior to your request-handling code. You can accomplish this using a Factory pattern. This pattern has its roots in the object-oriented design world. It instantiates new objects when the type is not known until runtime. Remember, in the last section you saw how a factory was used inside the request helper:

```
String action = (String) request.getParameter("action");
return ActionFactory.createAction(action);
```

This enables you to simply add new behaviors by adding them to the factory rather than modifying the request processing code in the servlet. To make this work, however, you need to define an interface for our command objects. I like to refer to command objects as actions, so I'll create an interface named Action. By coding to an interface rather than a specific class implementation, your request-handling code will never have to change when new behavior is added to the application as long as any new behavior implements the Action interface. Here are the base methods the Action interface defines:

```
/* Execute business logic */
public boolean execute(HttpServletRequest _req, HttpServletResponse _res)
  throws ServletException, IOException;

/* Return the page name (and path) to display the view */
public String getView();
```

```
/* Return a JavaBean containing the model (data) */
public Object getModel();
```

These methods, when implemented, will execute the business logic, return the JSP page name to be used as the view, and return a model to be used by the JSP to build its final output. To add new behavior to the application, you simply need to build a class that implements the Action interface and provide implementations for each of the methods defined by the interface.

The factory itself is implemented as an abstract class. You do this because the factory should never be instantiated. Its only purpose is to return objects that implement the Action interface. The only method you define in the factory is a static method that takes a String parameter telling it which action to return. The method then instantiates the appropriate object and returns it to the calling program (in this case, the request helper). Here's what the factory might look like:

```
public abstract class ActionFactory {

  public static Action createAction(String _action)
  {
    /* Return Action object */
    if (_action.equals("x")) {
      return new xAction();
    }
    if (_action.equals("y")) {
      return new yAction();
    }

    return null;
  }

}
```

The only problem with this approach to generating action objects is that new actions require the code to be recompiled. A more robust way would be to get a list of actions from an XML file or to pass in a fully qualified class name to the method and then use Java Reflection to instantiate the object. You'll do this in Chapter 11.

Resource Mapping Strategies

Once the request-handling framework is in place, your application needs a strategy for assigning actions to requests. Several strategies address this need. The

J2EE Patterns Catalog defines the Physical Resource Mapping strategy, Logical Resource Mapping strategy, and the Multiplexed Resource Mapping strategy.

The physical resource mapping strategy involves making requests to a specific physical resource name such as `http://myserver/myapp/servlet/controller`. The logical resource mapping strategy, on the other hand, maps logical names to physical resources using a configuration file. An example of this would be `http://myserver/myapp/controller`. This would point to a specific resource in the configuration file. If you wanted to change the resource acting as your controller, you would simply re-map the logical name in the configuration file. You configure these mappings in the `web.xml` file of your web application.

You still need a way to associate a specific action with the request. You can do this using the multiplexed resource mapping strategy. This is an extension to the logical resource mapping strategy in that it uses a logical name to specify the controller, but it adds another component to associate an action with the request. The logical mapping can be either a specific logical name or a particular pattern to be associated with a physical resource. For instance, `http://myserver/myapp/login.c` could be mapped to a controller by stating in the configuration file that all requests with a `.c` extension go to the controller servlet. In this case, the left side of the request, `login`, could be parsed out of it and used to specify the action.

Or, your request could simply be `http://myserver/myapp/controller?action=login`. This would associate the logical name `controller` with the servlet controller and pass in a parameter named `action` telling the servlet to create a `login` action. This is the most common and straightforward way to map requests to actions.

Applying the Front Controller Pattern

To apply this pattern, you're going to fill in the pieces of the request-handling framework that you began building in the previous sections. You'll then go back to the survey application you built in Chapter 5 and rebuild it using your new controller and request-handling framework.

Revisiting MVC: An Example

In Chapter 5, you built a survey application to illustrate the MVC framework. Although it was a big improvement over a standard JSP solution, there's lots of room for improvement. Specifically, it needs to be more extensible. If the application were to grow over time, as most do, it would become complex and difficult to add new behavior. This is where the new request-handling framework can be a big help. As you may recall, the example in Chapter 5 dealt with a simple login screen, then a data entry form, and finally a confirmation screen. For this example, you'll go through each step of the request-handling framework first, then you'll add the specific behaviors required by the application, and you'll finish by modifying the JSP pages to use the new controller.

Building the Request Helper

You'll start by building the request helper object. For these purposes, you'll implement the minimum functionality required by a request helper. The getAction method uses the ActionFactory that you'll create later to get an instance of the appropriate action object. Listing 7-1 shows what the request helper looks like.

Listing 7-1. ReqUtil.java

```
package jspbook.ch7;

import javax.servlet.*;
import javax.servlet.http.*;
import java.io.*;

public class ReqUtility {

  HttpServletRequest request;

  public ReqUtility(HttpServletRequest _req)
    throws ServletException, IOException
  {
    request = _req;
  }

  public Action getAction()
  {
    /* Use factory to create action based on request parms */
    String action = (String) request.getParameter("action");
    return ActionFactory.createAction(action);
  }

}
```

Defining the Action Interface

Before building the factory, let's take a look at the action objects that the factory
will generate. Each action object will implement the Action interface. This
enables the request-handling framework to remain unchanged as you add
new behaviors because it deals with the Action interface rather than any
concrete objects.

The Action interface defines three core methods and one helper method. The
core methods are the execute, getView, and getModel methods. In addition to
these, I added a helper method, setDatabase, to enable you to pass an existing
database connection into the object. This allows you to easily share database
resources. The execute method, when implemented, will perform any necessary
business logic needed to carry out the request. The getView and getModel methods are used to return the page and data necessary to present the results of the
action. Listing 7-2 shows what this interface looks like.

Listing 7-2. Action.java

```
package jspbook.ch7;

import javax.servlet.*;
import javax.servlet.http.*;
import java.io.*;
import java.sql.*;

public interface Action {

  /* Set Database Connection */
  public void setDatabase(Connection _db);

  /* Execute business logic */
  public boolean execute(HttpServletRequest _req, HttpServletResponse _res)
    throws ServletException, IOException;

  /* Return the page name (and path) to display the view */
  public String getView();

  /* Return a JavaBean containing the model (data) */
  public Object getModel();

}
```

Building the Action Factory

The factory you use to instantiate your Action objects is an abstract class with a single static method. The class is abstract because you never want it to be instantiated. The single static method, createAction, checks the name of the action passed into it and then instantiates the appropriate object, returning an object of type Action. Listing 7-3 shows what the factory looks like.

Listing 7-3. ActionFactory.java

```
package jspbook.ch7;

abstract class ActionFactory {

  public static Action createAction(String _action)
  {
    /* Return Action object */
    if (_action.equals("login")) {
      return new LoginAction();
    }
    if (_action.equals("submit")) {
      return new SubmitAction();
    }

    return null;
  }

}
```

Implementing the Application-Specific Behaviors

The big difference between this example and the one in Chapter 5 is that you implement the application logic as separate actions rather than inside of the controller code. There are two actions that need to be created, a login action and a submit action. You've essentially moved the same code from the previous example inside of the execute method of each action. The execute method performs its processing and updates class variables with necessary data. In the case of the login action, you store the user ID and the status of the login action. The getModel method assembles a CustomerBean object and updates these fields. This bean will be tagged onto the request attributes and used by the view to display the next page. The getView method returns the name of the page to display next. This is determined inside of the execute method and stored locally. Listing 7-4 shows what the login action looks like.

Listing 7-4. LoginAction.java

```java
package jspbook.ch7;

import javax.servlet.*;
import javax.servlet.http.*;
import java.io.*;
import java.sql.*;

import jspbook.ch7.CustomerBean;

public class LoginAction implements Action {

  private String view;
  private Connection dbCon;
  private String status;
  private String uid, pwd;

  public LoginAction() {}

  /* Set Database Connection */
  public void setDatabase(Connection _db)
  {
    dbCon = _db;
  }

  /* Execute business logic */
  public boolean execute(HttpServletRequest _req, HttpServletResponse _res)
    throws ServletException, IOException
  {
    uid = (String) _req.getParameter("UID");
    pwd = (String) _req.getParameter("PWD");

    /* Validate User */
    if (authenticate(uid, pwd)) {
      status = "success";
      view = "/WEB-INF/jsp/ch7/census.jsp";
    }
    else {
      status = "failed";
      view = "/ch7/login.jsp";
    }

    return true;
  }
```

```
/* Return the page name (and path) to display the view */
public String getView()
{
  return view;
}


/* Return a JavaBean containing the model (data) */
public Object getModel()
{
  /* Use the CustomerBean to return the status of the login */

  CustomerBean cBean = new CustomerBean();
  cBean.setUid(uid);
  cBean.setLoginStatus(status);
  return cBean;
}


/* Check if the user is valid */
private boolean authenticate(String _uid, String _pwd)
{
  ResultSet rs = null;
  try {
    Statement s = dbCon.createStatement();
    rs = s.executeQuery("select * from user where id = '"
            + _uid + "' and pwd = '" + _pwd + "'");
    return (rs.next());
  }
  catch (java.sql.SQLException e) {
    System.out.println("A problem occurred while accessing the database.");
    System.out.println(e.toString());
  }
  return false;
}


}
```

The submit action is similar to the login action. The only difference is in the code inside of the execute method. It records the survey data and updates a status field inside of the class. The CustomerBean is updated inside of the getModel method and the next page is set in the getView method. Listing 7-5 shows what the submit action looks like.

Listing 7-5. SubmitAction.java

```
package jspbook.ch7;

import javax.servlet.*;
import javax.servlet.http.*;
import java.io.*;
import java.sql.*;

import jspbook.ch7.CustomerBean;

public class SubmitAction implements Action {

  private String view;
  private Connection dbCon;
  private String status;

  public SubmitAction() {}

  /* Set Database Connection */
  public void setDatabase(Connection _db)
  {
    dbCon = _db;
  }

  /* Execute business logic */
  public boolean execute(HttpServletRequest _req, HttpServletResponse _res)
    throws ServletException, IOException
  {
    /* Submit Survey Data */
    if (recordSurvey(_req)) {
      status = "success";
      view = "/WEB-INF/jsp/ch7/thankyou.jsp";
    }
    else {
      status = "failed";
      view = "/WEB-INF/jsp/ch7/census.jsp";
    }

    return true;
  }

  /* Return the page name (and path) to display the view */
  public String getView()
```

```
  {
    return view;
  }

  /* Return a JavaBean containing the model (data) */
  public Object getModel()
  {
    /* Return the status of the action */
    CustomerBean cBean = new CustomerBean();
    cBean.setSubmitStatus(status);
    return cBean;
  }

  /* Using the CustomerBean, record the data */
  public boolean recordSurvey(HttpServletRequest _req)
  {
    CustomerBean cBean = new CustomerBean();
    cBean.populateFromParms(_req);
    return cBean.submit(dbCon);
  }

}
```

You now need to make a few changes to the CustomerBean that you used back in Chapter 5 to accommodate the new framework. These changes have to do with the way you retrieve the user ID and set it inside of the bean. You also need to add some status fields. This bean is retrieved inside of the JSP pages, and these status fields are checked before displaying each screen. Listing 7-6 shows what the CustomerBean looks like after making these changes.

Listing 7-6. CustomerBean.java

```
package jspbook.ch7;

import java.util.*;
import java.sql.*;
import javax.servlet.http.*;

public class CustomerBean implements java.io.Serializable {

  /* Member Variables */
  private String lname, fname, sex;
  private int age, children;
  private boolean spouse, smoker;
```

```
/* Helper Variables */;
private String uid ;
private String loginStatus, submitStatus;

/* Constructor */
public CustomerBean() {
  /* Initialize properties */
  setLname("");
  setFname("");
  setSex("");
  setAge(0);
  setChildren(0);
  setSpouse(false);
  setSmoker(false);
}

public void populateFromParms(HttpServletRequest _req) {
  // Populate bean properties from request parameters
  setLname(_req.getParameter("lname"));
  setFname(_req.getParameter("fname"));
  setSex(_req.getParameter("sex"));
  setAge(Integer.parseInt(_req.getParameter("age")));
  setChildren(Integer.parseInt(_req.getParameter("children")));
  setSpouse((_req.getParameter("married").equals("Y")) ? true : false);
  setSmoker((_req.getParameter("smoker").equals("Y")) ? true : false);
  setUid(_req.getParameter("uid"));
}

/* Accessor Methods */

/* Last Name */
public void setLname(String _lname) {lname = _lname;}
public String getLname() {return lname;}

/* First Name */
public void setFname(String _fname) {fname = _fname;}
public String getFname() {return fname;}

/* Sex */
public void setSex(String _sex) {sex = _sex;}
public String getSex() {return sex;}
```

```
/* Age */
public void setAge(int _age) {age = _age;}
public int getAge() {return age;}

/* Number of Children */
public void setChildren(int _children) {children = _children;}
public int getChildren() {return children;}

/* Spouse ? */
public void setSpouse(boolean _spouse) {spouse = _spouse;}
public boolean getSpouse() {return spouse;}

/* Smoker ? */
public void setSmoker(boolean _smoker) {smoker = _smoker;}
public boolean getSmoker() {return smoker;}

/* Helper Variables */
public void setUid(String _uid) {uid = _uid;}
public String getUid() {return uid;}

public void setLoginStatus(String _status) {loginStatus = _status;}
public String getLoginStatus() {return loginStatus;}

public void setSubmitStatus(String _status) {submitStatus = _status;}
public String getSubmitStatus() {return submitStatus;}

public boolean submit(Connection _dbCon) {

  Statement s = null;
  ResultSet rs = null;
  String custId = "";
  StringBuffer sql = new StringBuffer(256);

  try {
    // Check if customer exists (use uid to get custID)
    s = _dbCon.createStatement();
    rs = s.executeQuery("select * from user where id = '" + uid + "'");
    if (rs.next()) {
      custId = rs.getString("cust_id");
    }
```

```
    rs = s.executeQuery("select * from customer where id = " + custId);
    if (rs.next()) {
      // Update record
      sql.append("UPDATE customer SET ");
      sql.append("lname='").append(lname).append("', ");
      sql.append("fname='").append(fname).append("', ");
      sql.append("age=").append(age).append(", ");
      sql.append("sex='").append(sex).append("', ");
      sql.append("married='").append((spouse) ? "Y" : "N").append("', ");
      sql.append("children=").append(children).append(", ");
      sql.append("smoker='").append((smoker) ? "Y" : "N").append("'");
      sql.append("where id='").append(custId).append("'");
    }
    else {
      // Insert record
      sql.append("INSERT INTO customer VALUES(");
      sql.append(custId).append(",'");
      sql.append(lname).append("', '");
      sql.append(fname).append("', ");
      sql.append(age).append(", '");
      sql.append(sex).append("', '");
      sql.append((spouse) ? "Y" : "N").append("', ");
      sql.append(children).append(", '");
      sql.append((smoker) ? "Y" : "N").append("')");
    }
    s.executeUpdate(sql.toString());
  }
  catch (SQLException e) {
    System.out.println("Error saving customer: "
      + custId + " : " + e.toString());
    return false;
  }
  return true;
}

}
```

Building the Controller

Finally, you build the controller, which is implemented as a servlet. Inside of the doPost method, the request is wrapped inside of a request helper (ReqUtil). An action object is then created, the action is executed, and then the model is attached to the request. The request is then forwarded to the appropriate JSP page for display. Listing 7-7 shows what our controller looks like.

Listing 7-7. `Controller.java`

```java
package jspbook.ch7;

import javax.servlet.*;
import javax.servlet.http.*;
import java.io.*;
import java.sql.*;
import javax.naming.*;
import javax.sql.*;

public class Controller extends HttpServlet {

  private Connection dbCon;

  public void init()
  {
    /* Initialize shared resources */

    try {
      Context initCtx = new InitialContext();
      Context envCtx = (Context) initCtx.lookup("java:comp/env");
      DataSource ds = (DataSource) envCtx.lookup("jdbc/QuotingDB");
      dbCon = ds.getConnection();
    }
    catch (javax.naming.NamingException e) {
      System.out.println(
        "A problem occurred while retrieving a DataSource object");
      System.out.println(e.toString());
    }
    catch (java.sql.SQLException e) {
      System.out.println("A problem occurred while connecting to the database.");
      System.out.println(e.toString());
    }

  }
```

```java
public void doGet(HttpServletRequest _req, HttpServletResponse _res)
  throws ServletException, IOException
{
  /* Forward to doPost method */
  doPost(_req, _res);
}

public void doPost(HttpServletRequest _req, HttpServletResponse _res)
  throws ServletException, IOException
{

  /* Wrap request object with helper */
  ReqUtility reqUtil = new ReqUtility(_req);

  /* Create an Action object based on request parameters */
  Action action = reqUtil.getAction();

  /* Pass the database connection to the action */
  action.setDatabase(dbCon);

  /* Execute business logic */
  if (action.execute(_req, _res)) {

    /* Get appropriate view for action */
    String view = action.getView();

    /* Add the model to the request attributes */
    _req.setAttribute("model", action.getModel());

    /* Forward the request to the given view */
    RequestDispatcher dispatcher = _req.getRequestDispatcher(view);
    dispatcher.forward(_req, _res);

  }

}

public void destroy()
{
  /* Clean up shared resources */

  try {
    dbCon.close();
```

```
    }
    catch (java.sql.SQLException e) {
      System.out.println("A problem occurred while closing the database.");
      System.out.println(e.toString());
    }

  }

}
```

Modifying the JSP Pages

The JSP pages are essentially the same as they were in Chapter 5. The only difference is in how they retrieve the status of either the login action or the submit action. Now, they retrieve the `CustomerBean` from the request attributes and then get the status from the bean. Listing 7-8, 7-9, and 7-10 show what the JSP pages look like after making these changes.

Listing 7-8. `login.jsp`

```
<%@ page
        import="jspbook.ch7.CustomerBean"
        errorPage="myError.jsp?from=login.jsp"
%>

<html>
<head>
  <title>Quoting System Login</title>
</head>

<body bgcolor="#FFFF99">

<%@ include file="myHeader.html" %>

<form method="post" action="Controller?action=login">

<p align="center">
  <font face="Arial, Helvetica, sans-serif" size="6" color="#003300">
    <b><i>Login to Quoting System</i></b>
  </font>
</p>

<p> </p>
```

```jsp
<%      CustomerBean custBean = (CustomerBean) request.getAttribute("model");
        if (custBean != null) {
          String status = custBean.getLoginStatus();
          if (status != null && status.equals("failed")) {
%>
<center>
  <font color="#ff0000">Invalid login, please try again.</font>
</center>
<%      }
      }
%>


<table width="199" border="0" align="center" cellpadding="5">
  <tr>
    <td>
      <font face="Arial, Helvetica, sans-serif" size="2">User ID:</font>
    </td>
    <td><input type="text" name="UID"></td>
  </tr>
  <tr>
    <td><font face="Arial, Helvetica, sans-serif" size="2">Password:</font></td>
    <td><input type="password" name="PWD"></td>
  </tr>
  <tr align="center">
    <td colspan="2"><input type="submit" name="Submit" value="Login"></td>
  </tr>
</table>

</form>

<%@ include file="myFooter.html" %>

</body>
</html>
```

Listing 7-9. `census.jsp`

```
<!-- JSP Directives -->
<%@ page
        import="jspbook.ch7.CustomerBean"
        errorPage="myError.jsp?from=census.jsp"
%>

<html>
<head>
  <title>Insurance Quoting System</title>
</head>

<body bgcolor="#FFFF99">

<basefont face="Arial">

<%@ include file="/ch7/myHeader.html" %>

<form action="Controller?action=submit" method="post">

<br><br>

<%  CustomerBean custBean = (CustomerBean) request.getAttribute("model");
    String uid = "";
    if (custBean != null) {
      String status = custBean.getSubmitStatus();
      uid = custBean.getUid();
      if (status != null && status.equals("failed")) {
%>
<center>
  <font color="#ff0000">Error recording survey data, please try again.</font>
</center>
<br><br>
<%     }
    }
%>


<center><b>Enter personal information:</b></center>
<br><br>
<input type='hidden' name='uid' value='<%= uid %>'>
<table cellspacing="2" cellpadding="2" border="0" align="center">
<tr>
```

```
        <td align="right">First Name:</td>
        <td><input type="Text" name="fname" size="10"></td>
    </tr>
    <tr>
        <td align="right">Last Name:</td>
        <td><input type="Text" name="lname" size="10"></td>
    </tr>
    <tr>
        <td align="right">Age:</td>
        <td><input type="Text" name="age" size="2"></td>
    </tr>
    <tr>
        <td align="right">Sex:</td>
        <td>
          <input type="radio" name="sex" value="M" checked>Male</input>
          <input type="radio" name="sex" value="F">Female</input>
      </td>
    </tr>
    <tr>
        <td align="right">Married:</td>
        <td><input type="Text" name="married" size="2"></td>
    </tr>
    <tr>
        <td align="right">Children:</td>
        <td><input type="Text" name="children" size="2"></td>
    </tr>
    <tr>
        <td align="right">Smoker:</td>
        <td><input type="Text" name="smoker" size="2"></td>
    </tr>
    <tr>
        <td colspan="2" align="center"><input type="Submit" value="Submit"></td>
    </tr>
    </table>

<br><br>

</form>
<%@ include file="/ch7/myFooter.html" %>

</body>
</html>
```

Listing 7-10. `thankyou.jsp`

```
<!-- JSP Directives -->
<%@ page
        errorPage="myError.jsp?from=thankyou.jsp"
%>

<html>
<head>
  <title>Insurance Quoting System</title>
</head>

<body bgcolor="#FFFF99">

<basefont face="Arial">

<%@ include file="/ch7/myHeader.html" %>

<br><br>

<center>
Your survey answers have been recorded. Thank you for participating in this
survey.
</center>

<br><br>

<%@ include file="/ch7/myFooter.html" %>

</body>
</html>
```

Using Filters with a Front Controller

A big advantage to implementing the Front Controller pattern is that it central-
izes request handling. This creates the ability to perform common processing on
the request and the response. This can be accomplished inside of the controller
itself, but in many cases it's better done using filters (see Chapter 6 for a complete
discussion of filters). Filters enable you to declaratively plug in and out new functionality without interfering with the request-handling framework in much the
same way your ActionFactory allowed you to add new behavior to the application
with no modifications to the controller servlet.

Later in this book, you'll assemble all of the pieces you've built along the way and create a complete framework. You'll then develop a complete application using the framework. Inside of this framework, you'll use filters to handle user authentication.

Summary

This chapter was perhaps one of the more important pieces of this book. It laid the foundation for building a solid application framework. You'll see in the next few chapters how you build upon the request-handling mechanism you built in this chapter to create a robust and extensible framework for building web applications. In Chapter 11, you'll enhance this request-handling framework to include features such as logging, error handling, and database management.

CHAPTER 8

The View Helper Pattern

THE LAST PIECE of the request-handling framework to investigate deals with how the view adapts the data stored in the model for presentation. The View Helper pattern describes the ways this can be done using custom tags and JavaBeans to adapt the model to the presentation inside of the view. This chapter will discuss these methods and build a few useful view helpers that you can add to your own toolkit.

Defining the Pattern

The View Helper pattern specifies that you use helpers to adapt model data to the presentation layer of an application. Typically, the presentation layer contains several JSP pages. These pages consist of HTML code and images used to present content to the user. A problem arises, however, when these pages need to display dynamic content stored in the model. You'd probably like to avoid embedding Java code within these pages to display model data, so you need to employ some *helpers* to do the work for you.

Recall from the previous chapter that the controller servlet attaches the model to the request as an attribute. To get at this model from within the JSP page, you have two choices. You could embed Java code as JSP scriptlets, or you could use a helper to extract the data for you. In keeping with the idea of separating presentation from business logic, it makes sense to employ several helpers to adapt the model to the presentation rather than clutter the presentation code with Java code (see Figure 8-1).

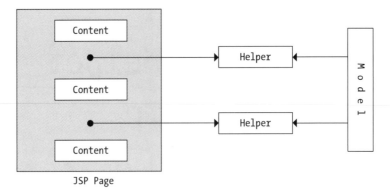

Figure 8-1. View Helper pattern

As you can imagine, helpers make it a lot easier for page designers to develop the presentation layer by replacing Java code with simple-to-use helpers. Of course, developers can only accomplish this if they publish a catalog of the helpers and describe how to use them. However, if the page designers develop their pages before the application is ready to give them a model for the helpers with which to work, then there's a problem. A useful technique to address this problem is to code into the helper a set of dummy data to display when no model is present. An alternate approach would be to provide a dummy model with which to work. Either way, the page designer should not be held up while waiting for the developers.

Using helpers has several advantages:

- Presentation components are standardized, creating a consistent look-and-feel for the application.

- Java code is abstracted away from the page designer, giving them an easy-to-use set of helpers to access the model.

- You can create helpers to display dummy data if no model exists, thus letting the page designer continue development regardless of the readiness of the application.

- Helpers provide a clean separation between presentation and business data by acting as intermediaries between the two.

Implementing View Helper Pattern Strategies

When developing helpers for JSP pages, you have two choices. You could use either JavaBeans or custom tags. Which you choose really depends on the type of data you're trying to adapt. Typically, you use JavaBeans to extract individual pieces of data, where custom tags are better suited toward working with sets of data. However, it's important to point out that you can use either choice for both types of data.

JavaBean Helper Strategy

You can implement helpers as JavaBeans within a JSP page. These helpers are typically easy to use when extracting and formatting single text items. The built-in JSP tags that enable you to work with JavaBeans are simple and intuitive to use. Using JavaBeans, as you may recall from Chapter 3, involves simply declaring the bean and referencing it later using the special tags as follows:

```
<!-- Declare bean -->
<jsp:useBean id="myBean" class="jspBook.util.myBean"/>

<!-- Get first name from bean -->
Hello <jsp:getProperty name="myBean" property="firstName"/>,
welcome to Acme Products online store!
```

JavaBeans can do more than simply retrieve data items from the model. They can also format specific data items, perform calculations, or even generate large blocks of content. Ideally, they're suited for simply retrieving data items using the built-in JSP tags. If you do much more with them, then your JSP may begin to get cluttered with too much Java code. In that case, you might consider encapsulating any additional behavior inside of a custom tag.

Custom Tag Helper Strategy

For more complex model adaptations, custom tags have the ability to embed Java code and perform several iterations over the data, while providing the page designer with a simple tag with which to work. I introduced custom tags back in Chapter 4, as I attempted to further separate the role of page designer from Java developer. To use custom tags, you write a class that extends either TagSupport or BodyTagSupport. You declare this class in a tag library descriptor like this:

```
<?xml version="1.0" encoding="ISO-8859-1" ?>
<!DOCTYPE taglib
  PUBLIC "-//Sun Microsystems, Inc.//DTD JSP Tag Library 1.2//EN"
  "http://java.sun.com/j2ee/dtd/web-jsptaglibrary_1_2.dtd">

<taglib>
  <tlib-version>1.0</tlib-version>
  <jsp-version>1.2</jsp-version>
  <short-name>myTags</short-name>
  <description>
    Tag library to support the examples in Chapter 8
  </description>
  <tag>
    <name>myTag</name>
    <tag-class>jspbook.ch8.myTag</tag-class>
    <body-content>JSP</body-content>
    <attribute>
      <name>myAttribute</name>
      <required>yes</required>
    </attribute>
</tag>
```

This tag is then referenced inside of the JSP page by first declaring it with the taglib directive and then by referencing the tag as follows:

```
<%@ taglib uri="/helpers" prefix="helpers" %>

<helpers:myTag myAttribute="some value">
  Body text ...
</helpers:myTag>
```

I prefer to use custom tags for most view helpers. They give the developer more access to the servlet context and offer some performance benefits when they're pooled within the application server. Another reason I like to use custom tags is that they're intuitive for a non-Java page designer. Their format is much like standard HTML tags, which by now have become second nature to most of us. Finally, you can use custom tags—once they're developed and debugged— across JSP pages in your application. If the tags are designed to be generic enough, you can package them as a tag library, which can be reused across applications.

Model Separation Strategy

Whether using custom tags or JavaBeans, it's sometimes useful to provide stand-alone helpers that can present a set of dummy data in place of the model when no model exists. This would enable the page designers to complete their work independent of the development team. To implement this strategy, the helper needs to check for the existence of a model and then uses either the real model or a static copy of the model to operate on (see Figure 8-2).

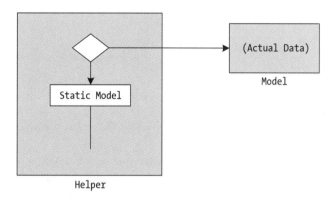

Figure 8-2. Model separation strategy

To make this work, the static model needs to be an exact replica of the real model. It's not always easy to keep these two in sync with each other. An alternate, and sometimes preferable, strategy is to have the development team build dummy data into their models so that the designer can do their work as if the real model exists, also ensuring that the model they're working with is always the correct one (see Figure 8-3).

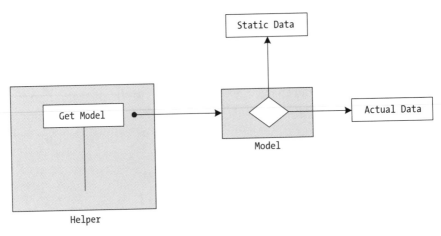

Figure 8-3. Alternate model separation strategy

Applying the View Helper Pattern

The following helpers you're going to build may be useful to you at some point, but at the least they should give you some ideas of ways you can apply the View Helper pattern to your own applications. The following items are implemented as custom tags and are declared in the `helpers.tld` file. This file is associated to the `/helpers` taglib URI inside of the `web.xml` file with an entry like this:

```
<taglib>
    <taglib-uri>/helpers</taglib-uri>
    <taglib-location>/WEB-INF/tlds/helpers.tld</taglib-location>
</taglib>
```

Formatting Text

I'll begin this section with a view helper for adapting numeric values to various date and currency formats. Although it may be simple to do this directly in the model, there are several reasons to format these values in the view instead. For instance, you may need to display the same value in various localized formats, or maybe the content will be accessed via multiple devices that require a different way to present the data.

You could encapsulate various formatting functions within a custom tag that reads the value to be formatted from its body and formats it based on an attribute you set in the tag. Here's how you would describe this tag in your tag library descriptor file, `helpers.tld`:

```
<tag>
  <name>FormatTag</name>
  <tag-class>jspbook.ch8.FormatTag</tag-class>
  <body-content>JSP</body-content>
  <attribute>
    <name>format</name>
    <required>yes</required>
    <rtexprvalue>true</rtexprvalue>
  </attribute>
</tag>
```

The model for this tag could be just about anything, but for this example you'll create a static JavaBean containing two Strings to hold a date value and a currency value. You'll set these from your JSP using the standard JSP setProperty tag. To accomplish this, of course, your JavaBean needs to define accessor methods for both String values. Listing 8-1 shows the code used to create this JavaBean.

Listing 8-1. `FormattingModel.java`

```
package jspbook.ch8;

import java.io.*;

public class FormattingModel implements Serializable {

  private String dateValue;
  private String currencyValue;

  public FormattingModel () {}

  /* Accessor Methods */
  public void setDateValue (String _date)
  {
    this.dateValue = _date;
  }

  public String getDateValue ()
  {
    return this.dateValue;
  }
```

```
public void setCurrencyValue (String _currency)
{
  this.currencyValue = _currency;
}

public String getCurrencyValue ()
{
  return this.currencyValue;
}

}
```

The tag itself is a simple body tag extending the BodyTagSupport class. All of the actual formatting code is inside of the formatValue method. This method is called from within the doAfterBody method once the value has been retrieved. The result of the formatValue method is written back to the page in place of the tag. Formatting of dates and currencies can be done using classes found in the java.text package. Specifically, you can make use of the SimpleDateFormat and DecimalFormat classes. The tag handler also provides a Locale object, along with an appropriate set method, to accommodate specific localization of the content. Because this tag is responsible for formatting date and currency values, it may be necessary to pass different locales to the formatting operations. Take a look at the following code in Listing 8-2, paying special attention to the formatValue method.

Listing 8-2. FormatTag.java

```
package jspbook.ch8;

import javax.servlet.http.*;
import javax.servlet.jsp.*;
import javax.servlet.jsp.tagext.*;

import java.io.*;
import java.util.*;

import java.text.*;

public class FormatTag extends BodyTagSupport {

  /* Locale object for internationalization of content */
  private Locale locale;
```

```
/* Tag Attributes */
protected int format;

/* Static Constants */
public final static int DATE_LONG = 0;
public final static int NUMERIC_DECIMAL = 1;
public final static int NUMERIC_ROUNDED = 2;
public final static int NUMERIC_CURRENCY = 3;

public FormatTag() {
  locale = Locale.getDefault();
}

public void setLocale(Locale locale) {
  this.locale = locale;
}

/* Process Tag Body */
public int doAfterBody() throws JspTagException {
  try {
    BodyContent body = getBodyContent();
    JspWriter out = body.getEnclosingWriter();

    /* Get Input Value */
    String textValue = body.getString().trim();

    /* Output Formatted Value */
    out.println(formatValue(textValue));
  }
  catch (IOException e) {
    throw new JspTagException(e.toString());
  }
  return SKIP_BODY;
}

/* Process End Tag */
public int doEndTag() throws JspTagException {
  return EVAL_PAGE;
}
```

```java
private String formatValue (String _input)
{
  String formattedValue = "";
  try {
    switch (format) {
      case DATE_LONG: {
        Calendar cal = Calendar.getInstance();
        cal.setTime(DateFormat.getDateInstance(
          DateFormat.SHORT).parse(_input));
        SimpleDateFormat df = new SimpleDateFormat("EEE, MMM d, yyyy");
        formattedValue = df.format(cal.getTime());
        break;
      }
      case NUMERIC_DECIMAL: {
        DecimalFormat dcf = (DecimalFormat) NumberFormat.getInstance(locale);
        dcf.setMinimumFractionDigits(2);
        dcf.setMaximumFractionDigits(2);
        formattedValue = dcf.format(dcf.parse(_input));
        break;
      }
      case NUMERIC_ROUNDED: {
        DecimalFormat dcf = (DecimalFormat) NumberFormat.getInstance(locale);
        dcf.setMinimumFractionDigits(0);
        dcf.setMaximumFractionDigits(0);
        formattedValue = dcf.format(dcf.parse(_input));
        break;
      }
      case NUMERIC_CURRENCY: {
        float f = Float.parseFloat(_input);
        DecimalFormat dcf = (DecimalFormat)
          NumberFormat.getCurrencyInstance();
        formattedValue = dcf.format(f);
        break;
      }
    }
  }
  catch (Exception e) {
    System.out.println(e.toString());
  }

  return formattedValue;
}
```

```
/* Attribute Accessor Methods */
public int getFormat ()
{
  return this.format;
}

public void setFormat (int _format)
{
  this.format = _format;
}

}
```

Finally, you have your JSP code. There's really nothing new here. The page declares a JavaBean to use as the model, sets values in the model, and displays those values in various formats. The formatting is done through the FormatTag, specified in the helpers.tld file, and declared in the JSP page using the taglib directive. Notice how you specify the format in an attribute of the custom tag. The format attribute should be set to an integer value inside the JSP page, corresponding to one of the static constants defined in the tag handler. To do this, the attribute is defined as allowing runtime expressions as values by setting the <rtexprvalue> element to true inside the tag descriptor. Listing 8-3 shows the code for the JSP page.

Listing 8-3. FormatHelper.jsp

```
<!-- Declare tag that we'll use as our helper -->
<%@ taglib uri="/helpers" prefix="helpers" %>

<html>
<head>
  <title>Text Formatting Example</title>
</head>

<body>

<basefont face="Arial">

<!-- Declare bean that will act as our model -->
<jsp:useBean id="myBean" class="jspbook.ch8.FormattingModel"/>

<jsp:setProperty name="myBean" property="dateValue" value="12/01/01"/>
<jsp:setProperty name="myBean" property="currencyValue" value="23500.253"/>
```

```
<!-- Display Formatted Values (using helper) -->
<center>

<h1>Various Date and Currency Formats</h1>

<br><br>
<table cellpadding="5">
  <tr>
    <th>Format</th>
    <th>Original Value</th>
    <th>Formatted Value</th>
  </tr>
  <tr>
    <td>Long Date</td>
    <td>
      <jsp:getProperty name="myBean" property="dateValue"/>
    </td>
    <td>
      <helpers:FormatTag format="<%= jspbook.ch8.FormatTag.DATE_LONG %>">
        <jsp:getProperty name="myBean" property="dateValue"/>
      </helpers:FormatTag>
    </td>
  </tr>
  <tr>
    <td>Decimal (NN.NN)</td>
    <td><%= myBean.getCurrencyValue() %></td>
    <td>
      <helpers:FormatTag format="<%= jspbook.ch8.FormatTag.NUMERIC_DECIMAL %>">
        <%= myBean.getCurrencyValue() %>
      </helpers:FormatTag>
    </td>
  </tr>
  <tr>
    <td>Integer (N,NNN)</td>
    <td><%= myBean.getCurrencyValue() %></td>
    <td>
      <helpers:FormatTag format="<%= jspbook.ch8.FormatTag.NUMERIC_ROUNDED %>">
        <%= myBean.getCurrencyValue() %>
      </helpers:FormatTag>
    </td>
  </tr>
```

```
<tr>
  <td>Currency ($N,NNN.NN)</td>
  <td><%= myBean.getCurrencyValue() %></td>
  <td>
    <helpers:FormatTag format="<%= jspbook.ch8.FormatTag.NUMERIC_CURRENCY %>">
      <%= myBean.getCurrencyValue() %>
    </helpers:FormatTag>
  </td>
</tr>
</table>
</center>

</body>
</html>
```

Figure 8-4 shows the results of formatting a date value and a numeric value using each of the different formats provided by the tag handler.

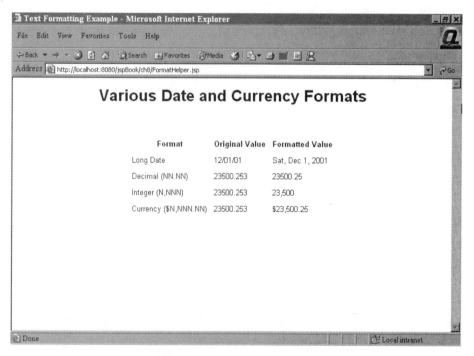

Figure 8-4. Format text helper example

Creating Menus

There can be an advantage in some cases to dynamically generate menus or simply collections of hyperlinks. The controller would execute the appropriate action, which in turn would generate a list of link items. The view, using a helper, would generate a formatted menu containing the links stored in the model.

As an example, the view will be a JSP page that will display a menu screen listing accessory items for a specific product. This is a good example of why you might need to dynamically generate menu screens. The user presumably clicks on a specific product in the company catalog and expects to see a list of accessories from which they can choose. This application pulls the necessary product information from the database and produces a set of product accessories to be displayed as hyperlinks within the view.

For this example, you'll skip the link generation part and simply provide a static model with which to work. The model will be a JavaBean containing a hashtable of link items with which to work. The hashtable will be keyed by the text to display, storing the links as values. You'll retrieve the links as a comma-delimited list and insert it inside of a custom tag. Listing 8-4 shows what the static model looks like.

Listing 8-4. MenuModel.java

```
package jspbook.ch8;

import java.io.*;
import java.util.*;

public class MenuModel implements Serializable {

  Hashtable links = new Hashtable();

  String list = "";

  public MenuModel()
  {
    /* Initialize model with sample values */
    links.put("Fold-away Keyboard", "/Controller?action=display&item=101");
    links.put("Standard Leather Case", "/Controller?action=display&item=102");
    links.put("Deluxe 3-pocket Case", "/Controller?action=display&item=103");
    links.put("Travel Cable", "/Controller?action=display&item=104");
    links.put("Stylus Pack", "/Controller?action=display&item=105");
    links.put("8MB Backup Module", "/Controller?action=display&item=106");
  }
```

```
/* Accessor Methods */
public void setList (String _list)
{
  this.list = _list;
}

public String getList ()
{
  StringBuffer csvList = new StringBuffer();

  /* Transform hash table into comma-separated list */
  Enumeration enum = links.keys();
  while (enum.hasMoreElements()) {
    String linkName = (String) enum.nextElement();
    String linkURL = (String) links.get(linkName);
    csvList.append(linkName).append(",").append(linkURL).append("\n");
  }

  return csvList.toString();
}

}
```

The helper you'll use is a custom tag that extends the BodyTagSupport class so that it can process the body content stored within its start and end tags. This custom tag needs to read in the list of link items and output a list of hyperlinks. It does this in the doAfterBody method, looping through each line of the body content and parsing out the link name and the link URL. Listing 8-5 shows what the code looks like for your helper class.

Listing 8-5. MenuTag.java

```
package jspbook.ch8;

import javax.servlet.http.*;
import javax.servlet.jsp.*;
import javax.servlet.jsp.tagext.*;

import java.io.*;
import java.util.*;

public class MenuTag extends BodyTagSupport {

  /* Tag Attributes */
  protected String links;
```

```
/* Process Tag Body */
public int doAfterBody() throws JspTagException {
  try {
    BodyContent body = getBodyContent();
    JspWriter out = body.getEnclosingWriter();

    /* Parse records and output as list of hyperlinks */
    BufferedReader contentReader = new BufferedReader(body.getReader());
    String record = "";
    while ((record = contentReader.readLine()) != null) {
      StringTokenizer st = new StringTokenizer(record, ",");
      while (st.hasMoreTokens()) {
        String linkName = st.nextToken();
        String linkURL = st.nextToken();
        out.println("<a href='" + linkURL + "'>");
        out.println(linkName + "</a>");
        out.println("<br><br>");
      }
    }
  }
  catch (IOException e) {
    throw new JspTagException(e.toString());
  }
  return SKIP_BODY;
}

/* Process End Tag */
public int doEndTag() throws JspTagException {
  return EVAL_PAGE;
}

/* Attribute Accessor Methods */
public String getLinks ()
{
  return this.links;
}

public void setLinks (String _links)
{
  this.links = _links;
}

}
```

Using this tag in the JSP is fairly simple, as intended. At the point you'd like to display the list of hyperlinks, you insert a custom tag to do the job for you. Inside the tag's body, you execute a small snippet of Java code to retrieve the comma-separated list of link items. Because you're executing Java code inside of the tag, it must be declared in our tag library descriptor file with the <bodycontent> tag containing the value JSP. Here's the full tag descriptor from the helpers.tld file and the code for the JSP page (see Figure 8-5 to see the results):

```
<tag>
  <name>MenuTag</name>
  <tag-class>jspbook.ch8.MenuTag</tag-class>
  <body-content>JSP</body-content>
</tag>
```

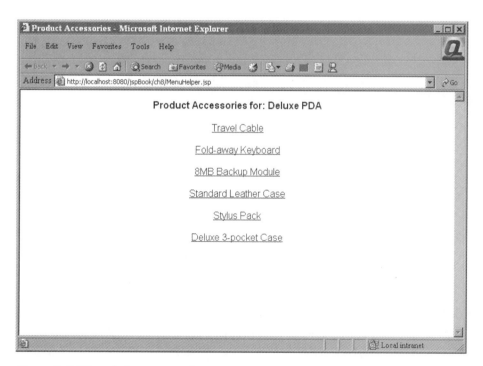

Figure 8-5. Menu helper example

Listing 8-6 shows the MenuHelper.jsp page. The menu items are retrieved inside of the MenuTag using the getList() method of the MenuModel JavaBean. The tag handler parses these items and outputs them as a list of hyperlinks.

Listing 8-6. `MenuHelper.jsp`

```
<!-- Declare tag that we'll use as our helper -->
<%@ taglib uri="/helpers" prefix="helpers" %>

<html>
<head>
  <title>Product Accessories</title>
</head>

<body>

<basefont face="Arial">

<!-- Declare bean that will act as our model -->
<jsp:useBean id="myBean" class="jspbook.ch8.MenuModel"/>

<!-- Display Product Accessory Links (using helper) -->
<center>

<b>Product Accessories for: Deluxe PDA</b>

<br><br>

<helpers:MenuTag>
  <%= myBean.getList() %>
</helpers:MenuTag>

</center>

</body>
</html>
```

Creating Custom List Formats

A common element of most web applications is a grouping of several related items displayed as a bulleted list. The standard HTML list element, using the `<ul>` tags, displays list items using a standard bullet. Using an appropriate helper to display the list enables you to customize the way the list is displayed. In this example, you're going to build a helper that adapts a list of items to a formatted list with a selection of three different list styles. Here's the descriptor for the tag:

```
<tag>
  <name>ListTag</name>
  <tag-class>jspbook.ch8.ListTag</tag-class>
  <body-content>JSP</body-content>
  <attribute>
    <name>format</name>
    <required>yes</required>
    <rtexprvalue>true</rtexprvalue>
  </attribute>
</tag>
```

The code for the tag is kind of a combination of the previous two examples. It defines the format attribute as in the FormatTag, and it processes its body content in much the same way as the MenuTag does. It's important to point out that there are many different ways a list can be formatted. You're simply double-spacing the list items and providing a choice of bullets. Listing 8-7 shows the code for the tag.

Listing 8-7. `ListTag.java`

```
package jspbook.ch8;

import javax.servlet.http.*;
import javax.servlet.jsp.*;
import javax.servlet.jsp.tagext.*;

import java.io.*;
import java.util.*;

public class ListTag extends BodyTagSupport {

  /* Tag Attributes */
  protected int format;

  /* Static Constants */
  public final static int BULLET_ORB = 0;
  public final static int BULLET_PLUS = 1;
  public final static int BULLET_ARROW = 2;

  /* Process Tag Body */
  public int doAfterBody() throws JspTagException {
    try {
      BodyContent body = getBodyContent();
      JspWriter out = body.getEnclosingWriter();
```

```java
        /* Parse records and output as formatted list */
        BufferedReader contentReader = new BufferedReader(body.getReader());
        String record = "";
        while ((record = contentReader.readLine()) != null) {
          if (record.trim().length() > 0) {
            out.println(formatListItem(record.trim()));
          }
        }

      }
      catch (IOException e) {
        throw new JspTagException(e.toString());
      }
      return SKIP_BODY;
    }

    /* Process End Tag */
    public int doEndTag() throws JspTagException {
      return EVAL_PAGE;
    }

    private String formatListItem (String _input)
    {
      StringBuffer listItem = new StringBuffer();

      /* Double-space the list */
      listItem.append("<br><br>");
      switch (format) {
        case BULLET_ORB: {
          listItem.append("<img src='images/orb.gif'>");
          break;
        }
        case BULLET_PLUS: {
          listItem.append("<img src='images/plus.gif'>");
          break;
        }
        case BULLET_ARROW: {
          listItem.append("<img src='images/arrow.gif'>");
        }
      }
      listItem.append("  ").append(_input);
```

```
    return listItem.toString();
  }


  /* Attribute Accessor Methods */
  public int getFormat ()
  {
    return this.format;
  }


  public void setFormat (int _format)
  {
    this.format = _format;
  }


}
```

In this example, you could have built a JavaBean to hold the model as you did in previous examples, but I think you get the idea of how you use these helpers to adapt actual model data to presentation code. So, in your JSP, you simply hard-code the list items into the tag bodies rather than pull the values out of a model. Listing 8-8 shows the code for the JSP page. See Figure 8-6 for a look at the formatted lists.

Listing 8-8. `ListHelper.jsp`

```
<!-- Declare tag that we'll use as our helper -->
<%@ taglib uri="/helpers" prefix="helpers" %>

<html>
<head>
  <title>List Examples</title>
</head>

<body>

<basefont face="Arial">

<center>

<h1>List Examples</h1>

<table width="600">
  <tr>
    <td valign="top" width="150">
```

```
          <helpers:ListTag format="<%= jspbook.ch8.ListTag.BULLET_ORB %>">
            High Card
            Pair
            Two Pair
            Three of a Kind
            Straight
            Flush
            Full House
            Four of a Kind
            Straight Flush
            Royal Flush
          </helpers:ListTag>
        </td>
        <td valign="top" width="150">
          <helpers:ListTag format="<%= jspbook.ch8.ListTag.BULLET_PLUS %>">
            Milwaukee Bucks
            Detroit Pistons
            Toronto Raptors
            Indiana Pacers
            Charlotte Hornets
            Cleveland Cavaliers
            Atlanta Hawks
            Chicago Bulls
          </helpers:ListTag>
        </td>
        <td valign="top" width="300">
          <helpers:ListTag format="<%= jspbook.ch8.ListTag.BULLET_ARROW %>">
            Chapter 1 - The History of Cheese
            Chapter 2 - The Many Faces of Cheese
            Chapter 3 - Love and Cheese
            Chapter 4 - Not Just for Mice
            Chapter 5 - So You're a Cheesehead ...
            Chapter 6 - The Perfect Cheese
            Chapter 7 - Cheddar is Better
            Chapter 8 - The Big Cheese
          </helpers:ListTag>
        </td>
      </tr>
    </table>

  </center>


  </body>
  </html>
```

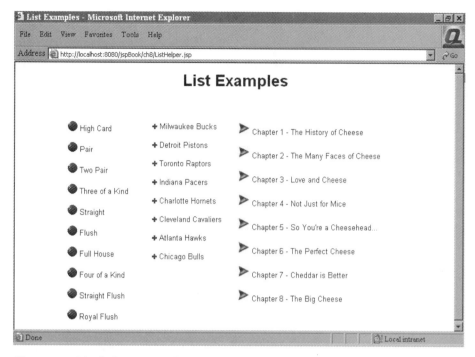

Figure 8-6. List helper example

Summary

This concludes the discussion of the J2EE presentation patterns as applied to JSP pages and Java servlets. When used in combination, they can produce a powerful request-handling framework for enterprise web applications. The next few chapters focus on proper software development techniques and procedures such as unit testing and automated deployment.

CHAPTER 9

Testing Techniques

A BOOK CLAIMING TO INCLUDE best practices would not be complete if it didn't cover perhaps the most important best practice of all: testing. I think you'll agree that most developers begin with good intentions, but when push comes to shove, testing efforts are often reduced to a couple of simple test cases done on the fly. I've been there many times myself. What I've learned over the years, however, is that conducting proper tests is not only essential to building quality software, it also saves time! That's right, it actually saves time by catching bugs earlier in development before they get buried so deep that it takes days just to replicate the bug, let alone the time it takes to fix it. This chapter will discuss proper testing techniques along with a primer on using the JUnit testing framework.

A different kind of testing you should do is *load testing*, which involves simulating several users accessing your application simultaneously. The kind of information you get from load testing helps to identify performance problems and gives you a chance to fix any bottlenecks before you deploy the application to the users. I'll discuss load testing and walk through using a load testing tool called JMeter.

Why Is Testing So Important?

Let's say two developers are working on a project. The first developer, Scott, writes methods A, B, and C. Scott tests the software and verifies that his methods work as expected. Now, Beth writes methods D and E. Beth tests the software and verifies that both methods work as intended. They release the software to the Quality Assurance (QA) department. Suddenly, QA discovers that a particular function is causing the application to return unexpected results. How could this be? Everyone tested their code and verified it was bug-free. Figure 9-1 illustrates this scenario and shows why the application is not functioning as it should.

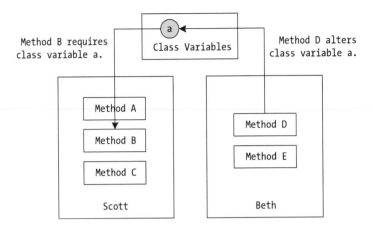

Figure 9-1. Development scenario without proper testing

Had Scott, the first developer, tested his code after the other methods were added, the problem would have been identified and corrected immediately. Apparently, method D modified a class variable that method B uses. Because method D is sometimes called prior to method B, the state of this variable is unknown when method B attempts to use it. This scenario gives us the perfect reason to perform *regression testing* with every introduction of new functionality into the software.

Understanding Regression Testing

Regression testing is the execution of a series of tests designed to validate each and every area of the software. These tests are executed as new functionality is added to the software. The idea is that each test should return the same results regardless of what new functionality has been introduced. This verifies that new code doesn't accidentally break existing code. Regression testing is always a good idea, but it becomes more important as the size of the project grows.

Breaking Regression Testing into Units

A regression test consists of several *unit tests*, which are usually simple tests designed to test the results of a single method or function. A *manual* unit test might consist of a developer running through the application in the role of an end user and validating that the new function produces the intended results with a specific set of input data. Although this works for our immediate purposes, it would be difficult to conduct this test for each and every function of the application every time something changes in the software.

Automated unit tests are typically scripts that pass a specific set of inputs into a specific method and test the results against a value known to be the correct result. If it fails the test, a message is written to a log file. These automated unit tests can be executed as a chain of tests each time the software changes. It's a good idea to include an automated regression test after each build of the software. For instance, let's say you have set up a build script using Ant (more on Ant in Chapter 10). This build script could kick off a series of unit tests upon successful completion of the build and report its results via a log file or even an email to the lead architect.

Building a Unit Testing Framework

Perhaps the biggest problem with unit testing is getting the developers to write the test scripts. Admittedly, this can be a real pain to do. To address this problem, you need to build a framework for conducting unit tests to make it as easy as possible for developers to focus strictly on testing their own code. Fortunately, a testing framework already exists for you to incorporate into your architecture. JUnit is a set of Java classes that combine to give you a simple, yet elegant, framework for conducting unit tests.

Using JUnit

JUnit is an open-source project and is freely available for anyone to use. You can obtain the JUnit package, as well as developer documentation, from the JUnit website (http://www.junit.org). To use JUnit, extract the downloaded file to the directory of your choice. Next, add the junit.jar file to your classpath. You're now ready to begin using JUnit.

The JUnit architecture is quite simple. Building a unit test involves writing a class that extends the TestCase class of the JUnit package. Each TestCase can include multiple tests within the class. When the TestCase is run, each method conforming to a testXXX() naming convention will be executed automatically. For instance, a test that checks an addition routine might be named testAdd(). These tests are executed in the order in which they appear in the code. To modify the order, or to only execute a specific set of tests, you can add each test method manually to the TestSuite using the addTest method of the TestSuite object. A TestSuite defines the tests to be executed. You typically set it by passing the current class as a parameter to the TestSuite constructor. An alternative would be to create a TestSuite using an empty constructor and then add each test case using the addTest method.

Before each test is run, the setUp method of the test case is executed. Upon completion of each test, the tearDown method is run. These methods perform initialization and cleanup activities for common objects in the *test fixture* of the TestCase. Each test within the TestCase class runs within its own test fixture. A test fixture is the context in which a test is run. For instance, you might want to instantiate and initialize a specific JavaBean that is required for each test. You could do this in the setUp method. It's then destroyed in the tearDown method to ensure that its state is cleared for the next test to be run (see Figure 9-2). This way, each test is run independent of each other. Each test case can have their own individual setUp and tearDown methods if they're written as separate TestCase classes and then added manually to the TestSuite using the addTest method of the TestSuite object, as described in the previous paragraph.

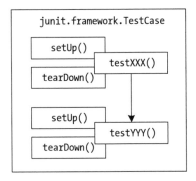

Figure 9-2. JUnit architecture

The only other method you need to do something with is the static method called suite. This method returns a TestSuite to be used by the TestRunner. In most cases, the TestSuite is simply the current class. If you wanted to nest your TestCases, you could define which TestCases, or TestSuites, to include in the current TestSuite. Either way, the TestRunner is called upon inside of the Main method of the class. Listing 9-1 shows the basic code behind a TestCase.

Listing 9-1. Skeleton Code for a TestCase

```
import junit.framework.*;

public class SkeletonTest extends TestCase {

  public SkeletonTest (String name)
  {
    super(name);
  }
```

```
/**
 * Sets up the test fixture.
 * (Called before every test case method.)
 */
protected void setUp () {}

/**
 * Tears down the test fixture.
 * (Called after every test case method.)
 */
protected void tearDown () {}

/**
 * Tests the XXX action of the application
 */
public void testXXX () {}

/**
 * Tests the YYY action of the application
 */
public void testYYY () {}

/**
 * Create a TestSuite object, including testXXX and testYYY
 */
public static Test suite ()
{
  TestSuite suite = new TestSuite(SkeletonTest.class);
  return suite;
}

/**
 * Run the TestSuite
 */
public static void main(String args[])
{
  junit.textui.TestRunner.run(suite());
}

}
```

This code is intended to give you a starting point for creating your own test cases. For it to do anything meaningful, however, you need to add some code to the appropriate testXXX method. Inside of this method, you can do whatever you like. The result of this method, though, should be some kind of comparison between an expected result and an actual result. To make these comparisons, and automatically report their results, you call either the assertEquals or assertTrue method. The assertEquals method takes the expected result, compares it to the actual result, and returns the result as a boolean value. The assertTrue method takes a single boolean argument and reports whether it passed or failed.

Now is a good time to walk through a simple example of a test case. Let's take the following method and write a test for it. This method is a simple add routine. It takes two integers as arguments and returns their sum. Here's the method:

```
public int addNumbers (int A, int B)
{
   return A + B;
}
```

This is obviously a simple example, but let's assume you need a unit test to validate the results of this method. The test code would set the values for A and B, execute the method, and compare the result with the expected result. Here's what the test code would look like:

```
public void testAdd()
{
   /* Set test values */
   int A = 25;
   int B = 35;

   /* Get result */
   SomeClass someClass = new SomeClass();
   int result = someClass.addNumbers(A, B);

   /* Compare result with expected result */
   assertEquals (60, result);
}
```

To try this, add the addNumbers method to a class and insert the testAdd method into the skeleton code in Listing 9-1. Although this is a trivial example, just imagine if this method performed calculations on a class variable rather than its own arguments. If the class variable is altered by a method added to the application in the future, this method may not work as expected.

Adding Unit Tests to Your Application Framework

Going back to the request-handling framework built in Chapter 7, let's write some code that allows you to test individual actions within the application. You'll start with the testing skeleton I showed you in the previous section (Listing 9-1). Each test you add will test a specific action. Remember, in this framework, each time the user submits a request, it's passed into the system as an *action*. To illustrate this, let's write a test for the login action.

To test the login action, you'll simply issue a request to the Controller servlet the same as if a user opened a browser window and attempted to log in to the application. Because this test is automated, however, you need to do this programmatically. You'll pass in a valid user ID and password combination and read in the results into a String object. The test will be successful if the string does not contain the 'action=login' string. If it does, then this means that the page returned from the action was the login page, indicating an incorrect login. There are better ways to do this, I'm sure, but it illustrates the concept well enough. A different way to test the results would be to embed testing flags inside of the JSP pages and check for those in the result string.

Your test script will go inside of the `testLoginAction` method. First, you need to construct the URL to which to connect. This URL will be the same as what you would type into the browser address box, with one exception. The UID and PWD form fields need to be passed along with the URL as form parameters. Here's how to build the URL:

```
String action = "login";
String UID = "apatzer";
String PWD = "apress";

StringBuffer servletName = new StringBuffer();
servletName.append("http://localhost:8080/jspBook/ch7/Controller");
servletName.append("?action=").append(action);
servletName.append("&UID=").append(UID);
servletName.append("&PWD=").append(PWD);
```

Next, try to connect to the URL using the `java.net.URL` object. You read in the results using an `InputStreamReader`. The results are then stored inside of a String variable. Finally, the `assertTrue` method is called to report whether the given string was inside of the result string. Here's what the rest of the method looks like:

```
try {
  URL url = new URL(servletName.toString());
  BufferedReader out = new BufferedReader(
    new InputStreamReader(url.openStream()));
  String line;
  while ( (line = out.readLine()) != null) {
    response += line;
  }
  out.close();
}
catch (Exception e) {
  System.out.println(e.toString());
}

/* If response page is the login page, then an error occurred */
assertTrue((response.indexOf("action=login")) <= 0);
```

Listing 9-2 shows what the entire code looks like.

Listing 9-2. TestFramework.java

```
package jspbook.util;

import junit.framework.*;

import java.net.*;
import java.io.*;

public class TestFramework extends TestCase {

  public TestFramework (String name)
  {
    super(name);
  }

  /**
   * Sets up the test fixture.
   * (Called before every test case method.)
   */
  protected void setUp () {}
```

```
/**
 * Tears down the test fixture.
 * (Called after every test case method.)
 */
protected void tearDown () {}

/**
 * Tests the login action of the application
 */
public void testLoginAction ()
{
  String action = "login";
  String UID = "apatzer";
  String PWD = "apress";

  String response = "";

  StringBuffer servletName = new StringBuffer();
  servletName.append("http://localhost:8080/jspBook/ch7/Controller");
  servletName.append("?action=").append(action);
  servletName.append("&UID=").append(UID);
  servletName.append("&PWD=").append(PWD);

  try {
    URL url = new URL(servletName.toString());
    BufferedReader out = new BufferedReader(
      new InputStreamReader(url.openStream()));
    String line;
    while ( (line = out.readLine()) != null) {
      response += line;
    }
    out.close();
  }
  catch (Exception e) {
    System.out.println(e.toString());
  }

  /* If response page is the login page, then an error occurred */
  assertTrue((response.indexOf("action=login")) <= 0);

}
```

```
public static Test suite ()
{
  TestSuite suite = new TestSuite(TestFramework.class);
  return suite;
}

public static void main(String args[])
{
  junit.textui.TestRunner.run(suite());
}

}
```

Testing for Performance

Once an application is complete, it should be tested for performance. You do this through something called *load testing*. Load testing an application uncovers performance bottlenecks by simulating a large number of simultaneous users and reporting detailed performance statistics.

A recent load test I conducted on an application showed me that after a certain number of users, the requests piled up and ran as if it were single-threaded and had to serve only a few users at a time. It turns out that the database connection pool I was using had a low threshold and was forcing requests to wait for the previous connections to be freed. By adjusting this setting, and re-running the load test, I was able to set the threshold to a more reasonable number. This is just one example of how load testing can improve your application.

Using JMeter

Another great piece of software from the Apache Group is JMeter. JMeter is a load testing tool written as a Java Swing application. As with all Apache projects, JMeter is open-source and therefore free to use. Just go to http://jakarta.apache.org and select the JMeter link along the left side of the page. You can download the software and access the documentation from this site.

Once you've downloaded the software and extracted it to your hard drive, go ahead and execute the /bin/jmeter.bat file. This will run the application and display the window shown in Figure 9-3.

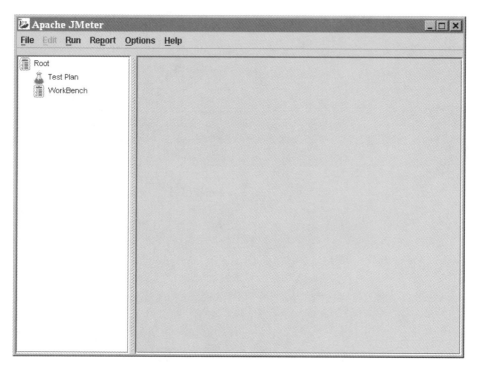

Figure 9-3. JMeter start screen

Basically, you create a test by adding a thread group to the test plan. A thread group is the top-level node for your tests. When a test is run, the thread group executes all of the tests contained within it and reports the results using a visualizer component. The thread group enables you to define the number of threads to run the test (simultaneous users). You can also specify a ramp-up time. This will space out the execution times of each test. For instance, if you enter 15 seconds for the ramp-up time and you have three tests to execute, each test will be executed five seconds apart from the other. Finally, you can specify the number of test iterations to execute (see Figure 9-4).

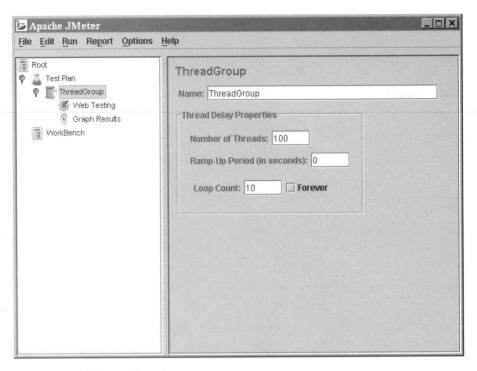

Figure 9-4. Adding a thread group

The next step is to add a test to the thread group. Right-click on the ThreadGroup node to view a context menu displaying components to add. Under the Add submenu, select the Generative Controller item. From here you can add an FTP, Web, or Database test. In this example, you'll add a web test (see Figure 9-5). From this screen, you specify the host name, port, protocol, method, and path. You can also add any form parameters you'd like to include in the request.

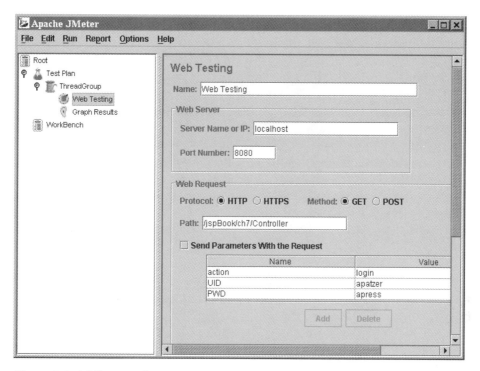

Figure 9-5. Adding a web test

Viewing the Results

To view the results of the test, you need to add a visualizer to the thread group. You have a choice of many different visualizers, but for this example add a simple graph. Right-click the thread group and add a listener. In this case, add a Graph Results listener. Now, you're ready to run the test. Go to the Run menu and select Start. See Figure 9-6 for a sample set of results.

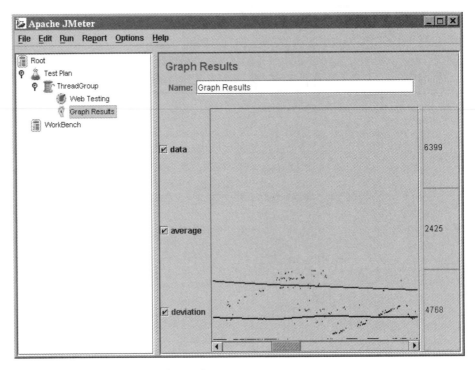

Figure 9-6. Viewing the graph results

Summary

This chapter discussed the importance of testing. Performing unit tests for each piece of functionality is a good habit to have. You can automate these unit tests and add them to a regression test. You usually run the regression test after each build to test that nothing broke as a result of new code being added. Once the application is complete, it should undergo some kind of load testing to assist in performance tuning. I've shown two great tools to assist in unit testing and load testing, JUnit and JMeter. Each tool should become part of your standard toolkit if similar tools are not already available to you. Chapter 10 will look at deployment techniques.

CHAPTER 10

Deployment Techniques

SOFTWARE PROJECTS OFTEN RUN INTO TROUBLE when there's no process in place to manage an application's deployment. Typically, the software is built and deployed through a series of manual tasks that, most of the time, is not even written down. Let's take a simple application as an example. Two developers are responsible for separate areas of the application, occasionally bumping into each other at integration points. Each developer compiles their code, runs simple tests (manually), and moves the source code either into a source control system or maybe just a common directory on a file server. Occasionally, a customer requires an updated version of the software. One of the developers packages the class files, updates their deployment descriptors, and copies it to the production application server.

You might be asking yourself what's wrong with this scenario. Certainly this has worked for you and several others in the past. However, several things can go wrong when a *repeatable process* is not in place to ensure consistency between application builds. A repeatable process is one that follows the same steps to build the software according to a specific configuration. For instance, over time the Java Development Kit (JDK) that one developer uses may have been updated several versions beyond what the other developer is using. A third-party library may have changed at some point and will not be correct when deployed to the customer. Or worse, one developer may have modified a deployment descriptor without letting the other developer know. I have even seen situations where the order of the classpath affects which version of a particular object is used at runtime (usually with XML parsers because they're included with many third-party libraries).

When an automated repeatable process is put into place at the start of development, you can be confident that each deployment is consistent with previous ones. In addition to an automated build process, it's necessary to have good source code control as well as a process for reviewing code changes and performing regression testing.

Fortunately, there's a great tool available to streamline the development process. Ant is a build tool from the Apache-Jakarta Project and is similar to the make utility in Unix. This chapter will provide an introduction to Ant and will discuss several techniques for automating deployment tasks. To bring everything together, the chapter will finish with an example that utilizes all of the techniques discussed to that point. It may seem a bit off topic to discuss deployment techniques in a JSP book, but it's a necessary component of any software project and certainly applies to the development of quality JSP-based applications.

Managing the Development Process

The development process can almost always be characterized as chaotic regardless of the size of the project or the experience of the people involved. With the right development framework in place, however, the chaos can be reduced to a more manageable size. A *development framework* is different from an *application framework*, which I discuss in the next chapter. A development framework is a combination of tools and processes aimed at streamlining the software development lifecycle.

A development framework consists of a source control management system, formal change procedures, code reviews, automated build scripts, and a testing framework for both regression and load tests (see Figure 10-1). I'll discuss each of these shortly, but first let's walk through a scenario using each of these components.

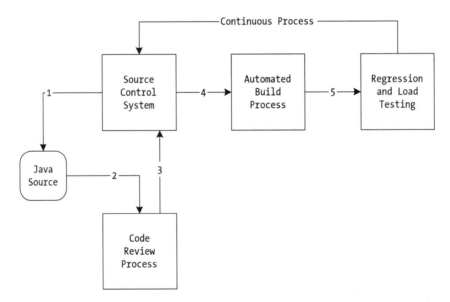

Figure 10-1. Development framework

Our developer, we'll call him Scott, needs to add a method to a Java class named QuoteEngine. First, he checks the source code out of the source control system to gain exclusive access to it. He then adds the new method to the class file, along with some code to test it, and compiles it. Once Scott is sure his method works as intended, he requests a code review with another developer. His code review goes well, so he proceeds to check the source code back into the source control system. At the end of the day, a system architect executes an automated build script that checks out all of the latest source code, compiles it, deploys it to a development server, and runs a complete regression test to verify changes to the application.

Once the development team reaches a particular milestone, they would *promote* the application from the development server to a testing server. Once the application has been thoroughly tested by a QA group, it's then moved to a stage environment for the end users to perform some testing or maybe some training. Finally, the application is moved into production.

If anything were to go wrong with the application, it would be pretty easy to isolate and fix it with minimal impact to the overall project. Without a formal development process and framework, bugs would have a way of creeping into an application and causing major headaches as they're tracked down and fixed.

Source Control

The software development process begins with good source code control. Source code should be maintained using a source code management system to track all changes to source code as well as protect against accidental overwrites. This becomes more important as the project team grows larger, but it's still recommended even for projects with a single developer. Even as a one-person development team, it's helpful to have the ability to roll back changes to a given point in time to help track down bugs.

Many different tools exist for source control. Popular commercial choices are Microsoft Visual SourceSafe and Starbase StarTeam. A great open-source alternative is the Concurrent Versions System (CVS). This has been a popular version control system and has been used extensively to manage other open-source projects with developers distributed around the globe. It's also easy to set up and to use. For more information, visit the http://www.cvshome.org web page.

Code Reviews

Before checking source code back into a version control system, the developers should review their code with another member of the project team or maybe a systems architect responsible for consistency among project teams. In addition to validating changes made to the code, code reviews are a good way to funnel information up to the project manager and let them know what changes are going into the system at any given time. The code review should answer the following questions:

- Does the code adhere to coding standards?

- Does the code take advantage of organizational best practices?

- Will the code conflict with other areas of the system?

- Has this code already been written somewhere else?

- Does the code work?

- Is there a better way to write this code (for instance, StringBuffers instead of Strings)?

To help facilitate a code review, you should create a standard form and use it regularly. Whenever a developer would like to check some code back into the version control system, they would print out this code review form and schedule a code review with another developer. Here's an idea of what a code review form might look like:

```
Project Name: Foobar Upgrade
Type of change: ____ New  __X__ Change Request # 1034


Change Description:
In response to a bug uncovered by the QA team, the Foobar application
needs to print out the phrase 'barfoo' instead of 'foobar'. Changes
had to be made in several places to accommodate the fix.


Files Affected:
FooBarMain.java
FooBarGUI.java
FooBarStringEngine.java


Review Items:
1. Does the code adhere to organizational coding standards?
2. Does the code work as intended?


Signoff:
To be included in build # __346a__
Developer _____ Date _____
Reviewer _____ Date _____
```

Automated Build Procedure

Each and every build of the system should follow a consistent and predictable procedure. This helps to minimize deployment problems that arise from inconsistent development environments. Typically, one or two team members are responsible for building the system and deploying the application. Sometimes, entire teams share the responsibility and set up a round-robin schedule including each team member. To ensure that each team member follows the same procedure, it's necessary to script the build so that it can be run automatically and monitored for errors by the developer doing the build.

You can script a build procedure in a few different ways. In a Unix-like environment, you could use the make utility to run your scripts. This is a heavily used tool for building C and C++ programs. In a Windows environment, the tool of choice has long been Windows batch files. Although each of these options might work okay, neither one was intended for Java development. The Apache-Jakarta Project has developed an open-source scripting tool called Ant that was made specifically for Java development. As you'll see in this chapter, Ant is a powerful and useful tool for not only automating your build, but for automating other tasks such as regression and load testing as well.

Testing Framework

As discussed in Chapter 9, testing your code is an important component of the development process. Using tools such as JUnit and JMeter to perform unit and load testing is vital to producing quality software in an efficient manner. As you'll see later in this chapter, you can even automate these tasks and attach them to the build process.

Change Management

A benefit of implementing a development framework such as the one introduced in this chapter is that it makes it much easier to handle problems that inevitably arise along the project lifecycle. Still, you need to implement a formal procedure for tracking bugs and managing change requests. Some source control systems include built-in bug tracking facilities. If your particular system does not include such functionality, then you can turn to one of several open-source alternatives such as Bugzilla (http://www.bugzilla.org).

Automating the Build Process with Ant

Ant is a Java-based scripting tool that automates tasks such as compiling and deploying an application. Ant is the result of a subproject within the Apache-Jakarta Project. Ant has gained industry-wide acceptance at a remarkable rate. In fact, you'll find that most Java-based open-source projects use Ant to script their build processes. Regardless of whether you use Ant on your own project, it's likely that you'll run into it sooner or later, so it pays to have a working knowledge of it.

To get the latest copy of Ant, go to the Apache-Jakarta Project website (http://jakarta.apache.org) and download the latest binary release. Extract the contents of the file to your hard drive. You'll need to add the /[path to ant]/ant/bin directory to your PATH environment variable. You'll also need to set the ANT_HOME and JAVA_HOME variables as well. Now you're ready to use Ant.

Creating a Simple Build Script

Ant scripts are XML files. These files can be called whatever you like, but the default name that Ant looks for is build.xml. To use a different name, you would simply specify the name when invoking the Ant script. For example, if your build script is App_build.xml, then you would run the script by typing in **ant App_build.xml** at the command prompt. If your build script were named build.xml, then you would simply type **ant** at the command prompt. Each of these examples assumes you're invoking Ant from the same directory that the build scripts reside in.

The first element defined inside of a build script is the <project> tag. This is where you give the project a name, specify a base directory for all of your virtual paths to work from, and tell the project which target to execute if none has been specified. Here's what the <project> tag looks like for a simple build script you'll put together in this section:

```
<project name="jspBook" default="dist" basedir=".">
```

This tag gives the name "jspBook" to the project, defines a default target of "dist," and sets the base directory to the current working directory. Each path specified throughout the build script will be attached to the current working directory if it's not explicitly defined. For example, the path /dist/classes would be resolved to /usr/local/development/projects/dist/classes if your current working directory is /usr/local/development/projects.

Ant works with your build script by executing targets defined within the file. A target is simply a tag that defines a set of actions to perform. Within the <target> tag, several child tags can be included to perform a variety of tasks.

The <target> tag itself requires a name and optionally can include other targets that need to run prior to executing the current target. This is an example of a target that requires the init target to run prior to execution:

```
<target name="compile" depends="init">
    <!-- Compile the java code from ${src} into ${build} -->
    <javac srcdir="${src}" destdir="${build}"
       classpath="/usr/local/development/j2ee/lib/j2ee.jar"
    />
</target>
```

When this target is executed, Ant sees that it requires the init target to execute before proceeding with the current target. Perhaps the init target creates the directories referenced within the compile target and populates them with the latest set of source code files. Therefore, the compile target would fail if the init target is not executed first. An entire chain of targets can be set up in this fashion, directing Ant to execute them in the correct order.

In the previous example, you saw the use of properties with the references to ${src} and ${build}. These are properties that have been set up earlier in the build script using the <property> tag. These are essentially global variables you can use throughout the build script. You've seen how to reference these properties using the ${property_name} syntax. You can define them using the following <property> tag:

```
<property name="src" value="work"/>
<property name="build" value="build"/>
```

These property tags associate the strings work and build with the properties labeled src and build. Again, you can reference these throughout the build script using ${src} and ${build} to substitute the corresponding string values in their place.

Ant has several tasks built in, as well as several more available as part of its optional .jar file you can add to your installation. Among the most common of these built-in tasks involve operations on the filesystem. The <mkdir> tag creates a directory. The <copy> tag, in conjunction with the <fileset> tag, moves files between directories. This is an example of creating a directory and then copying a set of files into that directory:

```
<mkdir dir="${temp}"/>
<copy todir="${temp}">
  <fileset dir="${src}"/>
</copy>
```

Other tasks commonly used are the `<tstamp>`, `<javac>`, and `<jar>` tags. The `<tstamp>` tag creates a timestamp that is later referenced as `${DSTAMP}`. The `<javac>` tag runs the Java compiler. The `<jar>` tag runs the Jar utility to create an archive of a specific set of files. Listing 10-1 shows a complete build file that utilizes each task discussed so far to compile all of the source code created for this book and archive it into a .jar file.

Listing 10-1. `build.xml`

```xml
<project name="jspBook" default="dist" basedir=".">

  <!-- Set global properties for this build -->
  <property name="src" value="work"/>
  <property name="build" value="build"/>
  <property name="dist" value="dist"/>

  <target name="init">
    <!-- Create the time stamp -->
    <tstamp/>
    <!-- Create the build directory used by compile -->
    <mkdir dir="${build}"/>
    <!-- Create the source directory and copy the source files into it -->
    <mkdir dir="${src}"/>
    <copy todir="${src}">
      <fileset dir="/usr/local/development/projects/jspBook"/>
    />
  </target>

  <target name="compile" depends="init">
    <!-- Compile the java code from ${src} into ${build} -->
    <javac srcdir="${src}" destdir="${build}"
        classpath="/usr/local/development/j2ee/lib/j2ee.jar
          :/usr/local/development/junit3.7/junit.jar"
    />
  </target>

  <target name="dist" depends="compile">
    <!-- Create distribution directory -->
    <mkdir dir="${dist}/lib"/>
    <!-- Create JAR file -->
    <jar jarfile="jspBook_${DSTAMP}.jar" basedir="${build}"/>
  </target>
```

```
<target name="clean">
  <delete dir="${build}"/>
  <delete dir="${dist}"/>
  <delete dir="${src}"/>
</target>

</project>
```

As you can see, the default target is dist, so Ant will go to that target and see that it depends on the compile target, which in turn depends on the init target. Therefore, the init target is executed first, then the compile target, and finally the dist target. The clean target is a special case. It should be executed once all the intended targets are finished. It's inside of this target that you clean up your working directories.

This build script was written to be used specifically with a Unix-like environment. The path names are formatted for use within such an environment rather than a Windows environment. I'll discuss how to write platform-neutral scripts shortly, but for now, just replace the path names with whatever is appropriate for your system.

To run this build script, be sure to first place the build.xml file in the directory from which you want to run the build. From that directory, at a command prompt, type in **ant** to execute the default target of the build.xml file. Again, be sure that you have set your ANT_HOME and JAVA_HOME environment variables appropriately. Also, include the /ant/bin directory in your PATH variable as well.

Integrating with Source Control

In the build script presented in the previous section, the source files were simply copied from one directory to a different directory. Ideally, the source code would be under the management of a source code control system rather than a directory in the filesystem. In that case, the code would need to be copied from a repository using the appropriate commands. Fortunately, Ant has a few built-in tasks that simplify interactions with source code control systems. In the standard built-in tasks, you can use the cvs task to interact with a CVS repository. In the optional built-in tasks (in the optional .jar file), tasks exist for PVCS, Microsoft Visual SourceSafe, and StarTeam. To illustrate the integration of Ant and source control, you'll use a CVS repository and the cvs task in Ant.

Before integrating CVS into the build script, let's step back and set up a CVS repository for the code. If you already have a CVS repository, or a different source control system, then simply skim over this section and make the appropriate modifications to integrate it with the Ant build script. To obtain CVS, go to their website (http://www.cvshome.org) and follow the download link to find the appropriate download for your platform. Go ahead and install CVS, following the installation instructions included with the download (or see the website for more details).

Creating a Repository

To create a CVS repository, you need to give it a location to store its files that maintain histories for source code managed within the repository. This is done using the cvs command, passing it a directory that will be home to the new repository, and adding the init argument to instruct CVS to create a new repository. In most cases, this repository will manage several projects, not just a single set of files. This is what the cvs command would look like for both a Windows and a Unix system:

```
Windows:
C:\> cvs -d :local:c:\development\cvs init

Unix (Linux):
> cvs -d /usr/local/development/cvs init
```

Now that the repository has been created, the next step is to create a project and add files to it. Once again, you'll use the cvs command to accomplish this. You'll still need to pass the location of the repository, but this time you'll use the import argument. The import argument causes CVS to copy all files under the current directory tree into the repository and creates special files inside of each folder to maintain historical records. The -m argument enables you to add a description of the project. The remaining arguments specify the project name, a username and a user-defined tag (which can be anything). Here's an example of this command:

```
Windows:
C:\development\project\jspBook> cvs -d :local:c:\development\cvs import
  -m "JSP Book Source Code" jspBook apatzer R1

Unix (Linux):
\usr\local\project\jspBook> cvs -d /usr/local/development/cvs import
  -m "JSP Book Source Code" jspBook apatzer R1
```

Your repository is now complete. You can check out source files (non-exclusive) using the checkout argument of the cvs command. To commit changes, you would use the commit argument and pass it the name of the file along with a description of what has been changed. There are several other commands that you might find useful but are not in the context of this book. Several CVS tutorials exist on the Internet, as well in as your local bookstore. Here are some examples of commands you might use:

```
C:\> cvs -d :local:c:\development\cvs checkout jspBook

C:\> cvs -d :local:c:\development\cvs commit -m
  "Added new connection pool." DataEngine.java

Note: log command displays a change history for a particular file
C:\> cvs -d :local:c:\development\cvs log jspBook DataEngine.java

Note: diff command displays differences between repository file and local copy
C:\> cvs -d :local:c:\development\cvs -Q diff -c
```

Integrating CVS with Ant

Ant provides a cvs task built into its standard set of tasks that enables you to check out an entire project and copy it to a working directory. Here's an example of the cvs task:

```
Windows:
<cvs cvsRoot=":local:c:\development\cvs"
    package="jspBook"
    dest="${src}"
/>

Unix (Linux):
<cvs cvsRoot="/usr/local/development/cvs"
    package="jspBook"
    dest="${src}"
/>
```

The cvs task takes the cvsRoot argument to specify the location of the CVS repository. The package argument names the project to check out of the repository. The dest argument states where the cvs task should place the files it checks out from the given project. Now that you have the ability to integrate with CVS, see Listing 10-2 for a complete build file that uses the cvs task rather than the copy task to move the source code into a working directory.

Listing 10-2. `build_cvs.xml`

```xml
<project name="jspBook" default="dist" basedir=".">

  <!-- Set global properties for this build -->
  <property name="src" value="work"/>
  <property name="build" value="build"/>
  <property name="dist" value="dist"/>

  <target name="init">
    <!-- Create the time stamp -->
    <tstamp/>
    <!-- Create the build directory used by compile -->
    <mkdir dir="${build}"/>
    <!-- Create the source directory and checkout the source files into it -->
    <mkdir dir="${src}"/>
    <cvs cvsRoot="/usr/local/development/cvs"
         package="jspBook"
         dest="${src}"
    />
  </target>

  <target name="compile" depends="init">
    <!-- Compile the java code from ${src} into ${build} -->
    <javac srcdir="${src}" destdir="${build}"
       classpath="/usr/local/development/j2ee/lib/j2ee.jar
          :/usr/local/development/junit3.7/junit.jar"
    />
  </target>

  <target name="dist" depends="compile">
    <!-- Create distribution directory -->
    <mkdir dir="${dist}/lib"/>
    <!-- Create JAR file -->
    <jar jarfile="jspBook_${DSTAMP}.jar" basedir="${build}"/>
  </target>

  <target name="clean">
    <delete dir="${build}"/>
    <delete dir="${dist}"/>
    <delete dir="${src}"/>
  </target>

</project>
```

Building WAR Files

The common way in which to deploy a J2EE web application is as a WAR file. A WAR file is simply an archive of a standard directory structure containing all of the necessary files and deployment descriptors. Most J2EE application servers provide web-based administration tools that will take a WAR file and automatically create the directory structure, copy the files over, and modify the server configuration to add the application.

The WAR file contains a root directory to store JSP and HTML files, a \WEB-INF directory to store the web.xml deployment descriptor, a \WEB-INF\classes directory for any servlets or other Java classes your application needs, and a \WEB-INF\lib directory to store supporting libraries on which your application depends. Of course, you can include more directories in this structure, but this is usually the minimum required by a web application. This is what a typical J2EE web application directory (and WAR file) might look like:

```
c:\tomcat\webapps\hellow\hello.jsp
c:\tomcat\webapps\hellow\images\hello.jpg
c:\tomcat\webapps\hellow\WEB-INF\web.xml
c:\tomcat\webapps\hellow\WEB-INF\classes\HelloEngine.class
c:\tomcat\webapps\hellow\WEB-INF\lib\helloUtils.jar
```

As you may have guessed, Ant provides a built-in task to build a WAR file. The war task can contain several different subtasks that are all aimed at copying the right files into their proper locations within the J2EE web application directory structure. The war task itself takes arguments to give the WAR file a name and a location and to specify a web.xml file to use. This is an example of a war task:

```
<war warfile="${dist}/hellow_${DSTAMP}.war" webxml="${src}/config/web.xml">
    <fileset dir="${build}/docroot"/>
    <lib dir="${build}/lib"/>
    <classes dir="${build}/classes"/>
</war>
```

The <fileset> task specifies which files should be copied into the document root of the WAR file. The <lib> task copies files into the \WEB-INF\lib directory. The <classes> task copies files into the \WEB-INF\classes directory. There are several more options for the war task. See the online documentation at the Ant website (http://jakarta.apache.org) for a more detailed description of building WAR files with Ant.

Precompiling JSP Pages

As you might recall from earlier chapters, the application server compiles JSP pages as needed into Java servlets. These servlets then service the original JSP requests as intended. Although this mechanism provides a great deal of flexibility in the development process, it sometimes can contribute to problems in the deployment process. Say, for instance, that your application consists of 100 JSP pages that will be accessed by several hundred users simultaneously. Unless you individually run through the application and access every page, these pages will be compiled as the users try to access them. This is an impractical solution, particularly in a production environment.

Besides performance issues, another reason this runtime compilation can be troublesome is that any compile-time errors will be presented to the application's end user. Perhaps the application server is missing some libraries necessary to perform the compilation, or maybe it's currently busy with several other processes and simply cannot handle compiling several hundred Java classes in its current state.

A solution to this problem is to compile the JSP files prior to deployment and avoid the entire runtime compilation process entirely. As you can imagine, a JSP file can't simply be compiled by the Java compiler. What would it do with all of that HTML code? First, the file needs to be converted into a source file for a Java servlet. Then, the new source file can be run through the Java compiler. The new class file is placed into the appropriate \WEB-INF\classes directory, and the web.xml file is updated with the new servlet definition.

This causes a bit of confusion when it comes to the names of the pages and how other pages will reference them. For instance, if you were originally calling the hello.jsp page, then the new page might be something like ...\servlet\hello. This can be cleared up by mapping the file intelligently in the web.xml file so that other pages can keep their original references to the new page intact.

Each application server has their own method and tools to perform the compilation of JSP files. The Tomcat server provides a tool called jspc that resides in the \tomcat\bin directory. Running it will give you a Java source file, which you will then need to compile. Using the right command-line options, it's possible to have the jspc tool generate a snippet of code to insert into the web.xml file for mapping the servlets. This is an example of running the jspc tool to convert a JSP file named index.jsp:

```
C:\tomcat\bin\jspc -uriroot . index.jsp
```

The uriroot argument specifies the root in which all references are based. In this case, it just uses the current directory. The result of this command is a file called index.java. If you try to compile it, you'll get a servlet object called `index.class`. Place this class in your `\WEB-INF\classes` directory and modify the `web.xml` file to reference it. If you'd like to place the servlet into a package structure, add a `-p package_name` argument to the `jspc` command. You would then need to place the servlet into the appropriate directory structure underneath the `\WEB-INF\classes` directory.

If precompilation of JSP files is important to you, then it would pay to invest time in scripting a process that would convert the file into the appropriate Java source code, compile it, and then generate the appropriate entries into the `web.xml` file. Ant would be a perfect tool to do this. At this time, there's a task already included with Ant's optional package that precompiles files for BEA WebLogic, and I'm sure there will soon be a task for using Tomcat's `jspc` command.

Accounting for Different Platforms

One advantage to using Ant to script your build procedure is that it's a Java-like environment that works together with the Java toolset to provide a familiar and platform-independent build scripting language. However, you have to watch out for a few things if your application truly requires a platform-independent build script. Specifically, the most common things to be careful of are inconsistent path names, tasks that are specific to a particular operating system, and anything that requires a specific location of a file or resource. Fortunately, Ant provides several tools for you to work around platform differences.

Path names can be troublesome to anyone trying to write a single script that needs to run on different platforms. Unix systems use forward slashes (/) to separate path elements and a colon (:) to separate items within a path. Windows systems use the backward slash (\) along with semicolons (;). One way you can address this issue is to use relative paths whenever possible. This is only a partial solution, however, because this will certainly not address all path issues.

Another thing you can do is set up paths using an Ant task like the `<path>` task and then passing the path to the `<pathconvert>` task to be formatted for the target operating system. The following snippet of Ant code sets a classpath using Windows syntax, then checks if the runtime environment is a Unix system and converts the classpath to a Unix-style syntax:

```
<target name="init">
  <path id="project.classpath">
    <pathelement path="c:\development\jars\j2ee.jar"/>
    <pathelement path="c:\development\jars\xerces.jar"/>
  </path>
  <condition property="unix_env">
    <and>
      <os family="unix"/>
```

```
      </and>
    </condition>
  </target>

  <target name="setenv" depends="init" if="unix_env">
    <pathconvert targetos="unix" property="project.classpath"
      refid="project.classpath"/>
  </target>

  <target name="compile" depends="setenv">
    <javac srcdir="${src}" destdir="${build}">
      <classpath refid="${project.classpath}"/>
    </javac>
  </target>
```

The <condition> task determines from which operating system the script is being run. If the condition is met, then the given property is set. The <target> element can decide whether to execute based on the existence of a given property. This can be useful to overcome the other issues with cross-platform build scripts and tasks unique to a specific operating system. By checking the host operating system and setting a property, it's possible to write a separate task for each individual operating system the script may run on. For instance, a task that precompiles a set of JSP files may need to be written as two separate tasks named jspc_bea and jspc_tomcat and called conditionally based on the existence of a particular property.

Summary

This chapter covered several items considered as best practices for not only Java and JSP development but software development in general. You should combine these best practices into a development process that encourages standardization and accountability. This process, along with a set of supporting tools, form a development framework that enables developers to be more efficient with the time and effort they contribute to a software development project.

An important piece of any development framework is the process for building and deploying the application. To avoid configuration headaches, you should script the build process and run it automatically on a regular basis. Ant, an open-source tool from the Apache-Jakarta Project, is a Java-based scripting tool that you can use to develop platform-independent build scripts. You can also use Ant to perform routine tasks such as unit testing, load testing, generating documentation, deployment, and staging.

CHAPTER 11

Application Frameworks

OVER THE COURSE OF DEVELOPING an application, there usually are quite a few tasks involved that have been done either in a prior application or even somewhere else in the current application. This is true of any software project, regardless of the language or platform. It would be nice to be able to look past these core tasks and focus on developing the application and not the basic plumbing on which it relies. This is where *application frameworks* come in.

An application framework is a set of core services that provide basic functionality, such as logging, database connectivity, security, and request handling, to name a few. Each of these components has been tested numerous times and in many cases has been used on several other projects. When you develop a new application, you build everything on top of the application framework. Consequently, developers can focus on tasks specific to the application, such as business domain objects and screen flows, without worrying about how to connect to the database or figuring out how they should log error messages.

This chapter will walk through the design, construction, and implementation of a lightweight framework for the development of web applications. It's considered to be lightweight because it contains only that which is necessary to provide a presentation framework with a few back-end services to provide for simple business logic and database access. You can extend it, however, to include other components required to develop enterprise applications, such as Enterprise JavaBeans (EJBs), JNDI lookups, and JavaMail.

Designing a Framework

When building a framework, you should put careful thought into its design to ensure it'll be usable in at least 80 percent of future projects. The other 20 percent where it's not usable is to be expected. There's always going to be something an application needs to do that's different from what the framework provides. With that said, how can you be sure your framework will work in most situations? Well, a good framework is one that evolves with each project. Therefore, the framework should be extensible while providing the core needs on which each application relies.

You should treat a framework as its own software project. Large enough companies even have entire teams devoted to the framework. An application framework should follow its own release cycle with no dependencies on any of the applications that use it. Project teams will treat the framework as any other third-party software package they use. For example, let's say a particular project is using the Xerces XML parser from the Apache Group. When a new release is available, the project team would typically evaluate the benefits along with any potential issues with upgrading to the new release prior to performing the upgrade. You should treat an application framework in the same manner, which means it needs to have the following characteristics:

- **Easily extensible**: The framework should be designed in such a way that it can easily be extended as new requirements arise.

- **Completely documented**: Each release of the framework should be accompanied by a complete set of documentation. This includes a set of HTML pages documenting the API, typically generated from the Javadoc utility. It also should include a set of release notes, allowing the user to evaluate what has changed before deciding to upgrade.

- **Simple to use**: If the framework is too complex, it'll be hard to gain acceptance by the developers, who may not use it. It might make sense for a developer to write their own custom code and sidestep the framework if they feel it's too difficult or clumsy to use.

Building a Web Application Framework

You should evaluate several existing application frameworks prior to constructing your own. Of these frameworks, the most popular is the Struts framework from the Apache Group. It's similar to the one presented in this chapter, except that it's much more complete and has been thoroughly tested by numerous developers. For more information on Struts, see their website (`http://jakarta.apache.org/struts/index.html`). The framework presented in this chapter will illustrate the concepts behind an application framework as well as provide a good start toward building your own complete, full-featured framework.

Designing the Framework

The framework will handle the core tasks of user authentication, logging, database connectivity, and request handling. In addition to these tasks, it'll begin to provide a set of presentation widgets in the form of custom tags. Most of these tasks will be pulled from previous chapters and combined to create an end-to-end solution for building web applications.

The first step is creating a separate project for the framework. This involves setting up a new packages structure and generating a new build script for deployment. Table 11-1 shows the package structure that will be used for the framework.

Table 11-1. Framework Packages

PACKAGE	DESCRIPTION
`jspbook.framework.security`	Authentication filter to authenticate users with each request
`jspbook.framework.logging`	Wrapper class to handle logging functions
`jspbook.framework.db`	Database helper classes
`jspbook.framework.request`	Classes that make up the request-handling framework
`jspbook.framework.ui.tags`	Custom tags acting as view helpers
`jspbook.framework.util`	Utility classes to perform tasks such as loading a set of application constants

The framework will have its own build script that will compile each of the classes in order (in other words, logging components should go first since they're used in other pieces of the framework), JAR them up into a distributable library, JAR up the source code, and generate the Javadoc pages and JAR those up as well. This will give the end users everything they need to start using the framework.

Documenting the Framework

To this point, all the code you've developed in this book has lacked Javadoc comments. Now that you'll distribute this code as a framework, it's essential that you also document it using the proper Javadoc syntax to enable the build script to generate a complete set of documentation automatically with each build.

Although there are many different things you can do with the proper Javadoc syntax, there are three specific areas that need to be covered for the documentation to be worth anything. First, just before each class definition, include a descriptive comment such as the following:

```
/**
 * One-line description of class
 *
 * <p>One or more paragraphs of usage notes</p>
 *
```

```
* @version 1.0
* @author  Andrew Patzer
* @since   JDK 1.3
*/
```

Notice how the comment is formatted. All Javadoc comments begin with a /** and end with a */. All text between these lines should begin with a single asterisk. The @version, @author, and @since comments are special fields that Javadoc converts into the appropriate sections of the finished documentation. The @version field is used to specify the version of the class. The @author field specifies the original developer that created the class. The @since field specifies the minimum version of the JDK required to use the class. The next area to be sure to comment is the class-level variables. Each of these will belong to a special section of the documentation and should be commented appropriately with a single comment preceding the variable declaration as follows:

```
/**
 * Counter to track usage statistics for pricing engine.
 */
private int counter = 0;
```

Finally, the other items that should be documented well are the individual methods belonging to the class. This documentation should be similar to that for class-level variables, only with greater detail. Here's an example:

```
/**
 * Validates a given user ID and password combination
 * against the user table in the quoting database. The
 * user ID and password should be taken from the request
 * object.
 *
 * @param _uid User ID
 * @param _pwd User Password
 *
 * @return Status of login authentication.
 */
public boolean isValidLogin(String _uid, String _pwd) {
```

The @param fields define each parameter passed in to the method. The @return field describes the value returned by the method. For more information on using Javadoc to document your code, visit http://java.sun.com/j2se/javadoc/writingdoccomments/index.html for a tutorial from Sun.

Logging Error and Debug Messages

A logging component of a framework is responsible for directing messages to a single log file, a system console, an email address, or even a pager. Messages could be error messages (exceptions), information messages, or debug statements. You can route each of these messages differently. For instance, debug statements are only important to a developer and can go to their own console or a local file. Errors might go to a log file located on a server, or they might get emailed to a system administrator.

This functionality is contained within a logging package from the Apache Group called log4j. Using log4j directly is okay for a simple project with only a few classes, but for anything larger, it pays to wrap the log4j functionality into a standard component of the framework. You can configure log4j from a property file or from within the code. For the purposes of this framework, you'll configure it within the code using a simple predefined layout and output it to a single text file. Listing 11-1 wraps the log4j functionality and gives the framework a standard logging component.

Listing 11-1. `Logger.java`

```
package jspbook.framework.logging;

import org.apache.log4j.*;
import java.io.IOException;

/**
 * Wrapper for Log4J logging utility
 *
 * <p>Wraps Log4J functionality</p>
 *
 * @version 1.0
 * @author  Andrew Patzer
 * @since   JDK 1.3
 */

public class Logger
{

  /**
   * Static constant for DEBUG log level
   */
  public static final int DEBUG = 0;
  /**
   * Static constant for INFO log level
   */
```

```java
public static final int INFO = 1;
/**
 * Static constant for WARN log level
 */
public static final int WARN = 2;
/**
 * Static constant for ERROR log level
 */
public static final int ERROR = 3;
/**
 * Static constant for FATAL log level
 */
public static final int FATAL = 4;

/**
 * Category to log messages to
 */
public static Category cat = Category.getInstance("framework");

static
{
  try {
    BasicConfigurator.configure(new FileAppender(
      new SimpleLayout(), "c:\\log.txt"));
  }
  catch (IOException e) {
    System.out.println(e.toString());
  }
}

/**
 * Static method to log messages
 */
public static void log(int _level, String _msg)
{
  switch (_level) {
    case DEBUG:
      cat.debug(_msg);
      break;
    case INFO:
      cat.info(_msg);
      break;
    case WARN:
```

```
        cat.warn(_msg);
        break;
      case ERROR:
     cat.error(_msg);
        break;
    case FATAL:
        cat.fatal(_msg);
        break;
    default:
        cat.warn("Problem using Logger class");
    }
  }
}
```

Building a Database Helper

Enterprise applications almost always reference a database, so you should take care to manage an application's interaction with the database. It should be managed by a single component to allow for greater control over user connections and query optimizations. Referring back to Chapter 7, Listing 7-7 uses a JNDI DataSource to manage connections to the database. This allows the application server to manage a pool of connections. Through this framework component, the DataSource object will get a connection and return it to the calling class.

The database helper component of the framework should be configurable through an external file in order to allow separate applications to specify their own DataSource configuration without having to modify the framework code. You can do this by creating a utility class that reads in a property file and then makes each property available through a static method. The AppConstants class, shown in Listing 11-2, creates a java.util.Properties object and exposes it through the static getProperty method.

Listing 11-2. AppConstants.java
```
package jspbook.framework.util;

import java.util.Properties;
import java.io.*;

import jspbook.framework.logging.Logger;

/**
 * Application Constants
 *
```

```
 * <p>Reads in application constants from a property
 * file and loads them into a java.util.Properties
 * object.</p>
 *
 * @version 1.0
 * @author  Andrew Patzer
 * @since   JDK 1.3
 */

public class AppConstants
{
  private static Properties appProps;

  public static String getProperty(String _property)
  {
    if (appProps == null) {
      try {
        appProps = new Properties();
        appProps.load(new FileInputStream(new File(
          System.getProperty("prop.file.dir"), "app.props")));
      }
      catch (IOException e) {
        Logger.log(Logger.ERROR, e.toString());
      }
    }
    return appProps.getProperty(_property);
  }
}
```

The app.props file is nothing more than a text file containing key-value pairs that will be read in to the Properties object and made available through the getProperty method. To use the CatalogDB DataSource, for instance, the app.props file would contain the following line:

```
dbName=jdbc/CatalogDB
```

The app.props file should be located in the \WEB-INF directory of the web application. In order to locate the app.props file, the AppConstants class retrieves the location of the file by accessing the prop.file.dir system property. This can be set as part of the startup script for your application server. The following script excerpt shows how you should modify the startup script for the Tomcat server to specify the prop.file.dir system property:

Relevant line of startup script before change:

```
%_STARTJAVA% %CATALINA_OPTS% -Dcatalina.base="%CATALINA_BASE%"
-Dcatalina.home="%CATALINA_HOME%"
org.apache.catalina.startup.Bootstrap %2 %3 %4 %5 %6 %7 %8 %9 start
```

After change:

```
%_STARTJAVA% %CATALINA_OPTS% -Dcatalina.base="%CATALINA_BASE%"
-Dcatalina.home="%CATALINA_HOME%"
-Dprop.file.dir=c:\development\tomcat4.0.2\webapps\catalog\WEB-INF
org.apache.catalina.startup.Bootstrap %2 %3 %4 %5 %6 %7 %8 %9 start
```

Listing 11-3 shows the code for the DBHelper component. Notice how the name of the DataSource is obtained using the AppConstants class.

Listing 11-3. `DBHelper.java`

```java
package jspbook.framework.db;

import javax.naming.*;
import javax.sql.*;

import java.sql.*;

import jspbook.framework.logging.Logger;

/**
 * Database helper object
 *
 * <p>Manages database connections by using a
 * single DataSource object to provide Connection
 * objects to calling classes. This allows the
 * application server to manage the connections
 * in a connection pool.</p>
 *
 * @version 1.0
 * @author  Andrew Patzer
 * @since   JDK 1.3
 */

public class DBHelper
{
```

```java
/**
 * Reference to a JNDI DataSource
 */
private static DataSource ds;

private static Context initCtx;
private static Context envCtx;

private static String dbName = AppConstants.getProperty("dbName");

/**
 * Using the DataSource object, gets a
 * database connection from the pool.
 */
public static Connection getConnection()
{
  if (ds == null) {
    try {
      initCtx = new InitialContext();
      envCtx = (Context) initCtx.lookup("java:comp/env");
      ds = (DataSource) envCtx.lookup(dbName);
    }
    catch (javax.naming.NamingException e) {
      Logger.log(Logger.ERROR,
        "A problem occurred while retrieving a DataSource object");
      Logger.log(Logger.ERROR, e.toString());
    }
  }

  Connection dbCon = null;
  try {
    dbCon = ds.getConnection();
  }
  catch (java.sql.SQLException e) {
    Logger.log(Logger.ERROR,
      "A problem occurred while connecting to the database.");
    Logger.log(Logger.ERROR, e.toString());
  }
  return dbCon;
}
}
```

Authenticating Users

Chapter 6 introduced filters. To manage access to the framework, a filter will be
put into place to intercept each web request and make sure the user has access
to the system. This involves setting a new variable in any HTML or JSP page using
the framework, `pageId`. This variable tells the filter from where the request is
coming. If it comes from the login page, then the filter should attempt to authenticate the user. If it comes from somewhere else, the filter should check the
session to see if the user has already been authenticated. Listing 11-4 shows
the code for this filter. Notice how it uses the logging and database components
of the framework.

Listing 11-4. `AuthenticationFilter.java`

```
package jspbook.framework.security;

import java.io.*;
import java.util.*;
import javax.servlet.*;
import javax.servlet.http.*;
import java.sql.*;

import jspbook.framework.logging.Logger;
import jspbook.framework.db.DBHelper;

/**
 * Filter to handle user authentication
 *
 * <p>Intercepts requests and validates users.
 * If the user is coming from the login page,
 * the filter attempts to authenticate the
 * user. If the user comes from somewhere else,
 * then the filter will check the session object
 * and validate that the user has already logged in.</p>
 *
 * @version 1.0
 * @author  Andrew Patzer
 * @since   JDK 1.3
 */

public class AuthenticationFilter implements Filter {
```

```java
/**
 * Static variable used to resolve the login page
 */
private static final String LOGIN_PAGE = "login.jsp";
/**
 * Stores the Filter Configuration
 */
private FilterConfig config = null;

/**
 * Called when Filter is put into service.
 */
public void init(FilterConfig _config)
  throws ServletException
{
  this.config = _config;
}

/**
 * Execution code for the filter.
 */
public void doFilter(ServletRequest _req, ServletResponse _res,
  FilterChain _chain) throws IOException, ServletException
{
  boolean success = true;

  /* Cast _req to HttpServletRequest and get a session */
  HttpServletRequest httpReq = (HttpServletRequest) _req;
  HttpSession session = httpReq.getSession();

  /* Get the pageId from the request parameters */
  String pageId = (String) httpReq.getParameter("pageId");
  if (pageId == null) {
    success = false;
  }

  /* Get uid and pwd from request parameters */
  String req_uid = (String) httpReq.getParameter("uid");
  String req_pwd = (String) httpReq.getParameter("pwd");

  /* If coming from login page, authenticate */
  if (pageId.equals("loginPage")) {
    if (authenticate(req_uid, req_pwd)) {
```

```java
          session.setAttribute("uid", req_uid);
      }
      else {
        success = false;
      }
    }
    else {
      String session_uid = (String) session.getAttribute("uid");
      if (session_uid == null || !session_uid.equals(req_uid)) {
        success = false;
      }
    }

    /* If login failed, set attribute in the request and forward to login page */
    if (!success) {
      _req.setAttribute("loginStatus", "failed");
      RequestDispatcher rd = httpReq.getRequestDispatcher(LOGIN_PAGE);
      rd.forward(_req, _res);
    }

    /* Continue with filter chain */
    _chain.doFilter(_req, _res);
}

/**
 * Check if the user is valid
 */
private boolean authenticate(String _uid, String _pwd)
{
  Connection dbCon = null;
  ResultSet rs = null;

  /* Get db connection, then validate user */
  try {
    dbCon = DBHelper.getConnection();
    Statement s = dbCon.createStatement();
    rs = s.executeQuery("select * from user where uid = '"
            + _uid + "' and pwd = '" + _pwd + "'");
    return (rs.next());
  }
  catch (java.sql.SQLException e) {
    Logger.log(Logger.ERROR,
```

```
        "A problem occurred while accessing the database.");
      Logger.log(Logger.ERROR, e.toString());
    }
    finally {
      /* Close database connection */
      try {
        dbCon.close();
      }
      catch (java.sql.SQLException e) {
        Logger.log(Logger.ERROR,
          "A problem occurred while closing the database.");
        Logger.log(Logger.ERROR, e.toString());
      }
    }
    return false;

  }


  /**
   * Reset the Filter configuration.
   */
  public void destroy()
  {
    config = null;
  }
}
```

Simplified Request Handling

Chapter 7 introduced a complete framework for handling web requests. To include it in your overall application framework, you have to make a few changes to include support for logging and the use of the central database component. Also, you'll see how the ActionFactory has been changed to allow for a clean separation between the framework and any application that uses the framework. You might recall that the ActionFactory required for Action classes to be hard-coded into the class. This is not flexible enough to allow for a separate deployment of the framework, so it has been changed to take in a new variable called actionClass. Using reflection, the ActionFactory loads the class and returns an instance to the controller servlet. Listings 11-5, 11-6, 11-7, and 11-8 show the code used to process requests.

Listing 11-5. `Controller.java`

```java
package jspbook.framework.request;

import javax.servlet.*;
import javax.servlet.http.*;
import java.io.*;
import java.sql.*;

import jspbook.framework.db.DBHelper;
import jspbook.framework.logging.Logger;

/**
 * Controller servlet to process all application requests
 *
 * <p>This class is used to provide an access point into
 * the framework. It should be declared as a servlet in
 * the application's web.xml file and mapped appropriately.</p>
 * <p>The Controller servlet uses a request-handling framework
 * to process web requests using a set of Action classes. To define
 * a new Action class, simply implement the Action interface
 * and add an entry to the ActionFactory class.</p>
 *
 * @version 1.0
 * @author  Andrew Patzer
 * @since   JDK 1.3
 */

public class Controller extends HttpServlet {

  /**
   *  Shared database connection
   */
  private Connection dbCon;

  /**
   * Initialize shared resources
   */
  public void init()
  {
    dbCon = DBHelper.getConnection();
  }
```

```
/**
 * Forward to doPost method
 */
public void doGet(HttpServletRequest _req, HttpServletResponse _res)
  throws ServletException, IOException
{
  /* Forward to doPost method */
  doPost(_req, _res);
}

/**
 * Process request using Action class and ReqUtility
 */
public void doPost(HttpServletRequest _req, HttpServletResponse _res)
  throws ServletException, IOException
{

  /* Wrap request object with helper */
  ReqUtility reqUtil = new ReqUtility(_req);

  /* Create an Action object based on request parameters */
  Action action = reqUtil.getAction();

  /* Pass the database connection to the action */
  action.setDatabase(dbCon);

  /* Execute business logic */
  if (action.execute(_req, _res)) {

    /* Get appropriate view for action */
    String view = action.getView();

    /* Add the model to the request attributes */
    _req.setAttribute("model", action.getModel());

    /* Forward the request to the given view */
    RequestDispatcher dispatcher = _req.getRequestDispatcher(view);
    dispatcher.forward(_req, _res);

  }

}
```

```
/**
 * Clean up shared resources
 */
public void destroy()
{
  try {
    dbCon.close();
  }
  catch (java.sql.SQLException e) {
    Logger.log(Logger.ERROR, "A problem occurred while closing the database.");
    Logger.log(Logger.ERROR, e.toString());
  }

}

}
```

Listing 11-6 shows the utility class that gets the action class above from the request parameters and return an action object.

Listing 11-6. ReqUtility.java

```
package jspbook.framework.request;

import javax.servlet.*;
import javax.servlet.http.*;
import java.io.*;

/**
 * Request helper utility
 *
 * <p>Used simply to extract the 'Action'
 * parameter and then return the appropriate
 * Action class using the ActionFactory. This
 * class could be used to assist with any
 * request handling activity that can be
 * offloaded from the servlet.</p>
 *
 * @version 1.0
 * @author  Andrew Patzer
 * @since   JDK 1.3
 */
```

```
public class ReqUtility {

  /**
   * Local copy of request object.
   */
  HttpServletRequest request;

  /**
   * Constructor. Used to set local request object.
   */
  public ReqUtility(HttpServletRequest _req)
    throws ServletException, IOException
  {
    request = _req;
  }

  /**
   * Use factory to create action based on request parms
   */
  public Action getAction()
  {
    String action = (String) request.getParameter("actionClass");
    return ActionFactory.createAction(action);
  }

}
```

Listing 11-7 shows the interface that all action objects must implement. This interface makes it possible for the controller servlet to act on new actions without modifying its code.

Listing 11-7. Action.java

```
package jspbook.framework.request;

import javax.servlet.*;
import javax.servlet.http.*;
import java.io.*;
import java.sql.*;
```

```
/**
 * Interface for Action objects
 *
 * <p>This interface is used to provide a generic
 * interface to Action objects, which are used to
 * implement a request action.</p>
 *
 * @version 1.0
 * @author   Andrew Patzer
 * @since     JDK 1.3
 */

public interface Action {

  /**
   * Set local database connection
   */
  public void setDatabase(Connection _db);

  /**
   * Execute business logic
   */
  public boolean execute(HttpServletRequest _req, HttpServletResponse _res)
    throws ServletException, IOException;

  /**
   * Return the page name (and path) to display the view
   */
  public String getView();

  /**
   * Return a JavaBean containing the model (data)
   */
  public Object getModel();
}
```

Listing 11-8 shows the factory class responsible for instantiating the appropriate action class. You do this using Java reflection to create a new instance of an action class based on the value passed in to the createAction method.

Listing 11-8. ActionFactory.java

```java
package jspbook.framework.request;

import jspbook.framework.logging.Logger;

/**
 * Factory class for Action objects
 *
 * <p>Generates an object that implements the
 * Action interface. The createAction method is
 * called from the ReqUtility object to instantiate
 * an Action object to handle a web request.</p>
 *
 * @version 1.0
 * @author  Andrew Patzer
 * @since   JDK 1.3
 */

abstract class ActionFactory {

  /**
   * Instantiate and return the appropriate
   * Action object
   */
  public static Action createAction(String _actionClass)
  {
    Class actionObj = null;
    Action action = null;
    try {
      actionObj = Class.forName(_actionClass);
      action = (Action) actionObj.newInstance();
    }
    catch (Exception e) {
      Logger.log(Logger.ERROR, e.toString());
    }

    return action;
  }
}
```

Common UI Components

Taken directly from Chapter 8, the FormatTag class provides a user interface component for formatting dates and numbers. With the addition of the logging component, Listing 11-9 shows the code for the custom tag.

Listing 11-9. FormatTag.java

```java
package jspbook.framework.ui.tags;

import javax.servlet.http.*;
import javax.servlet.jsp.*;
import javax.servlet.jsp.tagext.*;

import java.io.*;
import java.util.*;

import java.text.*;

import jspbook.framework.logging.Logger;

/**
 * JSP Tag that supports number formatting
 *
 * <p>The FormatTag is used to format a text
 * string into a valid Date, decimal, rounded,
 * or currency value. The format attribute is
 * set to a specific format and the body of the
 * tag is formatted accordingly.</p>
 *
 * @version 1.0
 * @author  Andrew Patzer
 * @since   JDK 1.3
 */

public class FormatTag extends BodyTagSupport {

  /**
   * Locale object for internationalization of content
   */
  private Locale locale;
```

```
/**
 * Tag attribute to format string
 */
protected int format;

/**
 * Static constant for date formatting
 */
public final static int DATE_LONG = 0;

/**
 * Static constant for number formatting
 */
public final static int NUMERIC_DECIMAL = 1;

/**
 * Static constant for number formatting
 */
public final static int NUMERIC_ROUNDED = 2;

/**
 * Static constant for currency formatting
 */
public final static int NUMERIC_CURRENCY = 3;

/**
 * Constructor. Assigns default locale to locale object.
 */
public FormatTag() {
  locale = Locale.getDefault();
}

/**
 * Accessor method for the locale variable.
 */
public void setLocale(Locale locale) {
  this.locale = locale;
}

/**
 * Process Tag Body
 */
public int doAfterBody() throws JspTagException {
```

```
  try {
    BodyContent body = getBodyContent();
    JspWriter out = body.getEnclosingWriter();

    /* Get Input Value */
    String textValue = body.getString().trim();

    /* Output Formatted Value */
    out.println(formatValue(textValue));
  }
  catch (IOException e) {
    throw new JspTagException(e.toString());
  }
  return SKIP_BODY;
}

/**
 * Process End Tag
 */
public int doEndTag() throws JspTagException {
  return EVAL_PAGE;
}

/**
 * Format text string into numeric format
 */
private String formatValue (String _input)
{
  String formattedValue = "";

  try {
    switch (format) {
      case DATE_LONG: {
        Calendar cal = Calendar.getInstance();
        cal.setTime(DateFormat.getDateInstance(
          DateFormat.SHORT).parse(_input));
        SimpleDateFormat df = new SimpleDateFormat("EEE, MMM d, yyyy");
        formattedValue = df.format(cal.getTime());
        break;
      }
      case NUMERIC_DECIMAL: {
        DecimalFormat dcf = (DecimalFormat) NumberFormat.getInstance(locale);
        dcf.setMinimumFractionDigits(2);
```

```
                dcf.setMaximumFractionDigits(2);
                formattedValue = dcf.format(dcf.parse(_input));
                break;
            }
            case NUMERIC_ROUNDED: {
                DecimalFormat dcf = (DecimalFormat) NumberFormat.getInstance(locale);
                dcf.setMinimumFractionDigits(0);
                dcf.setMaximumFractionDigits(0);
                formattedValue = dcf.format(dcf.parse(_input));
                break;
            }
            case NUMERIC_CURRENCY: {
                float f = Float.parseFloat(_input);
                DecimalFormat dcf = (DecimalFormat) NumberFormat.getCurrencyInstance();
                formattedValue = dcf.format(f);
                break;
            }
        }
    }
    catch (Exception e) {
        System.out.println(e.toString());
    }

    return formattedValue;
}

/**
 * Attribute accessor method for format attribute
 */
public int getFormat ()
{
    return this.format;
}

/**
 * Attribute accessor method for format attribute
 */
public void setFormat (int _format)
{
    this.format = _format;
}

}
```

Deploying a Framework

As mentioned at the beginning of this chapter, the framework is to be deployed as a separate project following its own release cycle. The completed framework should include JAR files containing the framework classes, framework source code, and framework documentation. The JAR file containing the classes can then be dropped into another application's \WEB-INF\lib directory and used immediately. To accomplish this, you should write an appropriate build script.

Creating the Framework's Build Script

Using Ant, as was introduced in Chapter 10, you can create a build script to deploy the framework, its source, and its documentation. In Chapter 10, the goal of the build scripts was to create a WAR file of a complete application. Because the framework is to be deployed as a library, the build script will be slightly different. This section will walk through the important changes to the build script.

First, the compile task should break out each package and compile it separately. This is done so that classes that depend on other framework components can be compiled after any dependent class have been compiled. Second, the dist task builds a JAR file containing the classes, not a WAR file for an entire application. It also builds a source JAR file as well as a documentation JAR file. The <javadoc> task includes a lot of information specifying exactly how the documentation should be organized. See the Ant website for more information on using the <javadoc> task (http://jakarta.apache.org/ant/index.html). Listing 11-10 shows the entire build script to compile and deploy the framework.

Listing 11-10. build.xml

```
<project name="framework" default="dist" basedir=".">

  <!-- Set global properties for this build -->
  <property name="src" value="working_files"/>
  <property name="build" value="build"/>
  <property name="dist" value="dist"/>

  <target name="init">
    <!-- Create the time stamp -->
    <tstamp/>
    <!-- Create the build directory used by compile task-->
    <mkdir dir="${build}"/>
  </target>
```

```
<target name="compile" depends="init">
  <!-- Compile the java code from ${src} into ${build} -->
  <path id="project.classpath">
    <pathelement path="C:\Development\j2ee1.3\lib\j2ee.jar"/>
    <pathelement path="C:\Development\log4j1.1.3\dist\lib\log4j.jar"/>
    <pathelement path="${build}"/>
  </path>
  <!-- Build framework in order -->
  <javac srcdir="${src}/jspbook/framework/logging" destdir="${build}">
    <classpath refid="project.classpath"/>
  </javac>
  <javac srcdir="${src}/jspbook/framework/db" destdir="${build}">
    <classpath refid="project.classpath"/>
  </javac>
  <javac srcdir="${src}/jspbook/framework/security" destdir="${build}">
    <classpath refid="project.classpath"/>
  </javac>
  <javac srcdir="${src}/jspbook/framework/request" destdir="${build}">
    <classpath refid="project.classpath"/>
  </javac>
  <javac srcdir="${src}/jspbook/framework/ui/tags" destdir="${build}">
    <classpath refid="project.classpath"/>
  </javac>
</target>

<target name="dist" depends="compile">
  <!-- Create distribution directories -->
  <mkdir dir="${dist}\lib"/>
  <mkdir dir="${dist}\docs"/>
  <!-- Create JAR files -->
  <jar jarfile="${dist}\lib\framework_${DSTAMP}.jar" basedir="${build}"/>
  <jar jarfile="${dist}\lib\framework_src_${DSTAMP}.jar" basedir="${src}"/>
  <!-- Create Javadoc -->
  <javadoc packagenames="jspbook.framework.*"
        sourcepath="${src}"
        defaultexcludes="yes"
        destdir="${dist}\docs"
        classpathref="project.classpath"
        author="true"
        version="true"
        use="true"
        windowtitle="Web Application Framework">
      <doctitle><![CDATA[<h1>Web Application Framework API</h1>]]></doctitle>
```

```
        <bottom><![CDATA[<i>Copyright &#169;
          2002 APress. All Rights Reserved.</i>]]></bottom>
        <group title="Request Handling Packages"
          packages="jspbook.framework.request.*"/>
        <group title="Database Helper Packages"
          packages="jspbook.framework.db.*"/>
        <group title="Logging Packages" packages="jspbook.framework.logging.*"/>
    </javadoc>
    <jar jarfile="${dist}\lib\framework_docs_${DSTAMP}.jar"
      basedir="${dist}\docs"/>
  </target>

</project>
```

Figure 11-1 shows a page taken from the API documentation generated by the <javadoc> task in the Ant build script created in Listing 11-10.

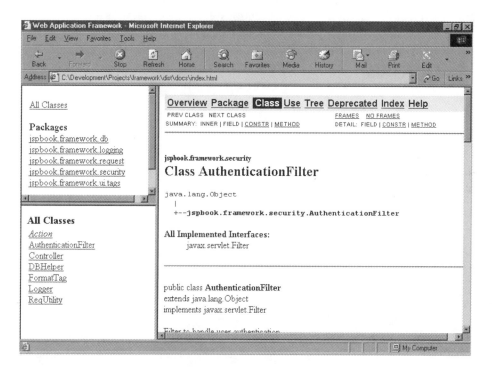

Figure 11-1. Javadoc output

Using the Framework

To use the framework, the first thing you need to do is add it to an application by dropping the JAR file into the \WEB-INF\lib directory. Place the log4j.jar file in that location as well. You will then need to modify the web.xml file to add the servlet definition for the controller servlet, the authentication filter, and the tag library for the user interface components. Once that's done, you need to add two variables, pageId and actionClass, to each page in the application. The pageId identifies the page that made the current request. The actionClass is the fully qualified class name of the action class that will process the page. In the next chapter, you'll build and deploy a sample application using this framework.

Summary

This chapter covered the importance of using an application framework and showed how to build one. The entire book has been leading up to the development of a reusable framework encapsulating a set of best practices and core components that should be present in any enterprise-ready web application. The next chapter will make use of this framework in a complete end-to-end web application.

CHAPTER 12

Putting It All Together

THROUGHOUT THE COURSE OF THIS BOOK, I've demonstrated several techniques in an attempt to describe a set of best practices for the development of JSP applications. This final chapter will use these techniques to build a complete web application to try and bring together what has been covered throughout the book in a single concrete example. Most importantly, though, this application can serve as a reference implementation of the framework developed in Chapter 11.

Building an Online Catalog

The application you'll be building in this chapter is a simple online catalog with a shopping cart. The catalog will contain items that corporations distribute as company promotions to clients and employees. I think everyone at some point in their career has received a coffee mug, fountain pen, or even a yo-yo sporting the company logo. This catalog will be displayed on a single page for simplicity.

The shopping cart will keep track of items the user wants to purchase. The user should be able to add and remove items to and from the shopping cart. Although this is not a complete e-commerce solution, it does cover enough functionality to demonstrate the application and development frameworks developed in previous chapters.

Designing the Application

This application will have three pages. The login page will authenticate the user. A catalog page will display the items in the catalog. The shopping cart page will display items the user has chosen to purchase. You'll use the framework developed in the last chapter to provide a request handling mechanism as well as facilities for logging, database connectivity, and security.

Using the framework, the only things you need to develop for your online catalog is a JSP page for each screen, along with an action to display the catalog and an action to manage the shopping cart (see Figure 12-1). Each action will populate a JavaBean that the corresponding JSP page will use to display the appropriate screen. Each screen will take advantage of the AuthenticationFilter of the framework to authenticate each request as it passes to the controller servlet.

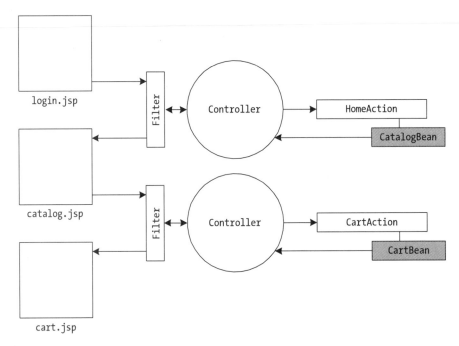

Figure 12-1. Online catalog system

Setting Up the Application

Before constructing the application, it's first necessary to perform a few tasks to set up the application and configure the framework. Once you've completed these tasks, you can develop and deploy the application pages and action classes. The first task to take care of is to create the database.

Creating the Database

The database for the online catalog application is simple, containing only two tables. The user table is necessary for use with the framework's authentication mechanism. The other table, product, holds all of the items in the catalog. Before creating these tables, let's first create the database using the following command:

```
c:\dev\mysql> bin\mysql
  mysql> CREATE DATABASE catalog;
  mysql> exit
```

Now that the database exists, add the user and product tables using the createCatalogDB.sql script as follows:

```
c:\dev\mysql> bin\mysql catalog < createCatalogDB.sql
```

This database script creates both the catalog and user tables. It then populates each table with sample data. The user that is added to the user table in this script is apatzer, but you can go ahead and change that to something more appropriate. Listing 12-1 shows the script used to create and populate the database.

Listing 12-1. createCatalogDB.sql

```
DROP TABLE IF EXISTS user;
CREATE TABLE user (
  uid varchar(10) not null,
  pwd varchar(10) not null,
  fname varchar(30),
  lname varchar(20)
);
INSERT INTO user VALUES
  ('apatzer', 'apress', 'Andrew', 'Patzer');
DROP TABLE IF EXISTS product;
CREATE TABLE product (
  prodid int not null,
  prodname varchar(30),
  proddesc varchar(150),
  price double(7,2)
);
INSERT INTO product VALUES (
  1,
  'Yo-Yo',
  'High-quality wooden yo-yo with your company
  name and logo imprinted on both sides.',
  3.50
);
INSERT INTO product VALUES (
  2,
  'Slinky',
  'Plastic slinky in the color of your choice with your
```

```
      company logo imprinted on closed slinky.',
      0.75
);
INSERT INTO product VALUES (
      3,
      'Envelope Cutter',
      'Small cutting tool for opening envelopes.
      Your company logo is imprinted on handle.',
      1.25
);
INSERT INTO product VALUES (
      4,
      'Padfolio',
      'Synthetic leather padfolio with company name
      and logo imprinted on cover.',
      9.50
);
INSERT INTO product VALUES (
      5,
      'Fountain Pen',
      'Attractive fountain pen sporting your company
      name on the cap.',
      1.20
);
INSERT INTO product VALUES (
      6,
      'Keychain',
      'Rubber keychain with your company name and
      logo imprinted in a variety of colors.',
      0.50
);
INSERT INTO product VALUES (
      7,
      'Ruler',
      'Wooden ruler with raised lettering containing
      your company name and logo.',
      0.25
);
INSERT INTO product VALUES (
      8,
      'Flashlight',
      'Metal flashlight in a variety of colors. Your
      company name and logo is imprinted on the handle.',
      5.0
);
```

Setting Up the Application Server

When deploying the application, you can manually create the directory structure and move the files into their appropriate locations, or you can assemble a WAR file in your build script and use the application server deployment tool to deploy the application (if your application server has such a tool). For this example, you'll create the directories and move the files manually to avoid differences in application server deployment tools.

First, create a \Catalog directory underneath the \webapps directory in your Tomcat's home directory. Inside of the \Catalog directory, add a \WEB-INF directory. Once you've created these directories, edit the server.xml file, and add the lines shown in Listing 12-2.

Listing 12-2. server.xml *Modifications*

```
<Context path="/Catalog"
  docBase="Catalog"
  crossContext="false"
  debug="0"
  reloadable="true">

  <Logger className="org.apache.catalina.logger.FileLogger"
    prefix="localhost_CatalogApp_log." suffix=".txt"
    timestamp="true"/>

  <Resource name="jdbc/CatalogDB" auth="SERVLET"
    type="javax.sql.DataSource"/>
  <ResourceParams name="jdbc/CatalogDB">
    <parameter>
      <name>driverClassName</name>
      <value>org.gjt.mm.mysql.Driver</value>
    </parameter>
    <parameter>
      <name>driverName</name>
      <value>jdbc:mysql://localhost:3306/catalog</value>
    </parameter>
  </ResourceParams>

</Context>
```

Next, you should create the web.xml file and add it to the \WEB-INF directory. Inside the web.xml file, just add a resource definition for the database you've just created. Listing 12-3 shows what the web.xml file looks like at this point.

Listing 12-3. `web.xml`

```
<?xml version="1.0" encoding="ISO-8859-1"?>


<!DOCTYPE web-app
    PUBLIC "-//Sun Microsystems, Inc.//DTD Web Application 2.3//EN"
    "http://java.sun.com/dtd/web-app_2_3.dtd">


<web-app>
  <!-- Describe a DataSource -->
  <resource-ref>
    <description>
      Resource reference to a factory for java.sql.Connection
      instances that may be used for talking to a particular
      database that is configured in the server.xml file.
    </description>
    <res-ref-name>
      jdbc/CatalogDB
    </res-ref-name>
    <res-type>
      javax.sql.DataSource
    </res-type>
    <res-auth>
      SERVLET
    </res-auth>
  </resource-ref>
</web-app>
```

Installing and Configuring the Framework

To use the framework with this application, you should add the `framework.jar` file to the `\WEB-INF\lib` directory. You need to make several additions to the `web.xml` file to install the framework. First, add a filter declaration for the AuthenticationFilter. Next, add a servlet declaration and mapping for the controller servlet. Finally, add the tag library descriptor to include the formatting tags found in the framework. Listing 12-4 shows these additions to the `web.xml` file.

Listing 12-4. Additions to `web.xml`

```
<filter>
  <filter-name>authFilter</filter-name>
  <filter-class>jspbook.framework.security.AuthenticationFilter</filter-class>
</filter>
```

```
<filter-mapping>
  <filter-name>authFilter</filter-name>
  <url-pattern>/Controller</url-pattern>
</filter-mapping>

<servlet>
  <servlet-name>Controller</servlet-name>
  <servlet-class>jspbook.framework.request.Controller</servlet-class>
</servlet>

<servlet-mapping>
  <servlet-name>Controller</servlet-name>
  <url-pattern>/Controller</url-pattern>
</servlet-mapping>

<taglib>
  <taglib-uri>/uitags</taglib-uri>
  <taglib-location>/WEB-INF/tlds/uitags.tld</taglib-location>
</taglib>
```

The framework contains a class called `AppConstants` that reads in a property file and makes it available to the rest of the application. You should create and save this property file, `app.props`, in the `\WEB-INF` directory. The property file needs just one property to begin with, the `dbName` property. Set it to `jdbc/CatalogDB` to match the data source in the `web.xml` file. Finally, modify the startup script for the application server to pass in a system property telling the framework the location of the `app.props` file. Here's an example of how to change the startup script (using Tomcat):

```
Relevant line of startup script before change:

%_STARTJAVA% %CATALINA_OPTS% -Dcatalina.base="%CATALINA_BASE%"
-Dcatalina.home="%CATALINA_HOME%"
org.apache.catalina.startup.Bootstrap %2 %3 %4 %5 %6 %7 %8 %9 start


After change:

%_STARTJAVA% %CATALINA_OPTS% -Dcatalina.base="%CATALINA_BASE%"
-Dcatalina.home="%CATALINA_HOME%"
-Dprop.file.dir=c:\development\tomcat4.0.2\webapps\catalog\WEB-INF
org.apache.catalina.startup.Bootstrap %2 %3 %4 %5 %6 %7 %8 %9 start
```

Setting Up the Development Environment

The development environment consists of a directory structure to place the project files in and a build script to compile and deploy the application. The directory structure to use for this project is as follows:

```
\Catalog
  \lib
  \working_files
```

The \lib directory should contain any supporting libraries necessary for compiling the application. In this case, the \lib directory should contain a copy of the framework.jar file. The \working_files directory is where the source code for the application will reside. The build script will create build and dist directories as needed. The build script is similar to those used in earlier chapters. Listing 12-5 shows the complete script used to build the application.

Listing 12-5. build.xml

```xml
<project name="catalog" default="dist" basedir=".">

  <!-- Set global properties for this build -->
  <property name="src" value="working_files"/>
  <property name="build" value="build"/>
  <property name="dist" value="dist"/>

  <target name="init">
    <!-- Create the time stamp -->
    <tstamp/>
    <!-- Create the build directory used by compile task-->
    <mkdir dir="${build}"/>
  </target>

  <target name="compile" depends="init">
    <!-- Compile the java code from ${src} into ${build} -->
    <path id="project.classpath">
      <pathelement path="C:\Development\j2ee1.3\lib\j2ee.jar"/>
      <pathelement path="C:\Development\log4j1.1.3\dist\lib\log4j.jar"/>
      <pathelement path="lib\framework.jar"/>
      <pathelement path="${build}"/>
    </path>
    <javac srcdir="${src}" destdir="${build}">
      <classpath refid="project.classpath"/>
    </javac>
  </target>
```

```
<target name="dist" depends="compile">
  <!-- Create distribution directories -->
  <mkdir dir="${dist}\lib"/>
  <mkdir dir="${dist}\docs"/>
  <!-- Create JAR files -->
  <jar jarfile="${dist}\lib\catalog_${DSTAMP}.jar" basedir="${build}"/>
  <jar jarfile="${dist}\lib\catalog_src_${DSTAMP}.jar" basedir="${src}"/>
  <!-- Create Javadoc -->
  <javadoc packagenames="catalog.*"
         sourcepath="${src}"
         defaultexcludes="yes"
         destdir="${dist}\docs"
         classpathref="project.classpath"
         author="true"
         version="true"
         use="true"
         windowtitle="Online Catalog Application">
    <doctitle><![CDATA[<h1>Online Catalog Application</h1>]]></doctitle>
    <bottom>
      <![CDATA[<i>Copyright &#169; 2002 APress. All Rights Reserved.</i>]]>
    </bottom>
  </javadoc>
  <jar jarfile="${dist}\lib\catalog_docs_${DSTAMP}.jar"
    basedir="${dist}\docs"/>
</target>

</project>
```

Creating Application Resources

The final preparation to make, as you move on to constructing the application, is to create some of the static resources used by JSP pages. These resources are the HTML header used by the JSP pages, the standard error page, and the images used by the application. These are the images that you need to create:

- **logo.gif**: Logo for display in leftmost column of top banner

- **hdr_bar.gif**: Background image for right column of top banner

- **viewcart.gif**: Button for home.jsp page

- **addtocart.gif**: Button for home.jsp page to accompany each catalog item

- **removefromcart.gif**: Button for cart.jsp to accompany each item in cart

267

The header HTML and error page are almost identical to those used in previous chapters. The header code is stored as and referenced by the name myHeader.html. Listing 12-6 shows what this code looks like.

Listing 12-6. myHeader.html

```
<table width="100%" border="0" cellspacing="0" cellpadding="0">
  <tr>
    <td width="187"><img src="images/logo.gif"></td>
    <td background="images/hdr_bar.gif"> </td>
  </tr>
</table>
```

The error page is called myError.jsp and contains the code shown in Listing 12-7.

Listing 12-7. myError.jsp

```
<%@page isErrorPage="true" %>

<html>
<head>
  <title>Trinkets Online - Error!</title>
</head>

<body>
<br>

<%@include file="myHeader.html" %>

<% String from = (String)request.getParameter("from"); %>

An error occurred on page <b><%= from %></b>.

<br><br>

The exception was:
<br>
<b><%= exception %></b>

<!-- Send exception report to administrator -->
<% System.out.println(exception.toString()); %>

</body>
</html>
```

Logging in to the Application

The login page simply collects the user ID and password of the user trying to access the application (see Figure 12-2). Each request made to the application passes through the AuthenticationFilter on its way to the controller servlet. The login page provides enough information to enable the user to be authenticated so that the filter will let all future requests flow through to the application.

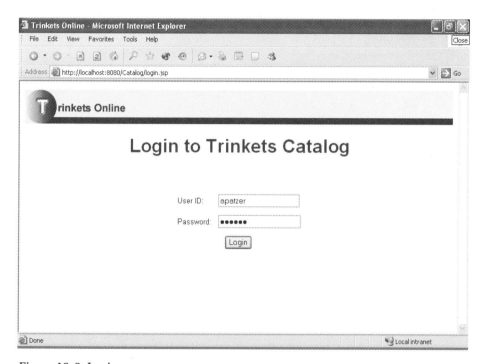

Figure 12-2. Login page

The code for the login.jsp page contains a simple form and a couple of hidden variables. These variables provide the filter and the controller with enough information to authenticate the user and forward them to the home page of the catalog. There's also a bit of code that checks to see if the user has arrived at this page as the result of a failed authentication attempt. If that's the case, a status message alerts the user to the failed attempt. Listing 12-8 shows the code for the login page.

Listing 12-8. `login.jsp`

```jsp
<%@ page
  errorPage="myError.jsp?from=login.jsp"
%>

<html>
<head>
  <title>Trinkets Online</title>
</head>

<body bgcolor="#FFFFFF">

<%@ include file="myHeader.html" %>

<form method="post" action="Controller">

<input type="hidden" name="pageId" value="loginPage"></input>
<input type="hidden" name="actionClass" value="catalog.actions.HomeAction"></input>

<p align="center">
  <font face="Arial, Helvetica, sans-serif" size="6" color="#0000CC">
    <b>Login to Trinkets Catalog</b>
  </font>
</p>

<p> </p>

<!-- Check login status and display message if login attempt failed. -->

<% String status = (String) request.getAttribute("loginStatus");
   if (status != null && status.equals("failed")) {
%>
<center>
  <font color="#ff0000">Invalid login, please try again.</font>
</center>
<%
  }
%>
```

```
<table width="199" border="0" align="center" cellpadding="5">
  <tr>
    <td>
      <font face="Arial, Helvetica, sans-serif" size="2">User ID:</font>
    </td>
    <td><input type="text" name="uid"></td>
  </tr>
  <tr>
    <td><font face="Arial, Helvetica, sans-serif" size="2">Password:</font></td>
    <td><input type="password" name="pwd"></td>
  </tr>
  <tr align="center">
    <td colspan="2"><input type="submit" name="Submit" value="Login"></td>
  </tr>
</table>

</form>

</body>
</html>
```

Viewing the Catalog

The first page the user sees upon successful login to the application is the home page displaying the entire set of items contained within the catalog (see Figure 12-3). To present this page, the controller will instantiate the HomeAction class, execute its business logic, and forward the user to the appropriate view. The HomeAction class retrieves the entire set of catalog items from the product table and stores them in a CatalogBean object. Listing 12-9 shows the code for the HomeAction class.

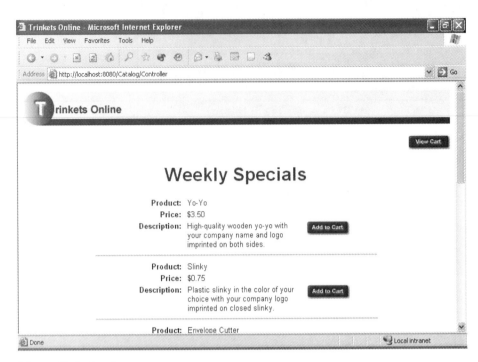

Figure 12-3. Catalog page

Listing 12-9. `HomeAction.java`

```java
package catalog.actions;

import javax.servlet.*;
import javax.servlet.http.*;
import java.io.*;
import java.sql.*;

import jspbook.framework.request.*;
import jspbook.framework.logging.*;
import catalog.beans.CatalogBean;

/**
 * Home action class used to display the home page of the catalog
 *
 * <p>Retrieves a list of catalog items, populates
 * a JavaBean, and returns the name of the page
 * to display the catalog.</p>
 *
 * @version 1.0
```

```
 * @author   Andrew Patzer
 * @since    JDK 1.3
 */

public class HomeAction implements Action
{

  /**
   *  Page to use to display data
   */
  private String view;
  /**
   *  Database connection
   */
  private Connection dbCon;
  /**
   *  JavaBean used to represent catalog items
   */
  private CatalogBean cBean;

  /**
   *  No-arg constructor used to initialize the JavaBean.
   */
  public HomeAction()
  {
    cBean = new CatalogBean();
  }

  /**
   *  Sets the database connection.
   */
  public void setDatabase(Connection _db)
  {
    dbCon = _db;
  }

  /**
   *  Retrieves the catalog items and populates JavaBean.
   */
  public boolean execute(HttpServletRequest _req, HttpServletResponse _res)
    throws ServletException, IOException
  {
    /* Retrieve list of catalog items and store in JavaBean */
```

```
        ResultSet rs = null;
        try {
          Statement s = dbCon.createStatement();
          rs = s.executeQuery("select * from product");
        }
        catch (SQLException e) {
          Logger.log(Logger.ERROR, "Error retrieving catalog items: " + e.toString());
        }

        cBean.populate(rs);

        /* Set the view */
        view = "home.jsp";

        return true;
      }


      /**
       *  Returns the page name used to display the view.
       */
      public String getView()
      {
        return view;
      }


      /**
       *  Returns a JavaBean containing the data necessary to display the view.
       */
      public Object getModel()
      {
        return cBean;
      }


    }
```

The CatalogBean class represents a set of items from the product table of the catalog database. It contains methods that allow an external entity to scroll through the set of items and access each one individually. Listing 12-10 shows the code for the CatalogBean.

Listing 12-10. `CatalogBean.java`

```java
package catalog.beans;

import java.io.*;
import java.util.*;
import java.sql.*;

import jspbook.framework.logging.*;

/**
 * JavaBean representing a catalog item
 *
 * <p>Stores the data representing an item
 * from the catalog database.</p>
 *
 * @version 1.0
 * @author   Andrew Patzer
 * @since    JDK 1.3
 */

public class CatalogBean implements Serializable
{

  /**
   *  Product ID
   */
  private int prodid;
  /**
   *  Product Name
   */
  private String prodname;
  /**
   *  Product Description
   */
  private String proddesc;
  /**
   *  Product Price
   */
  private double price;

  /**
   *  Stores all product ID's in the database
   */
```

```
    private ArrayList prodidList;
    /**
     *  Stores all product name's in the database
     */
    private ArrayList prodnameList;
    /**
     *  Stores all product description's in the database
     */
    private ArrayList proddescList;
    /**
     *  Stores all product price's in the database
     */
    private ArrayList priceList;

    /**
     *  Current row (used when displaying records)
     */
    private int currentRow;
    /**
     *  Row count (used to keep track of total rows
     */
    private int rowCount;
    /**
     *  Total rows (used to report the total number of items in the bean)
     */
    private int totalRows;

    /**
     *  No-arg constructor used to initialize the bean.
     */
    public CatalogBean()
    {
      /* Initialize arrayLists to hold recordsets */
      prodidList = new ArrayList();
      prodnameList = new ArrayList();
      proddescList = new ArrayList();
      priceList = new ArrayList();

      /* Initialize helper variables */
      currentRow = 0;
      rowCount = 0;
    }
```

```
/**
 *  Setter method for Product ID.
 */
public void setProdid (int _prodid) {this.prodid = _prodid;}
/**
 *  Getter method for Product ID.
 */
public int getProdid () {return this.prodid;}


/**
 *  Setter method for Product Name.
 */
public void setProdname (String _prodname) {this.prodname = _prodname;}
/**
 *  Getter method for Product Name.
 */
public String getProdname () {return this.prodname;}


/**
 *  Setter method for Product Description.
 */
public void setProddesc (String _proddesc) {this.proddesc = _proddesc;}
/**
 *  Getter method for Product Description.
 */
public String getProddesc () {return this.proddesc;}


/**
 *  Setter method for Product Price.
 */
public void setPrice (double _price) {this.price = _price;}
/**
 *  Getter method for Product Price.
 */
public double getPrice () {return this.price;}


/**
 *  Populates JavaBean with data from a JDBC result set.
 */
public boolean populate(ResultSet _rs)
{
  try {
    prodidList.clear();
```

```
                prodnameList.clear();
                proddescList.clear();
                priceList.clear();

                rowCount = 0;
                while (_rs.next()) {
                   prodidList.add(new Integer(_rs.getInt("prodid")));
                   prodnameList.add(_rs.getString("prodname"));
                   proddescList.add(_rs.getString("proddesc"));
                   priceList.add(new Float(_rs.getDouble("price")));
                   rowCount++;
                }
             }
             catch (Exception e) {
                Logger.log(Logger.ERROR, "Error populating Catalog Bean: " + e.toString());
                return false;
             }

             return true;
          }

          /**
           *  Resets the current row.
           */
          public void setStartRow(int _start)
          {
             if (_start < rowCount) {
                currentRow = _start;
             }
          }

          /**
           *  Returns the total number of items in the bean.
           */
          public int getTotalRows()
          {
             return this.rowCount;
          }

          /**
           *  Advances the bean to the next record.
           */
```

```
  public int nextRow()
  {
    if (currentRow <= rowCount) {
      /* Populate bean properties with current row */
      Integer tmpInt = (Integer)prodidList.get(currentRow);
      setProdid(tmpInt.intValue());
      setProdname((String)prodnameList.get(currentRow));
      setProddesc((String)proddescList.get(currentRow));
      Float tmpFloat = (Float)priceList.get(currentRow);
      setPrice(tmpFloat.doubleValue());
    }

    currentRow++;

    /* return currentRow*/
    return currentRow;
  }

}
```

The home.jsp page takes the CatalogBean and displays each record for the user to select and add to a shopping cart. You do this by looping through the CatalogBean and passing its values to the CatalogItem custom tag for display. Listing 12-11 shows the code for the home.jsp page.

Listing 12-11. home.jsp

```
<%@ page
   import="catalog.beans.CatalogBean"
   errorPage="myError.jsp?from=home.jsp"
%>

<%@ taglib uri="/catalogtags" prefix="cat" %>

<html>
<head>
  <title>Trinkets Online</title>
</head>

<body bgcolor="#FFFFFF">

<%@ include file="myHeader.html" %>
```

```
<p align="right">
  <a href="Controller?pageId=home&actionClass=
        catalog.actions.CartAction&action=view">
    <img src="images\viewcart.gif" border="0">
  </a>
</p>

<center>

<font face="Arial, Helvetica, sans-serif" size="6" color="#0000CC">
  <b>Weekly Specials</b>
</font>

<br><br>

<% CatalogBean cBean = (CatalogBean) request.getAttribute("model");
    if (cBean != null) {
      cBean.setStartRow(0);
      for (int i = 0; i < cBean.getTotalRows(); i++) {
        cBean.nextRow();
%>

<cat:CatalogItem
  prodid='<%= Integer.toString(cBean.getProdid()) %>'
  prodname='<%= cBean.getProdname() %>'
  price='<%= Double.toString(cBean.getPrice()) %>'
  proddesc='<%= cBean.getProddesc() %>'
/>

<hr width="500" align="center">

<%
    }
  }
%>

</center>

</body>
</html>
```

The CatalogItem tag takes the data from the CatalogBean and adapts it to a table row. The tag requires a tag library descriptor as well as an entry in the web.xml file. Listing 12-12 shows the catalogtags.tld file containing the necessary entries to describe the CatalogItem tag.

Listing 12-12. catalogtags.tld

```
<?xml version="1.0" encoding="ISO-8859-1" ?>
<!DOCTYPE taglib
    PUBLIC "-//Sun Microsystems, Inc.//DTD JSP Tag Library 1.2//EN"
    "http://java.sun.com/j2ee/dtd/web-jsptaglibrary_1_2.dtd">

<taglib>
  <tlib-version>1.0</tlib-version>
  <jsp-version>1.2</jsp-version>
  <short-name>catalogTags</short-name>
  <description>
    Tag library to support the case study in chapter 12
  </description>
  <tag>
    <name>CatalogItem</name>
    <tag-class>catalog.ui.tags.CatalogItem</tag-class>
    <body-content>JSP</body-content>
    <attribute>
      <name>prodid</name>
      <required>yes</required>
      <rtexprvalue>true</rtexprvalue>
    </attribute>
    <attribute>
      <name>prodname</name>
      <required>yes</required>
      <rtexprvalue>true</rtexprvalue>
    </attribute>
    <attribute>
      <name>price</name>
      <required>yes</required>
      <rtexprvalue>true</rtexprvalue>
    </attribute>
    <attribute>
      <name>proddesc</name>
      <required>yes</required>
      <rtexprvalue>true</rtexprvalue>
    </attribute>
  </tag>
</taglib>
```

The `CatalogItem` tag handler builds a table entry containing the product ID, product name, price, and product description by making three separate calls to the `printRow` method. Each call to this method builds a table row. The row to build is determined by a `switch` statement that evaluates the value passed into the method. Listing 12-13 shows the code for the `CatalogItem` tag handler.

Listing 12-13. `CatalogItem.java`

```java
package catalog.ui.tags;

import javax.servlet.http.*;
import javax.servlet.jsp.*;
import javax.servlet.jsp.tagext.*;
import java.io.IOException;
import java.text.*;

import jspbook.framework.logging.Logger;

/**
 * Custom Tag Extension representing a catalog item
 *
 * <p>Outputs a table row representing an item
 * in a catalog.</p>
 *
 * @version 1.0
 * @author  Andrew Patzer
 * @since   JDK 1.3
 */

public class CatalogItem extends TagSupport
{

    /**
     *  Product ID
     */
    protected String prodid;
    /**
     *  Product Name
     */
    protected String prodname;
    /**
     *  Product Price
     */
    protected String price;
```

```
/**
 *  Product Description
 */
protected String proddesc;

/**
 *  Processes the tag, outputting a formatted
 *  catalog item.
 */
public int doStartTag() throws JspTagException {
  try {
    JspWriter out = pageContext.getOut();
    out.println("<table width='500' border='0'>");
    out.println(printRow(1));
    out.println(printRow(2));
    out.println(printRow(3));
    out.println("</table>");
  }
  catch (IOException e) {
    Logger.log(Logger.ERROR, e.toString());
    throw new JspTagException(e.toString());
  }
  return SKIP_BODY;
}

/**
 *  Processes the end tag.
 */
public int doEndTag() throws JspTagException {
  return EVAL_PAGE;
}

/**
 *  Prints a single row of the catalog item.
 */
public String printRow(int _row)
{
  String col1 = "";
  String col2 = "";
  String col3 = "";

  StringBuffer htmlRow = new StringBuffer();
```

```
            switch (_row) {
              case 1:
                col1 = "Product:";
                col2 = prodname;
                col3 = "";
                break;
              case 2:
                col1 = "Price:";

                /* Format price */
                float f = Float.parseFloat(price);
                DecimalFormat dcf = (DecimalFormat) NumberFormat.getCurrencyInstance();
                col2 = dcf.format(f);

                col3 = "";
                break;
              case 3:
                col1 = "Description:";
                col2 = proddesc;

                /* Build link to cart action */
                StringBuffer tmpStr = new StringBuffer();
                tmpStr.append("<a href='Controller?");
                tmpStr.append("action=add&");
                tmpStr.append("prodid=").append(prodid).append("&");
                tmpStr.append("prodname=").append(prodname).append("&");
                tmpStr.append("price=").append(price).append("&");
                tmpStr.append("pageId=home&");
                tmpStr.append("actionClass=catalog.actions.CartAction'>");
                tmpStr.append("<img src='images/addtocart.gif' border='0'></a>");

                col3 = tmpStr.toString();
                break;
            }

        htmlRow.append("<tr>");

        /* Column 1 */
        htmlRow.append("<td width='150' align='right' valign='top'>");
        htmlRow.append("<b><font face='Arial, Helvetica, sans-serif' size='2'>");
        htmlRow.append(col1);
        htmlRow.append("</font></b></td>");
```

```
    /* Column 2 */
    htmlRow.append("<td width='200' valign='top'>");
    htmlRow.append("<font face='Arial, Helvetica, sans-serif' size='2'>");
    htmlRow.append(col2);
    htmlRow.append("</font></td>");

    /* Column 2 */
    htmlRow.append("<td width='116' valign='top'>");
    htmlRow.append(col3);
    htmlRow.append("</td>");

    htmlRow.append("</tr>");

    return htmlRow.toString();
}

/**
 *  Setter method for Product ID
 */
public String getProdid() {return prodid;}
/**
 *  Getter method for Product ID
 */
public void setProdid(String _prodid) {prodid = _prodid;}

/**
 *  Setter method for Product Name
 */
public String getProdname() {return prodname;}
/**
 *  Getter method for Product Name
 */
public void setProdname(String _prodname) {prodname = _prodname;}

/**
 *  Setter method for Product Price
 */
public String getPrice() {return price;}
/**
 *  Getter method for Product Price
 */
public void setPrice(String _price) {price = _price;}
```

```
/**
 *   Setter method for Product Description
 */
public String getProddesc() {return proddesc;}
/**
 *   Getter method for Product Description
 */
public void setProddesc(String _proddesc) {proddesc = _proddesc;}

}
```

Accessing the Shopping Cart

The shopping cart is managed using the CartAction class and is displayed using the cart.jsp page. Each item in the cart is displayed along with a Remove button, which removes a specific item from the cart. For this example, the only functionality the cart has is to add items to it, remove items from it, and view the contents of it. The first step in managing the shopping cart is to make a request to the CartAction class, along with a new form parameter called 'action'. This should be set to add, remove, or view as needed. Listing 12-14 shows the code for the CartAction class.

Listing 12-14. CartAction.java

```
package catalog.actions;

import javax.servlet.*;
import javax.servlet.http.*;
import java.io.*;
import java.sql.*;

import jspbook.framework.request.*;
import jspbook.framework.logging.*;
import catalog.beans.CartBean;

/**
 * Cart Action class to manage a shopping cart
 *
 * <p>Allows a user to view a cart, add items
 * to a cart, or remove an item from the cart.</p>
 *
 * @version 1.0
 * @author  Andrew Patzer
```

```
 * @since    JDK 1.3
 */


public class CartAction implements Action {

  /**
   *  Name of the page used to present the cart screen
   */
  private String view;

  /**
   *  Database connection object
   */
  private Connection dbCon;

  /**
   *  JavaBean representing the shopping cart
   */
  private CartBean cBean;

  /**
   *  No-args constructor
   */
  public CartAction() {}

  /**
   *  Sets the database connection
   */
  public void setDatabase(Connection _db)
  {
    dbCon = _db;
  }

  /**
   *  Execute the business logic.
   */
  public boolean execute(HttpServletRequest _req, HttpServletResponse _res)
    throws ServletException, IOException
  {
    /* Retrieve cBean from session, if it exists */
    HttpSession session = _req.getSession();
    cBean = (CartBean) session.getValue("cart");
    if (cBean == null) {
```

```java
    cBean = new CartBean();
  }

  /* Perform action */
  String action = _req.getParameter("action");
  String prodid = _req.getParameter("prodid");
  String prodname = _req.getParameter("prodname");
  String price = _req.getParameter("price");

  if (action.equals("add")) {
    cBean.add(prodid, prodname, price);
  }

  if (action.equals("remove")) {
    cBean.remove(prodid);
  }

  /* Write cBean back to session */
  session.putValue("cart", cBean);

  /* Set the view */
  view = "cart.jsp";

  return true;
}

/**
 *  Return the name of the page used to display the data.
 */
public String getView()
{
  return view;
}

/**
 *  Return a JavaBean containing the model (data).
 */
public Object getModel()
{
  return cBean;
}

}
```

Each item stored in the cart is represented by the CartBean class. This bean stores items much like the CatalogBean does. It contains a similar mechanism for navigating through the set of items it contains. Listing 12-15 shows the code for the CartBean class.

Listing 12-15. CartBean.java

```java
package catalog.beans;

import java.io.*;
import java.util.*;
import java.sql.*;

import jspbook.framework.logging.*;

/**
 * JavaBean representing a shopping cart
 *
 * <p>Stores the product id, product name,
 * and product description of each item
 * stored in the shopping cart.</p>
 *
 * @version 1.0
 * @author   Andrew Patzer
 * @since    JDK 1.3
 */

public class CartBean implements Serializable
{
  /**
   *  Product ID
   */
  private String prodid;
  /**
   *  Product Name
   */
  private String prodname;
  /**
   *  Product Price
   */
  private String price;

  /**
   *  List of Product ID's stored in cart
```

```
      */
    private ArrayList prodidList;
    /**
     *  List of Product name's stored in cart
     */
    private ArrayList prodnameList;
    /**
     *  List of Product price's stored in cart
     */
    private ArrayList priceList;

    /**
     *  Pointer used to display items in order
     */
    private int currentRow;

    /**
     *  No-args constructor used to initialize the bean.
     */
    public CartBean()
    {
      /* Initialize arrayLists to hold recordsets */
      prodidList = new ArrayList();
      prodnameList = new ArrayList();
      priceList = new ArrayList();

      /* Initialize helper variables */
      currentRow = 0;
    }

    /**
     *  Setter method for Product ID.
     */
    public void setProdid (String _prodid) {this.prodid = _prodid;}
    /**
     *  Getter method for Product ID.
     */
    public String getProdid () {return this.prodid;}

    /**
     *  Setter method for Product Name.
     */
    public void setProdname (String _prodname) {this.prodname = _prodname;}
    /**
```

```
 *  Getter method for Product Name.
 */
public String getProdname () {return this.prodname;}


/**
 *  Setter method for Product Price.
 */
public void setPrice (String _price) {this.price = _price;}
/**
 *  Getter method for Product Price.
 */
public String getPrice () {return this.price;}


/**
 *  Inserts item into cart.
 */
public boolean add(String _id, String _name, String _price)
{
  try {
    prodidList.add(_id);
    prodnameList.add(_name);
    priceList.add(_price);
  }
  catch (Exception e) {
    Logger.log(Logger.ERROR, "Error populating CartBean: " + e.toString());
    return false;
  }

  return true;
}


/**
 *  Removes an item from the cart.
 */
public void remove (String _id)
{
  int index = prodidList.indexOf(_id);
  prodidList.remove(index);
  prodnameList.remove(index);
  priceList.remove(index);
}


/**
 *  Resets the current row.
```

```
  */
  public void setStartRow(int _start)
  {
    if (_start < prodidList.size()) {
      currentRow = _start;
    }
  }


  /**
   *  Returns the total number of items in the cart.
   */
  public int getTotalRows()
  {
    return prodidList.size();
  }


  /**
   *  Advances the bean to the next item in the shopping cart.
   */
  public int nextRow()
  {
    /* Populate bean properties with current row */
    setProdid((String)prodidList.get(currentRow));
    setProdname((String)prodnameList.get(currentRow));
    setPrice((String)priceList.get(currentRow));

    currentRow++;

    /* return currentRow*/
    return currentRow;
  }

}
```

The cart is displayed using the cart.jsp page. The cart.jsp page simply displays each item stored in the CartBean object. It uses the FormatTag of the framework to format the price field as a currency value. Listing 12-16 shows the code for the cart.jsp page.

Listing 12-16. cart.jsp

```
<%@ page
    import="catalog.beans.CartBean"
    errorPage="myError.jsp?from=cart.jsp"
%>
```

```
<%@ taglib uri="/uitags" prefix="uitags" %>

<html>
<head>
  <title>Trinkets Online</title>
</head>

<body bgcolor="#FFFFFF">

<%@ include file="myHeader.html" %>

<center>

<font face="Arial, Helvetica, sans-serif" size="6" color="#0000CC">
  <b>Items in Cart</b>
</font>

<br><br>

<table width="400" border="0">

<% CartBean cBean = (CartBean) request.getAttribute("model");
   if (cBean != null) {
     cBean.setStartRow(0);
     for (int i = 0; i < cBean.getTotalRows(); i++) {
       cBean.nextRow();
%>
  <tr>
    <td width="100">
      <a href="Controller?pageId=home&actionClass=catalog.actions.CartAction
        &action=remove&prodid=<%= cBean.getProdid() %>">
        <img src="images\removefromcart.gif" border="0">
      </a>
    </td>
    <td align="left" width="200"><%= cBean.getProdname() %></td>
    <td width="100">
      <uitags:FormatTag format="NUMERIC_CURRENCY">
        <%= cBean.getPrice() %>
      </uitags:FormatTag>
    </td>
  </tr>
<%
    }
```

```
      }
%>

  <tr>
    <td colspan="3" align="center">
      <a href="Controller?pageId=cart&actionClass=catalog.actions.HomeAction">
        Return to Catalog</a>
    </td>
  </tr>
</table>

</body>
</html>
```

Figure 12-4 shows what the shopping cart might look like after selecting a few items. Clicking a Remove button will remove the item and redisplay the cart. Notice how the item prices are formatted as currency using the FormatTag View Helper class developed in Chapter 11.

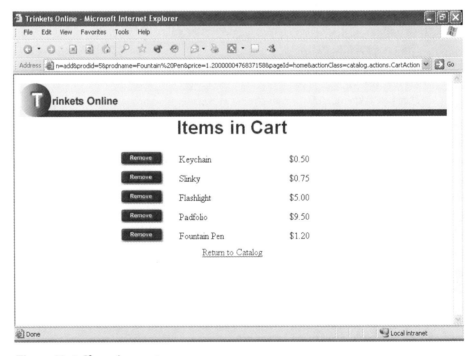

Figure 12-4. Shopping cart

Summary

This book has presented a set of examples and best practices that can be applied to almost any software development project that utilizes JavaServer Pages and J2EE technologies. In Chapters 1 and 2, you learned the basics of using JSP to effectively manage sessions, handle errors, navigate between pages, and process form data. You also learned techniques to make your JSP pages more modular and reusable.

Chapters 3 and 4 showed you several techniques to achieve role separation between programmer and page designer. Using JavaBeans to encapsulate page data, as well as business logic, takes away much of the Java code that typically clutters up an HTML page. This makes it easier for the page designer to concentrate on the presentation of the page while the Java programmer takes care of the application logic behind the page. Custom tag extensions are another tool designed to further separate HTML content from Java code. Custom tags provide a familiar format that page designers should be comfortable working with because they closely resemble that of HTML tags.

Chapters 5 through 8 introduced several design patterns to apply to JSP development to create a robust and extensible presentation tier. Each of these patterns build upon the Model-View-Controller (MVC) pattern, separating application data and navigation code from the user interface layer of the application. Using these patterns, it's possible to build a complete request-handling framework capable of supporting many different applications.

Chapters 9 and 10 introduced several concepts and techniques used to build a development framework consisting of unit testing, load testing, source control, and automated application builds. Each of these components greatly contributes to the success of a software development project, regardless of the technology used. It's important to create this development framework, wrap a set of processes around it, and enforce its use on every software project.

Chapters 11 and 12 built an application framework using many of the techniques discussed throughout the book. The framework developed in Chapter 11 should serve as a starting point for further development of a framework that will meet the needs of your organization. You've seen in Chapter 12 how easy it is to build an application when using a framework. As you extend this framework to meet your needs, your future development projects will become easier and easier.

Index

Apress Titles

ISBN	PRICE	AUTHOR	TITLE
1-893115-73-9	$34.95	Abbott	Voice Enabling Web Applications: VoiceXML and Beyond
1-893115-01-1	$39.95	Appleman	Dan Appleman's Win32 API Puzzle Book and Tutorial for Visual Basic Programmers
1-893115-23-2	$29.95	Appleman	How Computer Programming Works
1-893115-97-6	$39.95	Appleman	Moving to VB. NET: Strategies, Concepts, and Code
1-59059-023-6	$39.95	Baker	Adobe Acrobat 5: The Professional User's Guide
1-893115-09-7	$29.95	Baum	Dave Baum's Definitive Guide to LEGO MINDSTORMS
1-893115-84-4	$29.95	Baum, Gasperi, Hempel, and Villa	Extreme MINDSTORMS: An Advanced Guide to LEGO MINDSTORMS
1-893115-82-8	$59.95	Ben-Gan/Moreau	Advanced Transact-SQL for SQL Server 2000
1-893115-91-7	$39.95	Birmingham/Perry	Software Development on a Leash
1-893115-48-8	$29.95	Bischof	The .NET Languages: A Quick Translation Guide
1-893115-67-4	$49.95	Borge	Managing Enterprise Systems with the Windows Script Host
1-893115-28-3	$44.95	Challa/Laksberg	Essential Guide to Managed Extensions for C++
1-893115-39-9	$44.95	Chand	A Programmer's Guide to ADO.NET in C#
1-893115-44-5	$29.95	Cook	Robot Building for Beginners
1-893115-99-2	$39.95	Cornell/Morrison	Programming VB .NET: A Guide for Experienced Programmers
1-893115-72-0	$39.95	Curtin	Developing Trust: Online Privacy and Security
1-59059-008-2	$29.95	Duncan	The Career Programmer: Guerilla Tactics for an Imperfect World
1-893115-71-2	$39.95	Ferguson	Mobile .NET
1-893115-90-9	$49.95	Finsel	The Handbook for Reluctant Database Administrators
1-59059-024-4	$49.95	Fraser	Real World ASP.NET: Building a Content Management System
1-893115-42-9	$44.95	Foo/Lee	XML Programming Using the Microsoft XML Parser
1-893115-55-0	$34.95	Frenz	Visual Basic and Visual Basic .NET for Scientists and Engineers
1-893115-85-2	$34.95	Gilmore	A Programmer's Introduction to PHP 4.0
1-893115-36-4	$34.95	Goodwill	Apache Jakarta-Tomcat
1-893115-17-8	$59.95	Gross	A Programmer's Introduction to Windows DNA
1-893115-62-3	$39.95	Gunnerson	A Programmer's Introduction to C#, Second Edition
1-59059-009-0	$49.95	Harris/Macdonald	Moving to ASP.NET: Web Development with VB .NET
1-893115-30-5	$49.95	Harkins/Reid	SQL: Access to SQL Server
1-893115-10-0	$34.95	Holub	Taming Java Threads
1-893115-04-6	$34.95	Hyman/Vaddadi	Mike and Phani's Essential C++ Techniques
1-893115-96-8	$59.95	Jorelid	J2EE FrontEnd Technologies: A Programmer's Guide to Servlets, JavaServer Pages, and Enterprise JavaBeans
1-893115-49-6	$39.95	Kilburn	Palm Programming in Basic
1-893115-50-X	$34.95	Knudsen	Wireless Java: Developing with Java 2, Micro Edition
1-893115-79-8	$49.95	Kofler	Definitive Guide to Excel VBA
1-893115-57-7	$39.95	Kofler	MySQL
1-893115-87-9	$39.95	Kurata	Doing Web Development: Client-Side Techniques
1-893115-75-5	$44.95	Kurniawan	Internet Programming with VB

ISBN	PRICE	AUTHOR	TITLE
1-893115-38-0	$24.95	Lafler	Power AOL: A Survival Guide
1-893115-46-1	$36.95	Lathrop	Linux in Small Business: A Practical User's Guide
1-893115-19-4	$49.95	Macdonald	Serious ADO: Universal Data Access with Visual Basic
1-893115-06-2	$39.95	Marquis/Smith	A Visual Basic 6.0 Programmer's Toolkit
1-893115-22-4	$27.95	McCarter	David McCarter's VB Tips and Techniques
1-59059-021-X	$34.95	Moore	Karl Moore's Visual Basic .NET: The Tutorials
1-893115-76-3	$49.95	Morrison	C++ For VB Programmers
1-893115-80-1	$39.95	Newmarch	A Programmer's Guide to Jini Technology
1-893115-58-5	$49.95	Oellermann	Architecting Web Services
1-59059-020-1	$44.95	Patzer	JSP Examples and Best Practices
1-893115-81-X	$39.95	Pike	SQL Server: Common Problems, Tested Solutions
1-59059-017-1	$34.95	Rainwater	Herding Cats: A Primer for Programmers Who Lead Programmers
1-59059-025-2	$49.95	Rammer	Advanced .NET Remoting
1-893115-20-8	$34.95	Rischpater	Wireless Web Development
1-893115-93-3	$34.95	Rischpater	Wireless Web Development with PHP and WAP
1-893115-89-5	$59.95	Shemitz	Kylix: The Professional Developer's Guide and Reference
1-893115-40-2	$39.95	Sill	The qmail Handbook
1-893115-24-0	$49.95	Sinclair	From Access to SQL Server
1-893115-94-1	$29.95	Spolsky	User Interface Design for Programmers
1-893115-53-4	$44.95	Sweeney	Visual Basic for Testers
1-59059-002-3	$44.95	Symmonds	Internationalization and Localization Using Microsoft .NET
1-59059-010-4	$54.95	Thomsen	Database Programming with C#
1-893115-29-1	$44.95	Thomsen	Database Programming with Visual Basic .NET
1-893115-65-8	$39.95	Tiffany	Pocket PC Database Development with eMbedded Visual Basic
1-893115-59-3	$59.95	Troelsen	C# and the .NET Platform
1-59059-011-2	$59.95	Troelsen	COM and .NET Interoperability
1-893115-26-7	$59.95	Troelsen	Visual Basic .NET and the .NET Platform
1-893115-54-2	$49.95	Trueblood/Lovett	Data Mining and Statistical Analysis Using SQL
1-893115-68-2	$54.95	Vaughn	ADO.NET and ADO Examples and Best Practices for VB Programmers, Second Edition
1-59059-012-0	$49.95	Vaughn/Blackburn	ADO.NET Examples and Best Practices for C# Programmers
1-893115-83-6	$44.95	Wells	Code Centric: T-SQL Programming with Stored Procedures and Triggers
1-893115-95-X	$49.95	Welschenbach	Cryptography in C and C++
1-893115-05-4	$39.95	Williamson	Writing Cross-Browser Dynamic HTML
1-893115-78-X	$49.95	Zukowski	Definitive Guide to Swing for Java 2, Second Edition
1-893115-92-5	$49.95	Zukowski	Java Collections
1-893115-98-4	$54.95	Zukowski	Learn Java with JBuilder 6

Available at bookstores nationwide or from Springer Verlag New York, Inc. at 1-800-777-4643; fax 1-212-533-3503. Contact us for more information at sales@apress.com.

Apress Titles Publishing SOON!

ISBN	AUTHOR	TITLE
1-59059-022-8	Alapati	Expert Oracle 9i Database Administration
1-59059-039-2	Barnaby	Distributed .NET Programming
1-59059-019-8	Cagle	The Graphical Web
1-59059-015-5	Clark	An Introduction to Object Oriented Programming with Visual Basic .NET
1-59059-000-7	Cornell	Programming C#
1-59059-014-7	Drol	Object-Oriented Flash MX
1-59059-033-3	Fraser	Managed C++ and .NET Development
1-59059-038-4	Gibbons	Java Development to .NET Development
1-59059-030-9	Habibi/Camerlengo/Patterson	Java 1.4 and the Sun Certified Developer Exam
1-59059-006-6	Hetland	Practical Python
1-59059-003-1	Nakhimovsky/Meyers	XML Programming: Web Applications and Web Services with JSP and ASP
1-59059-001-5	McMahon	Serious ASP.NET
1-893115-27-5	Morrill	Tuning and Customizing a Linux System
1-59059-028-7	Rischpater	Wireless Web Development, 2nd Edition
1-59059-026-0	Smith	Writing Add-Ins for .NET
1-893115-43-7	Stephenson	Standard VB: An Enterprise Developer's Reference for VB 6 and VB .NET
1-59059-032-5	Thomsen	Database Programming with Visual Basic .NET, 2nd Edition
1-59059-007-4	Thomsen	Building Web Services with VB .NET
1-59059-027-9	Torkelson/Petersen/Torkelson	Programming the Web with Visual Basic .NET
1-59059-018-X	Tregar	Writing Perl Modules for CPAN
1-59059-004-X	Valiaveedu	SQL Server 2000 and Business Intelligence in an XML/.NET World

Available at bookstores nationwide or from Springer Verlag New York, Inc. at 1-800-777-4643; fax 1-212-533-3503. Contact us for more information at sales@apress.com.